T5-BPY-365

'TWIXT THE CUP AND THE LIP

Psychological and Socio-Cultural Factors Affecting Food Habits

MARGARET CUSSLER *and* MARY L. DE GIVE

New Introduction by Margaret Cussler

CONSORTIUM PRESS

WASHINGTON, D.C.

Library of Congress Cataloging in Publication Data

Cussler, Margaret.
'Twixt the cup and the lip.

Includes bibliographical references.
1. Food habits--Southern States. 2. Diet--Southern States. I. De Give, Mary L., joint author. II. Title.
[GT2860.C8 1972] 301.5'2 73-129963
ISBN 0-8434-0157-5

MANUFACTURED IN THE UNITED STATES OF AMERICA

TO OUR RESPECTIVE MOTHERS

Margaret King Cussler *and* Gertrude Westmoreland de Give

NEW ISSUES IN CHANGING FOOD HABITS

Some 30 years ago, Professor Carle C. Zimmerman suggested to two of his students that malnutrition might be considered a suspect in the enervation of persons living in coastal North Carolina.[1] We discovered that he had been right, and in probing more deeply comparing this tobacco-growing area with a cotton-growing area and finally with an area of small farms growing and consuming a wide variety of foodstuffs that a whole complex of variables intervened between the availability of food and the consumption of nutritional diet.[2]

Today we are newly discovering that people are hungry and malnourished in the United States – ten million people. How many such persons there are no one knows exactly, according to the Surgeon-General of the U.S. Public Health Service.[3] We are told, however, by *Hunger, U.S.A.*[4] and the more authoritative nationwide dietary studies of

1. C. C. Zimmerman, *The Changing Community* contains the first description of this type of community. (1938) His data were later drawn upon by G. C. Homans in *The Human Group*, Harcourt, Brace, 1950, among others.

2. Margaret Cussler and Mary L. de Give, *'Twixt the Cup and the Lip: Psychological and Socio-Cultural Factors Affecting Food Habits*, Twayne Publishers, 1952. Shorter published accounts of studies by the authors in food habits in 1941 and 1942 appeared in "The Effect of Human Relations on Food Habits in the Rural Southeast", *Applied Anthropology*, (April-June, 1942), pp. 13-18. Synopses of all the studies and an apprasisal of them are to be found in publications of the Committee on Food Habits, National Research Council, Washington, D.C.: *The Problem of Changing Food Habits*, Bulletin No. 108, (October, 1943), pp. 109-112, No. 111 (January, 1945), pp. 47, 56-57.

3. *Hearings*, p.44.

4. The main criticism of *Hunger, USA* seems to center on first, the assumption that there is a causal relationship between poverty and malnutrition, and second, that the 256 counties designated as Emer-

Dr. Arnold Schaefer that pockets of malnutrition exist throughout the United States, among the aged, adolescents, the urban ghetto-dwellers, the migrants, the rural poor, and to some extent among the well-to-do.

It is disturbing to find that Beaufort County, N.C. thirty years later when studied by the U.S. Department of Agriculture was *still* ranked at the bottom *D* grade (from 27-30% with poor diets).[5]

We know moreover, that, as Professor Zimmerman had long suggested, it was fallacious to subsidize farmers in restricting their production.[6] As one result farming is no longer the "family farm" but big business. Dr. Margaret Mead suggests that the Department of Agriculture be moved into the Department of Commerce. The list of 'surplus' commodities has not been well received, even as give-aways, either at home or abroad. Dr. Schaefer's National Nutritional Survey indicated that, if Texas results were indication, less than 10% of the $3000 for a family of four and under were receiving food stamps and commodities.[7] Furthermore, many of the items are not nutritionally valuable and need to be fortified to make them so.

Granted that the emergency nature of the World War II period, combined with the efforts of singularly gifted nutritionists, health educators and social scientists, produced some short-range victories. Vitamins were sold, almost oversold, with the result that foods fortified with vitamins helped to dispel pellagra and beri-beri. I would guess, however, that many cases are simply undiagnosed, to judge from the preliminary findings of the National Nutrition Survey. Granted that the combined efforts of the government and private food companies in the United States and

gency Hunger Counties included rural and urban families on the same bases, although rural families are in a better nutritional position. See *Hunger, USA*, New American Press, 1968, and *Hearings before the Select Committee on Nutrition and Human Needs of the U.S. Senate*, pp. 211 ff.

5. See *Hearings*, *ibid.*, p. 483.

6. C. C. Zimmerman, "Pathological Economics and Agriculture", *Rural Sociology*, June, 1956.

7. *Hearings*, p. 347.

of FAO overseas produced for the 1940's and early 1950's a remarkable climate of interest in seeing that people were well-fed. Some countries still had large peasant populations where protein deficiency did not show up on a subsistence farm.[8]

Unfortunately, population began to win its race with the food supply.[9] Mechanized farmers needed fewer helpers so that a double nutritional hazard developed: the huge farms produced a single cash crop, and the former rural share croppers migrated in hordes to the ghettos. The sons of the small farmers wanted to be 'professionals'. In the U.S. there was still an oversupply of food, indeed, in the 1960's there was for many an affluent society. It was thought that the problems centered on over-nutrition and obesity and that malnutrition was a dead issue. Thus, many who had learned the lessons of the 1940's felt that the nutrition situation was well in hand, whereas actually the United States suffered a regression. This situation was brought to light in the most recent surveys. It was true that obesity, lack of exercise, arteriosclerosis and a diet high in saturated fat was evidence of the malnutrition of the middle and upper classes.

The new deficiencies are only partially documented. However, we know that exotic diseases like marasmus and kwashiorkor are not confined to Ghana or India; we have cases right here among Indians and other rural poor. Dr. Michael Latham, Professor of International Nutrition in Cornell University fears that there are probably hundreds of undiagnosed cases.[10] Most of all, we know that much of the food eaten by some malnourished groups, the poor, the aged, the adolescents is protein-deficient. Also, iron deficiency anemia has been widely found. In the South, parasites exacerbated the effect of a poor dietary.

Somewhat puzzling to Senator McGovern's Select Com-

8. C. C. Zimmerman, "The Traditional Rural Village", unpublished p. 19.

9. C. C. Zimmerman, "The Population Explosion", unpublished article, p. 2.

10. *Hearings*, p. 45 and *Hearings*, p. 442.

mittee on Nutrition and Human Needs was the discovery that the food stamp plan was being only partially utilized by those for whom the bonus foods were intended. Why did only 10% out of ten million take advantage of food stamps that would increase purchasing power from $50 to $100 a month for a four-person family?

There were many answers. The commodities had low prestige – being 'surplus' made them inherently suspect. Or a poor family had to make an inordinate initial investment to be issued stamps, a system which was at variance with hand-to-mouth customs. Or local officials required many forms as proof of indigence, or made themselves available at inconvenient times.

All sorts of social mechanisms have been proposed for bettering the nutrition of the ten million Americans. For example, it has been generally agreed that person-to-person persuasion will prove to be successful. But who is to do the persuading – the nutritional aides employed by the Office of Economic Opportunity who "speak the language of the poor"? – Or should the nutrition educators represent the most knowledgeable and authoritative persons who can be secured?

Another issue has to do with making some surplus foods such as corn more advantageous nutritionally. In the 1940's flour had been fortified with vitamins. Now, for protein and iron deficient food, fortification is an obvious solution. For example, iodine has long fortified salt; lysine can double the protein in bread, a soybean drink which contains protein has 20 to 25% of the soft drink market in Hong Kong; amino acids may be added to pasta.

The catch then and the catch now is that nobody apparently wants to eat what is good for him. To the newer social scientists, it comes as a striking discovery that ". . . foods need to be considered in social-psychological aspects. . ."[11] People seem to be motivated (as had been true in the 1940's) by a desire to consume food and drinks which are prestigious. That is, in 1941 and 1942 store-

11. D. Gottlieb and P. Rossi, *Bibliography of Food Habit Research*, 1958.

bought and processed foods had more prestige for the rural sharecropper in the Southeast than his own home-produced eggs and butter. What you served to neighbors or to the parson was often the landlord's idea of quality food.[12]

In 1970, the dwellers in the urban ghettos of *Tally's Corner* or *La Vida* are undoubtedly still choosing carbonated drinks and convenience foods. What the prestige foods of a decade from now will turn out to be is a matter for speculation. The probability is that they will be foods in short supply, rather than surplus foods.

The issue is, then, how far do you depend upon nutrition education and economic means to salvage the ten million malnourished. Dr. Schaeffer says forthrightly that poverty and ignorance are the two culprits. I would suspect that money, wisely distributed, may prevent *hunger*, but not malnutrition. I would also wonder what disadvantages to society and even to the hungry persons might attend the billion and a half presently requested. Secretary Freeman calculated in 1969 that if a free school lunch were given to every child that the cost would be about four billion dollars a year.[13] Obviously these amounts are not hay. Could a Malnutrition Mafia develop around this sum? Can the food companies who undertake to fortify the foods be depended upon to keep consumer costs to a minimum?

As for nutrition education, I would hope that the overfed middle class and the 'beautiful' people would themselves hasten to choose the protein and iron-rich foods. If they do, these will be the prestige foods sought after by the malnourished as symbols of vertical mobility. If, on the contrary, we urge upon the poor, or anyone, a special series of food items on the ground that it is good for them and all they can afford, we are shrouding those foods with a taboo as surely as in any primitive religious tribe.

The topics for food habits research suggested by Margaret Mead have a wider series of variables: agricultural, economic, socio-cultural, educational, food-handling, and dietary

12. *'Twixt the Cup and the Lip*, *op. cit.*, pp. 110 ff.
13. *Hearings*, p. 239.

planning.[14]

Finally I believe I would follow the teaching of my mentor if I made the following suggestions in summary. First, the time is now to stop restricting farm production and to subsidize unwanted products. Second, fortification at minimum cost seems immediately practicable. So-called nutrition education may take decades if it is successful at all. Free breakfasts, free school lunches and, for adults, direct supplies of food made available in census tracts where need really occurs without red-tape for individuals seem fast remedies.

There is one caution. We know that malfeasance has occurred in Vietnam. It is troubling to hear, "Poverty is Out and Hunger is In". The billions at stake in the hunger program must find their way to the ultimate recipients.

A fierce interagency battle waged between Agriculture and Health, Education, and Welfare, seems likely to be resolved in favor of the latter. We would all be more comfortable if the administering agency would be somehow apolitical, or at least freed from too close political association. In any case sociological realists know that social change, even in food habits, has unexpected results.

July 1970

Margaret Cussler
University of Maryland

14. Margaret Mead, *Food Habits Research: Problems of the 1960's*, Natural Academy of Science, National Research Council Publication 1225, Washington, D.C., 1964, p. 22.

Acknowledgments

This study is the result of a photosynthesis of several different elements, the source of each one of which we are grateful to acknowledge.

The first element, in point of time, came from one of our Harvard professors, Dr. Carle C. Zimmerman, who had anticipated the national interest in the subject of food habits when he sent us to Seaford, North Carolina—a one-crop (tobacco) area—in the summer of 1940 to investigate the role of nutrition in the cultural changes in that community. For his original faith in us, and the first opportunity to explore this subject, we thank him profoundly. We are also indebted to him for an introduction to the sociology of the family, the community, and rural sociology—all of which have contributed to our understanding of the subject-matter of this book.

The second element was provided by Dr. M. L. Wilson. In addition to his indispensable service as Director of Extension, United States Department of Agriculture, he had also taken on the duties of Director of the National Nutrition Program, which was administered by the Nutrition Division, Office of Defense Health and Welfare Services, Federal Security Agency. Having seen the Seaford study, in November, 1941, he employed us and sent us back to Seaford, where we already had a benchmark, to evaluate the degree of success of the National Nutrition Program in such a community. Being aware of the importance of the socio-cultural element in nutrition and the scarcity of information on it, Dr. Wilson then sent us from Seaford to German Flats, South Carolina—where a live-at-home type of economy is prevalent—to observe the effects of a totally different cultural tradition—that of a group of descendants of German and Swiss colonists—upon the present-day nutrition of the community. We then went to Thoms County, Georgia, one of the best examples of a cotton economy we could find—to develop and observe a test county nutrition program, and to make a more intensive study of the local food habits in their relation to the culture and society. While unpublished reports on all three of these communities are in the files of the Nutrition Division (see footnote 3, Chapter 1), it is upon the data secured in Thoms County through the intensive methods used there that this study is largely based. To Dr. M. L. Wilson, therefore, must go our principal gratitude for the opportunity to develop further this subject of food habits. In the field of government administration, his great kindness and helpfulness, which manage to exist without jeopardizing his deep wisdom or effectiveness, distinguish him among his colleagues.

A third element consisted of the incalculable stimulation and insights which came to us in the person of Dr. Margaret Mead, who, while being Associate Curator of Anthropology, American Museum of Natural History, was also at that time Executive Secretary of the Committee on Food Habits of the National Research Council. This was established shortly after the National Nutrition Conference was called by President Roosevelt in May, 1941, to develop systematically the cultural and social aspects of nutrition. When the scores are totalled by time, we believe it will be found that no one has done so much to open up this "undeveloped area" of food habits, and push it to its full potentialities for the understanding and amelioration of nutritional problems, as has Margaret Mead. Besides the general ideological debt we owe her—not only with regard to this subject, but with regard to the whole subject of culture in general, and of personality and culture—there is a strongly-felt and gladly acknowledged personal debt for the gifts so freely given. In the early stages of this study she contributed greatly to its conceptual clarification, and also lent us important collateral material from her own library. She kept us in touch with the developing field of food habits research by inviting us to the meetings of the Committee on Food Habits and mailing us all the literature it issued. She read the field notes for this study and urged its publication. Dr. Patricia Woodward of the Committee on Food Habits has also earned our gratitude for her great helpfulness.

A fourth element entered into the photosynthesis of this work when Dr. Talcott Parsons of the Sociology Department, now the Department of Social Relations, Harvard University, generously consented to act as adviser to us, during Dr. Zimmerman's absence with the Army, when we were preparing this material for our doctoral theses at Radcliffe College. He, too, helped us to sharpen the edges of our conceptualizations of the problem, and turned what could have been a discouraging period into one of intellectual stimulation and hopefulness. We are permanently grateful to him for his interest and succor at that stage. Dr. Parsons also first oriented us in the subject of social structure, and from his memorable class on social institutions was derived our understanding of many of the social phenomena encountered in this study.

Dr. Forrest E. Clements, as Head of the Division of Special Surveys in the Bureau of Agricultural Economics, United States Department of Agriculture, has been directing some memorable pioneer studies in the field of consumer preferences. Since many of these are large-scale, we have drawn considerably upon them for validation of some of our own data.

In addition, there are the able scientists and government administrators in Washington who gave generously of their advice, among whom we wish especially to thank Dr. Hazel Stiebeling of the Bureau of Human Nutrition and Home Economics, Agricultural Research Administration, United States Department of Agriculture; Dr. Carl Taylor, Chief of the

Division of Rural Life and Welfare of the Bureau of Agricultural Economics, United States Department of Agriculture, and several members of his staff at that time, including Dr. Douglas Ensminger and Dr. John Provinse.

We also express thanks to our research assistants and secretaries in the field, Lois Nichols and Luna Mae Ivey, and, for her help in the preparation of this condensed version of our studies, Anna Quillen. There are our delightful landladies in Seaford and Westmore, Mrs. Lorena Godley, Miss Drucy Gaines, and Mrs. Mollie Brown, as well as our estimable hosts in German Flats, Mr. and Mrs. Harry Bauknight. Then, there were the many gracious and helpful public figures and leading citizens who facilitated our study. And finally, there were our many informants—necessarily nameless, but each one of whom remains sharp in our minds for the warm hospitality and generosity, the wit and the wisdom, which flowed from all of them so naturally.

College Park
Maryland

MARGARET CUSSLER
MARY L. DE GIVE

Contents

Acknowledgments 7

1 : FIRST OF ALL 17

The Problem So Far, 17—Source of Field Data and Method, 22.

2 : THEORIES OF FOOD IDEAS AND ATTITUDES 29

Attitudes toward Abstemiousness and Gluttony, 29—Food Regarded as a Source of Danger: Taboos, 30—Food and Social Interaction, 31—Meat as a Center of Emotional Disturbance, 32—The Prestige of Processed Foods, 35—Purity and Light Color in Foods, 36—Rarity and Cost and Effort, 36—Distinctions between Children's and Adults' Food, 36—Distinctions between Men's and Women's Food, 37—Distinctions between Rural and Urban Food, 37.

3 : IT'S A MATTER OF TASTE 41

The Individual and the Foodways, 41 — Shock Treatment, 44 — Temperature, 46 — Taste and Flavor, 46—Texture, 46—Appearance, 47—Evidence of Conflict: Discrepancy between Values and Practice, 50—Conflicts of Value: Nation and Region, 50—Conflicts within the Region, 51—Those Who Leave, 52 — Sanctions, 52 — Verbatim Case Material and the Foodways, 53.

4 : THE TRANSMISSION OF THE FOODWAYS: SOCIAL FACTORS 56

Adequacy of the Diet, 56—Adequacy of Nutritutional Information, 57—Back to the Land, 60—Routine of the Day, 61—Social Relations which Alter the Foodways, 62 — Cash Crops and Storebought Food, 63—Class Differences and the Food Pattern, 63—Family Relations and Food, 65—Informal Agencies for Transmitting the Foodways, 68—Race Relations, 71—Episodic Relations, 72.

5 : THE TRANSMISSION OF THE FOODWAYS (continued): HOW CHANGE OCCURS 79

Spreading the News, 79—Other Lines of Communication, 81—Periodicals, 81—Radio, 84—Motion Pictures, 84—Studies in the Effectiveness of Techniques, 85—The Dynamics of Food Habits, 89—Change through Outside Contacts, 89—Change Through Local Contacts, 91—The Function of Individual Preferences in the Process of Change, 91.

6 : TRADITION IN THE FOODWAYS 95

Anglo-Saxon Heritage, 95—Religious Background, 97—Attitude toward Living-at-home Practices, 99—Tradition in the Foodways, 101.

7 : SCIENCE TELLS US 105

Conflicts in Cultural Values: Tradition vs. Science, 105—Accent on Formal Education, 108—Rural Expression of Urban Superiority, 109—Rural Attitudes toward Urban Foodways: "Storebought" Foods, 110—Sale of Home-Grown Food Products, 110—Qualities Attributed to Purchased Food, 111—Negative Attitudes toward Rural Foodways, 112.

8 : THE CATERING PATTERN 116

Affability in Social Relations, 117—Visiting and Hospitality, 118—Freedom from Restrictions of Work and Time, 119—Catering to Family Food Preferences, 122—Sunday Dinner, 125.

9 : SOCIAL DISTINCTIONS IN THE FOODWAYS 129

10 : THE PREACHING AND THE PRACTICE 136

Standards for Food, 138—Nutritional Know-How, 139 — Disregarding the Nutritional Ideal, 140 — Rationalizations of Dietary Deficiencies, 141—Lack of Gardens and Garden Failures, 142—Wheat, 143 Canning, 143—Health, 144.

11 : FOODS WHICH SEEM EMOTION-CENTERED 147

Anxiety and Digestion, 148—Foods with Special Powers, 151—Highly Esteemed Foods, 152—"Such as Have Need of Milk, and not of Strong Meat," 153 —One Man's Meat, 154—Sweets, 156—A Food Carrying a Particular Aversion: English Peas, 157—"Light" and "Heavy" Foods, 158—Urban, Refined, Packaged and Purchased Foods, 159.

12 : IMPLICATIONS FOR FOOD POLICY 163

From out of the South, 163—Shifts in Consumption, 166—Foods for New Types of Families, 167—Food for an Aging Population, 168—Some Questionable Assumptions, 168.

APPENDICES

APPENDIX A : MAP AND DOCUMENTARY PHOTOGRAPHS 177

1 : Documentary Photographs 177
2 : Map of the Southeast showing general location of the three communities studied 192

APPENDIX B : OUTLINE USED IN INTENSIVE INTERVIEWS 193

APPENDIX C : EXAMPLE OF CASE MATERIAL SECURED BY INTENSIVE INTERVIEWS WITH ONE INFORMANT USING OUTLINE IN APPENDIX B 198

APPENDIX D : SUMMARY OF CENSUS DATA AVAILABLE FOR THOMS COUNTY, GEORGIA 229

APPENDIX E : DESCRIPTIVE DETAILS OF THE FOOD HABITS OF THE NEIGHBORHOODS OF WESTMORE AND GLEN, THOMS COUNTY, GEORGIA 232

Table I : The Food Supply 233

Table II : Basic Summer Diet 246

Table III : Seasonal Deviations from the Basic Diet 246

Table IV : Class Deviations from the Basic Diet 247

Table V : Racial Deviations from the Basic Diet 249

Table VI : Individual Deviations from the Basic Diet 250

Table VII : Circumstantial Deviations from the Basic Diet 251

Table VIII : Foods and Remedies for Diseases and Diseases Caused by Foods 254

Table IX : Trends in Food 255

Table X : Typical Menus in Westmore 256

INDEX 257

'TWIXT THE CUP AND THE LIP

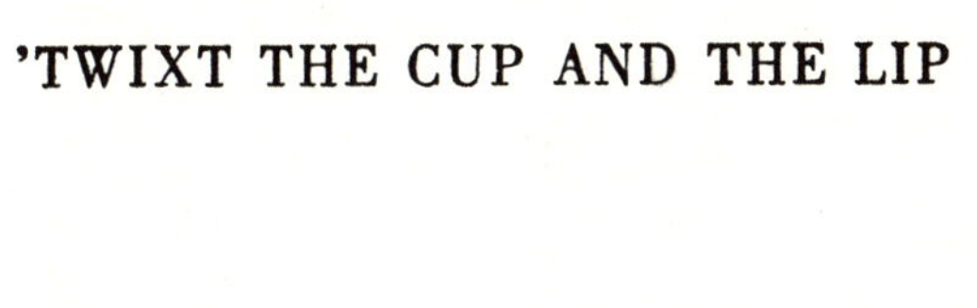

1

First of All–

Nutritionists are constantly discovering, with wonder and alarm, that man, that rational creature, often behaves unreasonably. The earth has yielded her fruits, and the secrets of her fruits, in "the new knowledge of nutrition." The food analyst took a long, close look at the universal aliment and found calories, vitamins, and minerals. He said, reversing Brillat-Savarin, "Tell me what you are, and I will tell you what you should eat." But it was not to be that easy.

Indeed, the area of food choices has seemed an area of great unreason. When they asked the British, "What would be your chief complaint about food at the moment [April, 1946], that it is monotonous and without variety, or that you do not get enough of it?", complaints focused on the monotony rather than the lack of food.[1] In this country, the whims and vagaries of consumers have been the despair of food processors. In time of war, the planning at desk and laboratory for Army messes is hampered by regional and personal tastes. Civilian point-rationing programs have to be constantly adjusted in the light of mysterious x-factors.

Nor did the consumer mend his ways in peacetime. There was still a great deal of apparent lack of logic in his food choices. But this time, with the rise of market research and the refinement of interviewing techniques, there was an attempt to find out just what this fellow, the consumer, wanted, anyway. So the questions were formulated, the sample was chosen, and the interviewers knocked on doors.

"In general," asked the interviewer disarmingly in one national survey, "why do you use fresh grapefruit?" The answer may be illuminating:

Why, we feel that it helps to give us an appetite. (Any other reason?) No, that's all I know. (How does it help to give you an appetite?) Oh, I just never thought much about it. I just don't know. (Any idea?) [Giggle—Giggle] I know I ought to try to help you out but I just never thought much about why we eat them—we just do.

Or, as Respondent 856, a rural Negro widow, said, "I have never ate either one, so I couldn't ruther about either one."

Thus it was evident that one of the major difficulties in consumer preference studies was the inarticulateness of the consumer. Even when you went to him at infinite trouble and expense and asked, he often couldn't tell you *why* he liked what he liked. A food taste is hard to explain; most people "just never thought much about it." The foodways are so profoundly a part of the folkways that they are accepted without conscious consideration.

Yet in spite of the difficulties, the area should not remain uncharted; study of food preferences should be carried forward. The world over, food and sex are major concerns, nor can we tell who will be the Freud of food. Moreover, there is reason to believe that food is particularly important to Americans. At any rate, the very bountifulness and scope of the table set in America means that here food choices are not restricted by a hand-to-mouth economy—and therefore that the range of factors affecting the American's choices of a particular food may be the more easily studied.

Doubtless it will be long before the psychological and socio-cultural factors affecting the food pattern are fully explored. It may be long before social science reveals, as science often does, the reasons behind apparent irrationality, the order in apparent disorder. At any rate, the task set here is a comparatively limited one. What are the psychological and socio-cultural factors affecting the food pattern—especially as they can be observed in one region, the rural South?

While the rural Southern dietary is specifically recorded here (see tables in Appendix E), it was rather the whole food pattern that was observed. The food pattern comprehends a number of elements associated with food aside from the dietary itself, such as food production, distribution, consumption, storage, preparation, choices, and attitudes in relation to food.

In many primitive societies the relation between the food pattern and the wider socio-cultural pattern is very obvious and direct; in fact, they are almost identical. For example, Radcliffe-Brown reports that social activity and social values for the Andaman Islanders center around securing food.[2] In modern societies the problem of survival becomes less directly concerned with food, shelter, and clothing. Securing these generally implies an occupation, but this may be so specialized as to have little direct connection with food-getting. Besides, in his capacities as husband, father, club-member, as well as bread-winner, an individual may be still further removed from the physical means of survival.

Similarly, a multitude of middlemen intervene between the producer and the consumer. Continents may stretch between the place of origin of a food and its point of consumption. Days, weeks, even years elapse between the harvest and the meal. Thus the relation between the food pattern and the socio-cultural pattern is by no means direct.

The rural Southern community described in this study is neither a primitive society nor a modern society, but one intermediate between the two. Here are the strong primary relationships of blood and emotion, but, at the same time, reliance upon distant cotton and tobacco markets. Here is the traditional preoccupation with the soil coincident with the technology, attitudes, and arts of a far more sophisticated society.

In this folk society of the rural South, then, we may expect to find no such identification between the food pattern and other elements as one would expect in an extremely simple community. On the other hand, the food pattern is much more directly associated with the wider socio-cultural pattern than it is in a modern urban society. The choice of this intermediate group was fruitful in its revelations about a relationship which is not too obscured.

The diet of this region is not conditioned solely by man's biological equipment, nor by the climate, soil, type of agriculture, nor by the social or economic system. All these factors affect the food pattern and are affected by it. It is probable that, more than all these, the traditional and contemporary attitudes and values of the local culture influence the food pattern. The local culture sifts and selects until only certain foods remain open to individual choice. These, too, are ranked more or less definitely until the final choice available for an individual's acceptance or rejection on the basis of individual experience is relatively limited, for often these experiences are themselves subconsciously colored by the common sentiment about certain foods. Thus, specific values basic to the culture of the South such as *tradition, respect for science, affability,* and *social distinction* have their counterparts in various aspects of the foodways. Documentation of these values, in both the general culture and in the foodways, is submitted as they become explicit in the verbatim case material.

We must note that the foodways in the area of our study may be far different from the foodways in the United States or the world as a whole. Furthermore, within this area, there are differences in personal tastes and values, and accordingly in diet, between persons of different classes, races, occupations, ages, and stages of health or disability, even though there is continual pressure upon all these deviant persons to conform to the general foodways.

These discrepancies become more important in the light of the League of Nations' assumption that the allocation of food budgets is a matter of intelligent choices. "Intelligent" in respect to what?—the values of one's family, one's class, one's caste, the neighborhood, the nation, or something more inclusive than all of these? It is true that these discrepancies constantly tend to disappear, but the evidence here indicates that there is a serious difference at present between local dietary practice and scientific theory.

It must be admitted that science is a major sanction in our culture. How people *should* eat has become a great new science entrusted to persons whose relations with farmers and housewives take on an encyclical authority. Indeed, the authority of science endows certain foods with the same kind of *mana,* or special supernatural power, as was attributed to certain articles of diet in primitive societies. Other food items are as rigidly tabooed.

Now that vitamin preparations have become popular and some foods enriched by legal dictum, doubters have appeared. Recalling that the official recommendations of nutritionists have done rather an about-face within twenty-five years, sceptics hold that the contemporary "newer knowledge of nutrition" may be followed by a "newer, newer knowledge of nutrition." Although the American Medical Association officially supports efforts for better nutrition, individual members have protested against some of the implications of the official policy. Some doctors feel that the techniques for appraising vitamin deficiency are still not far enough developed to justify scientific recommendations as to what is or is not the proper food to eat.

Beyond pointing out some doubts with respect to nutritional science, we cannot decide here whether certain foods rightly deserve this scientific sanction or disapproval. But it does make a tremendous difference what foods are so regarded, how far the people of a given area are aware of the current scientific view of these foods, and whether, being so aware, they change their eating habits accordingly. Whether the individual concerned is a sophisticated urban dweller who cannot secure butter in wartime, or a rural sufferer from pellagra in the South who cannot buy yeast or liver at the only accessible store, it is not only the so-called food deficiency itself but also the feeling about the deficiency which becomes significant.

Source of Field Data and Method

Findings based upon original research were derived from time spent in the field in the rural South in Seaford Township, North Carolina, German Flats, South Carolina, and Thoms County, Georgia, in 1940-1942, and from briefer participation in two consumer preference studies: on one of which, in Nelson County, Kentucky (1948) one of the authors (Margaret Cussler) acted as Study Director, and on the other in Prince Georges County, Maryland (1949) she acted as consultant.[8]

Several of these communities were originally chosen because they afforded characteristics in contrast to others in the series. Seaford is a rural coastal community, formerly of considerable political and religious significance in colonial Carolina, but now more devoted to its past glories than its future expectations. Its cash-crop tobacco sharecroppers may be contrasted with the live-at-home diversified farmers of German Flats, South Carolina. In turn, the people of Thoms County, Georgia, with a large proportion of long-term tenants, considered cotton their main crop, but were notable for their readiness to support soil conservation programs, bond drives, and the like. Both Nelson County in Kentucky and Prince Georges County in Maryland tended to prosper, partly because of contiguous industry, the former in the distilleries, the latter in the suburban area around Washington, D.C. Since much of the data was collected at a time when the National Nutrition Program was in its initial stages, we had the rare opportunity of making these observations during an extremely dynamic period.

The rural region from which most of the material is derived is a colorful one. The returning Southerner first notices the chinaberry trees green against the brown farmhouses perched on their stilts above the ground. At the roadside, this ground shows rust-red through trailing honeysuckle and, now, kudzu vines. It is a land where the tempo of affairs is slowed —a Negro lounges on top of a high-piled load of corn he is taking to the local mill to be ground into meal. Even in June the day soon grows hot, and men and mules are up early, stepping carefully between the rows of young cotton plants. By midday, the screen door of the general store at the cross-roads has squeaked open and shut many times, for this is a major place of talk and trade. In the little towns, the sun, beating down on the wide, flat buildings along Main Street, finds nobody about—only the rasping cry of the cicada swells and fades away in the stillness. At length the sun is spent, dusk comes, and squares of light show here and there along the road. This is the time to make excuse to take a walk, down to the meeting at the church, to the store to make a purchase that *could* have waited, or just to breathe the scent of honey-suckle when a breeze comes up.

Our studies were not nutrition studies as such, for they are the province of trained nutritionists or medical personnel, and of government bureaus, college departments, laboratories, and foundations devoted exclusively to nutrition research and education. Having no trained nutritionist or doctor with us, and finding it impossible to attempt a direct medical evaluation of the nutritional status of the population, we had to use an indirect method, i.e., we estimated the nutritional adequacy of the diet by analyzing it in terms of the nutritive value of the foods eaten compared with the dietary allowances recommended by the National Research Council. These were originally worked out in connection with our first Seaford study, and are given there in tabular form. In the subsequent studies, we did not seek to establish the nutritional status so laboriously, but applied inductively the criteria of nutritional adequacy developed in the first study. Our own appraisals of nutritional status of the population were checked against the experience of medical men working on the subject, such as Dr. D. F. Milam and Dr. J. M. Ruffin of Duke University; Dr. I. H. Moore of Sparta, Georgia; Dr. Lucy Morgan of the United States Public Health Service; Dr. Wilkins and his research associate, Miss French Boyd; and others.

The techniques used in all of our studies were more qualitative than quantitative, though in the first two Seaford studies our method was more an extensive survey, in which the population of Seaford Township was systematically checked by interviewing the occupants of every tenth house along every road, using a prepared questionnaire, while in the Thoms County study we used both the extensive survey in the two neighborhoods studied and the repeated intensive personal interview with several informants. This latter method especially reveals those subtler aspects of the food pattern in a culture than could be reached by any other method. The later consumer preference studies on citrus and cantaloupe made use of current techniques in mass sampling, interviewing, and coding.

The facts thus gained were cross-checked by reference to census materials, annual reports of various government agencies, and other local surveys, as well as interviews with persons occupying significant roles in the society, such as the county agent, the doctor, the country storekeeper, the preacher, the Negro school superintendent, and teachers.

While in the field we lived on farms and were introduced to the people of the locality by persons of established standing in the community—a very important precaution in any community research. We were not strictly participant-observers in that we openly stated our purpose and took notes and photographs. Nevertheless, we did participate as fully as possible in such community activities as church services, Ladies' Aid and Missionary Society meetings, P. T. A. and Home Demonstration Club meetings, church picnics, tobacco-barn parties, square dances, swimming and fishing trips, and Farm Bureau and other civic meetings. We eventually came to know almost every family in the two neighborhoods of Thoms County we were studying.

One of the dangers which field research in so highly stratified a society as the rural South entails is that the informants chosen and the contacts made may be mainly among the White owner class. Correction for this possible error was made by choosing informants proportionally among Whites and Negroes, owners, sharecroppers, and wage-laborers. The classifications which were used were those of race and agricultural class.[4] Class of land tenure does not invariably denote social and economic status, but we found it roughly useful for distinguishing social class. Where we do venture to qualify a classification, as when we say "a White landowner (low class)," the estimate is based upon the position which that person actually occupies in the social scale in the eyes of others in the community.

After choosing informants for the intensive interviewing, one of us visited them regularly with a stenographer who took down in shorthand a verbatim record of all that was said. While following a topic outline (see Appendix B), we tried to keep the interviews as "open-ended" as possible, leaving plenty of chance for free association of ideas. The whole interview situation became highly informal, with the stenographer sitting unobtrusively and forgotten in a corner. In this way a range and depth of material was secured from the informants that could have been gotten in no other way.

Documentary photography provided a device for securing supplementary data on the physical milieu, and also provided some insights into the social and cultural milieu.[5] Besides a collection of still shots, a movie in color and sound, *You Can't Eat Tobacco,*[6] depicting socio-economic factors affecting nutrition in the rural, one-cash-crop South, was produced in the course of these studies. An additional advantage proved to be the entrée which photography gave to homes when it was desirable to check the behavioral pattern with regard to food against the ideal pattern. Also, the popularity of local showings of scenes from local movies facilitated continued work in the community.

It was early recognized that there were possible difficulties inherent in the multiple role of field researchers, government representatives, and members of the White race. For example, the role of government representative might have limited the persons chosen for informants, the type of information secured, and the interpretation of the results. The very recognition of such dangers was a principal safeguard. As a matter of fact, the role of government representatives enabled us to cut across local group barriers and take advantage of considerable freedom, especially in interviewing Negro informants. Also, working as women with women informants on a topic so closely associated with women's traditional work appears to have its advantages, especially since our broader interest in the whole food pattern and the folkways afforded us general contacts. Finally, a certain advantage lay in the fact that one author, as a Northerner, could check her objective observations against her Southern colleague's intimate subjective familiarity with the culture.

NOTES

1. British Institute of Public Opinion, April, 1946.
2. A. Radcliffe-Brown, *The Andaman Islanders* (Cambridge, University Press, 1922), p. 277
3. Seaford, North Carolina, was originally chosen by Dr. Carle C. Zimmerman for study as one of a series of community personality studies because, although once the capital of the colony, it is now an isolated village of about 300 inhabitants, and shows many characteristics of a retrogressive community. Unpublished studies have been made for Dr. Zimmerman of its history (Charles Reynard), its literature (Margaret T. Cussler), as well as a published account in *Interrelations between the Cultural Pattern and Nutrition,* Mary L. de Give and Margaret T. Cussler, United States Department of Agriculture, Extension Service Circular 366 (August, 1941). The authors studied

Seaford in July-August, 1940, and November-February, 1941-42. Later materials on Seaford were compiled in an unpublished study for the Nutrition Division, Office of Defense Health and Welfare Services, Federal Security Agency, *Some Cultural Factors Affecting the Nutritional Situation*, Margaret T. Cussler and Mary L. de Give, and in a published account: "Let's Look It in the Eye," *Consumer's Guide* (March 15, 1942).

Field study of German Flats, near Columbia, South Carolina, was carried on in February-March, 1942, and compiled in an unpublished study for the Nutrition Division, *Home Grown Food and Homely Virtues*, Margaret T. Cussler and Mary L. de Give.

Field study of Thoms County, Georgia, extended from March to mid-June, 1942, and was reported principally in two unpublished doctoral theses written by the authors for Radcliffe College (Harvard University) in 1943: *Social Interrelations and Food Habits in the Rural Southeast*, Mary L. de Give, and *Cultural Sanctions of the Food Pattern in the Rural Southeast*, Margaret T. Cussler. Part of the research was also reported in an unpublished manual written for the Nutrition Division, June, 1942: *From Cotton to Calories: What a Southeastern Rural County Nutrition Committee Can Do in the National Nutrition Program.*

Shorter published accounts of all these studies appeared in: "The Effect of Human Relations on Food Habits in the Rural Southeast," *Applied Anthropology*, (April-June, 1942), pp. 13-18, and in "Foods and Nutrition in Our Rural Southeast," *Journal of Home Economics*, 35:380-382, 1943. Synopses of all the studies and an appraisal of them are to be found in publications of the Committee on Food Habits, National Research Council, Washington, D. C.: *The Problem of Changing Food Habits*, Bulletin of the National Research Council, No. 108, (October, 1943), pp. 109-112, and *Manual for the Study of Food Habits*, Bulletin of the National Research Council, No. 111 (January, 1945), pp. 47, 56-57.

Statements about any of the communities studied are supported in these more detailed studies. Statistical data are to be found in Appendix D.

The consumer preference studies in which Dr. Cussler participated in the summers of 1948 and 1949, the published accounts of which are forthcoming, are tentatively titled: *Consumer Preferences Regarding Citrus Fruit* (Division of Special Surveys, Bureau of Agricultural Economics, United States Department of Agriculture) and *Consumer Preferences Regarding Cantaloupe* (Maryland State Department of Markets).

4. Landowner: one who owns rural farm land.
   Tenant: one who rents rural farm land for farming and supplies his own equipment.
   Sharecropper: one who farms someone else's land for shares (usually half the crop), and is supplied the horse, fuel, work-stock, tools, seed, and half the fertilizer by the landlord.
   Wage-laborer: one who works on a farm for wages.
5. The uses of documentary photography in sociological research have

been described in an article by the authors, "The Innocent Eye," in *Rural Sociology* (September, 1942), pp. 335-337, and also in two articles by Margaret T. Cussler, "Film-Making as a Focus of Social Forces in an Indian Tribe," in *Rural Sociology* (September, 1946), pp. 362-65 and "Documentary Films and the Scientist-Producer," in *American Anthropologist*, n. s. (April-June, 1948). An account of how the movie, *You Can't Eat Tobacco,* came to be made appeared in an article by the authors, "Cine-Camera Surveys the Sharecropper," *Home Movies*, 440 (October, 1944), pp. 410-411. Probably the most outstanding demonstration of the use of photography in cultural analysis is to be found in a publication by Gregory Bateson and Margaret Mead, *Balinese Character* (New York Academy of Sciences, 1942).

6. Distributed by New York University Film Library.

2

Theories of Food Ideas and Attitudes

Among all the different ideas attached to foods at various times and in various cultures, certain ideas recur consistently. There is little evidence that these foodways have developed in either chronological or evolutionary order. But the reappearance of similar taboos and sanctions makes them significant. There will be occasion later to compare these theories with the prevailing food customs in the local areas studied.

Always linked with the universal process of eating is the factor of social approval or disapproval of various foods. It is difficult to attempt a logical explanation of social approval or disapproval with regard to food. The origin of such attitudes is indeed largely emotional in many instances rather than logical. And what appears to be logical or reasonable to us might seem the opposite to the originators of the food attitude in question. The effort here is directed toward gathering into some order the universal theories which have surrounded food through the centuries.

Attitudes toward Abstemiousness and Gluttony

Ascribing superior qualities to the ascetic, and inferior qualities to the gluttonous, is typical of the traditional attitude toward overeating and undereating found in our own and many older societies. Many of the major religions of the world, including Christianity, Judaism, Taoism, Buddhism, Zoroastrianism, and Islam, establish periods of restriction in food or restricted foods which indicate that food is felt to be carnal. Among classic writers, disapproval for intemperate eating is voiced by Aristotle,[1] Pliny,[2] Porphyry,[3] Tertullian,[4] Cicero,[5] and Lucian.[6] The Biblical proverb that "the glutton shall come to poverty,"[7] and the association of religious ceremonies with fasting, found expression in the dietary restrictions of Lent, Fridays, and yearly fast days.

However, it does not seem logical to suppose with Spencer[8] and Westermarck[9] that eating beyond that amount which is biologically necessary is associated with lower stages of culture, while temperance and asceticism are associated with advanced societies. For one thing, what observers of primitive societies called "eating to excess" may actually have only seemed so, in view of the irregularity of the food supply and the lack of storage facilities among certain tribes. These circumstances required that the food on hand had to be eaten to be saved. Thus, in the Southern cotton and tobacco areas, a period of plenty during the autumn after the harvest is followed by a period of food scarcity, roughly from December to April.

It has often been indicated that primitive social structure is not necessarily simple social structure, and in the same way primitive ideas about food are often exceedingly complex. The number of foods forbidden absolutely or at certain times must impose a kind of abstemiousness which could challenge that of the most sophisticated culture.

Food Regarded as a Source of Danger: Taboos

Apart from the feeling that eating all foods and too much food is not so commendatory as eating certain foods in moderation, positive and negative feelings have grown up about certain items of the diet. In most cultures, for example, there are taboos against eating human flesh, horsemeat, cats, dogs, and rats. These taboos are only relaxed under the stress of disaster, and particularly of famine. Sorokin has given historical evidence of the disappearance of food taboos under the pressure of famine, and instances of "the modifications of ideas, beliefs, convictions, ideologies, and speech reactions effected by hunger."[10] In the disaster of famine, a starving individual will eat anything nutritious, as well as such objects as clay, powdered stone, and bark which may give him a feeling of satisfaction.

But in situations falling short of the severity of famine, the negative feeling toward food in general or toward specific foods often flourishes. In this connection, the belief of the Ewe-speaking peoples of the Slave Coast, that the indwelling spirit leaves the body and returns to it by the mouth, is cited by Frazer as the explanation of the "source of danger" attitude toward eating.[11] Thus, a man must be careful about opening his mouth, lest while his own spirit has gone out, a homeless spirit take advantage of the absence to enter the body through the open mouth. Many primitive peoples are ashamed to be seen eating, and eat hastily without looking at one another or speaking, seeming to feel that the mouth must be protected from this danger.

A positive attribute, a kind of supernatural power, attaches to foods as they are used to mark the passage from one state of life into another: that is, in baptism, wedding, funeral, and other ceremonies. This special power seems most often attributed either to the staple foods like meat, millet, or yams, or to rare foods such as turtles or grubs, and less to foods ranging between these two values. Frazer believes that positive power and negative taboos indicate the savage's desire or fear of acquiring attributed qualities.

Food and Social Interaction

The dangerous supernatural force associated with certain foods is often dispelled by the purifying influence of a ritualistic meal which serves as reassurance to the individual. The successful completion of hunting, fishing, herding, and gardening efforts is often marked by some sort of social observance in eating, ranging from a simple family meal to a Thanksgiving celebration for a whole nation.

Even in primitive societies, and certainly among today's interdependent civilized nations, the effort to secure food usually requires cooperative effort. Even the relative simplicity of hunting, fishing, herding, and gardening require cooperation among members of the family unit or the community in most instances. And as eating is so intimately associated with the family unit, eating together often implies a kind of kinship. Perhaps the taboo against inter-racial dining in the South is so much stronger than against inter-class dining because of this connotation of implied kinship.

In any case, for whatever purpose, securing food and eating together does entail an intensifying of communication and an increase of the rate of interaction to a degree found in no other act repeated so constantly.

Meat as a Center of Emotional Disturbance

When Shakespeare wished to concoct a witches' brew in *Macbeth* which should outrage every moral sensibility, he made rich use of the nauseating emotions associated with various kinds of animal substances:

FIRST WITCH
Round about the cauldron go;
In the poison'd entrails throw.
Toad, that under cold stone
Days and nights has thirty-one
Swelter'd venom sleeping got,
Boil thou first i' the charmed pot.

SECOND WITCH
Fillet of a fenny snake,
In the cauldron boil and bake;
Eye of newt and toe of frog,
Wool of bat and tongue of dog,
Adder's fork and blind-worm's sting,
Lizard's leg and howlet's wing,

For a charm of powerful trouble
Like a hell-broth boil and bubble.

THIRD WITCH Scale of dragon, tooth of wolf,
Witches' mummy, maw and gulf
Of the ravin'd salt-sea shark,
Root of hemlock digg'd i' the dark,
Liver of blaspheming Jew,
Gall of goat and slips of yew
Silver'd in the moon's eclipse,
Nose of Turk and Tartar's lips,
Finger of birth-strangled babe
Ditch-deliver'd by a drab,
Make the gruel thick and slab:
Add thereto a tiger's chaudron,
For the ingredients of our cauldron.

SECOND WITCH Cool it with a baboon's blood.
Then the charm is firm and good.[12]

It is immediately noticeable in this review that only an occasional item is of other than animal character or derivation.

Why is it that the idea of eating rats, cats, dogs, grubs, and horses offends many people in the world (though not all) more than eating the bark of trees, poisonous fungi, or clay?

One of the chief anthropomorphic and animistic explanations advanced is that man recognizes the kinship between himself and everything else in nature that lives, and feels guilt in violating that kinship by slaughter. Under the same principle, pets in our society are banned as sources of food, and even sometimes cattle and poultry which have been expressly raised for food.[13] Less believable is the explanation that meat aversion is conditioned by the primitive belief that what one eats becomes part of oneself, because that would not explain the preference for pork over squirrel, for instance. Nor does regard to the diet of the animal in question seem to have much weight. We say in disapproval, "He eats like a pig," but we do not show the same disapproval in "He eats pork."

Analysis of food taboos and of religious dietary restrictions as well as scientific controversy shows that collective approval or disapproval has centered about the eating of meat to a degree far out of proportion to its nutritive value. Where it is not censured, meat ranks high among preferred foods.

But just as asceticism has been associated with the highest good, vegetarianism has also acquired a connotation of special value. Many religions besides Christianity place restrictions on meat-eating, especially for holy men on special occasions. Robert Burton, in summarizing the opinion of the classics, calls beef "A strong and hearty meat which breeds gross melancholy blood . . . good for such as are sound but unfit for such as lead a resty life." He also casts doubts upon the digestibility of pork, goat, hare, fowl, and fish.[14]

In a now famous experiment, V. Stefansson proved that a person could live at least one year on an exclusively meat diet. During the course of his experiment, he described himself as the bane of hostesses. Their desire to press other morsels upon him for hospitality's sake finally compelled him to present the following sample menu along with the acceptance of a dinner invitation:

> *Hors d'œuvres*
>
> Caviar served on slices of white chicken breast, each about the size and thickness of a fifty-cent piece.
>
> *Soup*
>
> Broth made by boiling meat—in some cases bone.
>
> *Fish*
>
> Any kind of fish boiled or baked; if fried, then in bacon fat.
>
> *Entrée*
>
> Lamb chops. (Most hostesses preferred to garnish with bacon.)
>
> *Dessert*
>
> Gelatin, solely of meat origin and made according to a recipe.
>
> *Demi-tasse*[15]

That meat ranks high as a preferred food in contrast to soups and vegetables was indicated in a study of 123,000 man meals in 38 mess halls, to see what soldiers left on their plates to be thrown away. While 52 per cent of the soup and 38 per cent of the edible vegetables were discarded, only 18 per cent of the edible meats reached the garbage can.[16]

The Prestige of Processed Foods

Processed foods are often felt to be more healthful, and in this way more desirable, than foods consumed in a natural state, particularly since such foods are often presented with some sort of covering. Packaged, canned, wrapped foods, and bottled liquids at present have become endowed with the connotation of the pure, the sanitary, and the healthful.

While home-raised food is highly prized in the South, some handlers of food have been observed to have a distaste for products which they handle, as a dairyman for milk, or a farmer for pork, or a corn-grower for corn-on-the-cob. Yet, where this occurred in the South, it was noticeable that there might be an even greater acceptance of and liking for milk by the dairyman, if it was canned; of ham by the farmer, if it was "store-bought," boiled ham; and of corn, if it reappeared in the form of corn meal.

The process of changing the appearance of foodstuffs involves techniques which are indices to the complexity of civilizations. Milling by the use of a hand pestle produces a flour more like the original grain than the product of elaborate modern milling processes. Refined flours, elaborate recipes, sauces, dehydrated foods, polished rice, hydrogenated vegetable oils, refined sugars, and refined lard represent modern developments in processing which, in spite of scientific opposition, are felt by many persons to be superior to foods in a more natural state.[17] The feast of Lucullus, with molded birds and elaborate pastries, shows us how culinary artifice assumes prestige in the sophisticated Roman society. Burton recapitulates the long list of classic authors' warnings against such unrefined foods as roots, raw herbs and salads, and fruits.[18]

Purity and Light Color in Foods

It is significant that much effort in connection with the processing and refining of foods has been directed toward lightening their color. Flour, for example, has undergone elimination of the yellow wheat germ as well as of the bran, and moreover, it is often chemically bleached. The most sought-after grades of rice are the most polished. White sugar is preferred to brown, and light syrup and honey to darker varieties.

Rarity, Cost, and Effort

As has been said, supernatural qualities often attach to rare foods obtainable only after great effort, like the Andaman Islanders' turtles. In a capitalistic society, the high price of a food implies both effort and rarity. This is one reason why purchased foods are in such repute among the rural Southerners. They represent expenditure of hard-won cash. Since cash is hard to come by, few such foods can be bought, but the few that are add variety to a monotonous diet. Canned pineapple, grapefruit, salmon, and spaghetti come within this category.

Distinctions between Children's and Adults' Food

Certain foods have been considered especially suitable for children as distinguished from those suitable for adults. The character of these foods has been closely connected with the character of the society. A child-centered society like ours is likely to reserve for children its purest foods, its most processed, premasticated pabulum, whatever is rare, expensive, light-colored, packaged, and vegetarian, in accordance with the values previously outlined. This food is administered under the conditions considered optimum for good digestion, at regular intervals.

Distinctions between adult and children's food may result in a revolt by the child against his victuals, so that he may insist upon coffee, for instance, in place of milk as an indication of maturity. It would thus be unfortunate if all especially nourishing foods were relegated to the province of childhood. Fortunately, however, the pleasant associations of maternal solicitude appear to have overcome such a tendency of lasting revolt against children's food.

Distinctions between Men's and Women's Food

Distinctions between men's food and women's food have been made to a lesser extent. Many more distinctions giving preference to men in the time of eating, conditions of eating, and the choice of food exist, for instance, among the Todas, the Chinese, the Eskimos, the Tikopia, and the Navaho. In modern American society, foods like steak, roast beef, potatoes, and apple pie are quite frequently considered "men's food," in contrast to salads, whipped-cream concoctions, and soufflés, which are associated with women. Such distinctions do not seem to operate with much constraint upon individual tastes and are not well formulated. As might be expected in the predominantly authoritarian family society of the South, men are often given first choice of foods and control the store purchases. They seem less inclined to experiment with new foods, preferring those which are "old-timey."

Distinctions between Rural and Urban Food

Among rural residents, the food of villagers and urban dwellers has acquired positive sanction. It is paradoxical that this should be so in the matter of food where the advantages so obviously lie in rural hands.[19]

Summary

The sanctions attached to food have not been developed to serve exclusively utilitarian or rational goals, at least as far as we can discover. While the sources and goals of such ideas are not to be explained through reason, the theories surrounding food habits tend to group themselves in strongly positive or negative patterns.

Widely held are the ideas that discriminating choice is preferable to lack of discrimination, that food has a dangerous magical force for ill as well as for good, that certain foods must be avoided and others eaten. The numerous taboos in connection with food, in use among both primitive and sophisticated cultures, are relaxed in proportion to the existence of hunger and famine.

Food has been an agency for social interaction in its production, preparation, and consumption. It has been the starting point for intensified communication of all sorts, in ritual, family, and kinship situations and on occasions of ordinary hospitality.

Positive and negative attitudes have seemed to center most around meat, among all the items of diet. Positive sanctions have attached to vegetarian foods while meat has often been proscribed. Most culturally banned foods to which particular revulsion attaches are of animal origin. This has been variously explained as an instance of man's innate regard for life in any form, his disinclination to eat anything similar to himself, and his distaste at the unclean habits of animals; but such theories must remain speculations.

Changing the appearance of food usually involves complex techniques proportionate to the degree of civilization, so that highly milled and refined foods hold an approved position.

The fact that a food is *rare* often makes it prized, and this often implies higher cost in modern societies.

Aside from the widely held attitudes toward food, there are attitudes that are characteristic of *modern urban civilization* chiefly, and concepts that are significant chiefly in the region of the rural South. Among the former are the preferences for light-colored foods over dark-colored, adult over children's foods, men's over women's, scientifically sanctioned foods over "unscientific" foods. In the rural South, there is, among other attitudes, much stress on urban as opposed to rural, purchased as opposed to home-raised food, and food associated with the White owners as opposed to that of the Negro members of lower classes. Later sections of the study will state and document many other such food attitudes.

These distinctions are not strictly adhered to in any one cultural area. Individual variations take place; taboos are weakened under the exigency of crises; new foods and food techniques are introduced; and changes in the mores occur which serve to weaken or strengthen the preferential position of individual foods.

At first glance, there seems to be no order in the chaos of dietary customs. Every edible food has been eaten at some time, somewhere, with social approval, and each of these foods has been somewhere proscribed. What intelligible groupings one can make are highly tentative. Such patterns prove nothing; they tell us little that is positive; but they suggest much.

NOTES

1. Aristotle, *Ethica Nicomachea* III, 10, 10. ". . . since it belongs to us in that we are animals, not in that we are men."
2. Pliny, Libr. 11, c. 52.
3. *De Abstinentia,* 11, 44.
4. *De Oratione,* 19.
5. *De Officiis,* 30.
6. *De Luctu.*
7. Proverbs 23:21.
8. Herbert Spencer, *Principles of Sociology* (New York: 1891-1897), Vol. I, p. 80: "The progress from the less intelligent to the more intelligent and the most intelligent among the *Vertebrate* is similarly accompanied by increasing ability in the selection of food."
9. Edward Westermarck, *The Origin and Development of the Moral Ideas* (London: Macmillan and Co., Ltd., 1908), Vol. II, p. 291.
10. Pitirim A. Sorokin, *Men and Society in Calamity* (New York: E. P. Dutton and Co., 1942), Chapter III.
11. Sir James G. Frazer, *The Golden Bough* (New York: Macmillan and Co., 1927), p. 198.

12. *Macbeth,* Act IV, Scene 1, ll. 4-38.
13. Cf. Sir John Mandeville in *Fable of the Bees*:
"... some people are not to be persuaded to taste of any creatures they have daily seen and been acquainted with, whilst they were alive; others extend their scruple no further than to their own poultry, and refuse to eat what they fed and took care of themselves; yet all of them will feed heartily and without remorse on beef, mutton, and fowls, when they are bought in the market."
(Cited by Westermarck, *The Origin and Development of the Moral Ideas,* Vol. II, p. 329.)
14. Robert Burton, *The Anatomy of Melcancholy* [1651] (London: William Tegg and Co., 1894), p. 141.
15. Vilhjalmur Stefansson, *Not by Bread Alone* (New York: The Macmillan Company, 1946), p. 74.
16. Roy F. Hendrickson, *Food "Crisis"* (New York: Doubleday, Doran, 1943).
17. James Rorty and Phillip Norman, *Tomorrow's Food* (New York: Prentice Hall, Inc., 1947), Chapter 10.
18. Burton, *op. cit.,* pp. 143, 144.
19. Valuable works that should be cited in connection with this discussion are: Richard O. Cummings, *The American and His Food* (Chicago: The University of Chicago Press, 1940) and Mark Graubard, *Man's Food: Its Rhyme or Reason* (New York, Macmillan, 1943).

3

It's a Matter of Taste: The Individual and the Foodways

The discussion here centers about that relationship which has been variously called the individual and society, personality and culture, heredity and environment,—elements which are not opposed, though they have often been so treated. Part of this relationship is the more specific tie-up between individual food habits and the general foodways.

Even at the stage of birth, the individual in a pure state of individuality can scarcely be found. Prenatal environmental influences have already been at work upon him. The individual is born with a certain physical equipment, reflexes, intellectual potentialities, and probably with some specific inherited tendencies, though these are so complex in nature that they are only now being seriously studied. All of these individual capacities are significant in relation to food habits. It is obvious, for instance, that good or poor digestion, the existence of allergies, and the rate of metabolism directly concern food choices. The degree of intelligence may determine the access an individual has to scientific information about food or the economic and occupational status to which he may attain in order to procure food. Finally, however hot the argument may rage over inherited tendencies, we can probably agree that the degree of an individual's receptivity to outside influences affects the conventionality or unusual nature of his diet. Concerning this, Dr. Arnold Gesell says:

We recognize that it is artificial to set up a dichotomy, but I think it is profitable to realize that our problems begin with the organism itself. By the organism, I am thinking of that bundle of protoplasm which is called a baby. The baby was once a fetus. In a certain sense the problems of food habits and food cravings begin as far back as the prenatal period, because the appetites and cravings of the mothers, which vary from pregnancy to pregnancy, are themselves a biological indication of specific nutritional conditions in the fetus. Very little is known of this very important subject. More will be known in time because certain feeding problems undoubtedly are postponed residuals of faulty maternal hygiene.[1]

One of the major questions that has been posed is whether or not food selections are made on the basis of biological need. Does a child's vehement rejection or preference in respect to liver or cake represent a striking instance of Nature's wisdom in achieving a balanced diet for the individual? Can you trust a cow to choose the most vitamin-rich pasturage? Will a rickets-ridden rat show a preference for Vitamin D foods? To answer this, psychologists have devised some ingenious rat cafeterias in which a choice of items is available. The choices have been recorded, as well as the intensity of preference as indicated by the speed with which rats ran toward various food samples, and the relative time spent in exploring the sample.

On the basis of repeated experiments with rats, Paul Thomas Young believes that food selections probably do not reveal needs because: 1. Marked food preferences develop when no known metabolic benefit is being provided, as indicated by rats preferring water sweetened with saccharin to plain water. 2. The quantity of a particular foodstuff that is consumed varies markedly with characteristics other than its chemical constitution. 3. If foodstuffs are presented under optimal conditions, an animal may eat to excess, and poisons, if pleasant, are eaten. 4. When there is a need, as in the case of rickets, rats fail to show a preference for foods rich in Vitamin D. Young concludes by adding, "Our work leads to the view that rats accept foods which they *like* (find enjoyable) and that foods differ in the degree to which they arouse immediate enjoyment."[2]

If rats become obese or scrawny in the sinful course of eating what they like rather than what is good for them, people do, too. But the next question that arises is, just what are the qualities about a given food item that make it desirable? Here, of course, we are considering *psycho-physical qualities* as distinguished from values derived from social or cultural sources.

Proverbially, it's all a matter of individual taste, not a matter for disputing or further inquiry. "One man's meat is another man's poison." And to a certain degree it is scientifically accurate to note that individuals differ widely in the physical characteristics of their taste buds. When one person likes three lumps of sugar in his coffee and another, one, it is likely that the difference in their thresholds for the perception of sweetness is at least one factor involved. In addition, physical changes in the perceptors of taste take place in old age as opposed to infancy in the course of the life of a given person. Interviewers know how often people answer when asked *why* they like a particular food, "Oh, I don't know—I just like the taste, the flavor, I guess."

Is such an answer a dead end? Or are there certain physical qualities about foods which seem pleasing to enough people sufficiently often to tell us something of what is behind such vague terms as taste or flavor? In a pioneer discussion of this point in *The Origin of Food Habits,* H. D. Renner points out the range of the physical properties involved in the process of eating:

> We are seated at a table; on the table, immediately in front of us, is a dish exhaling odours. We perceive the odours before beginning to eat, more intensely when the dish is hot than when it is cold. (There are people who claim that by this time they know whether they are going to like the dish or not.) Now we take a spoon or fork and raise some of the food to our mouth, passing it under the nostrils in so doing. Thus

bringing the food nearer our nose, we intensify the effect on our sense of smell. By the time the food enters the mouth, the nose is already familiar with almost all that can be perceived in the way of smell from this food. There are of course a few exceptions, as, for instance, if we eat any form of orange peel. The molar teeth work like a press in squeezing out volatile oils, thus making them even more perceptible than before. But as a rule a constant stream of odours reach the nose before the mouth, so that by the time they are inside the mouth they are already in an atmosphere partly accustomed to them.[8]

Likewise, when an informant in the rural South was asked why she preferred white grapefruit to the pink variety, she answered:

They ain't got as many seeds in them. The pink ones are lousy with seeds. Then the white ones don't have that old tough heart in them. You can peel the white kind and pull slabs off just like oranges.

One begins, then, to understand that liking is not a matter of biological need, nor of the taste alone, but a rich interplay of physical properties of foods, such as temperature, taste and flavor, texture, and appearance. These will be discussed later in more detail.

Shock Treatment

Much emphasis has been laid on the effect of certain physical shocks on food aversions. For example, the trauma involved in sudden weaning is often referred to. While it is interesting to speculate whether a person early deprived of the breast will, as an adult, prefer to eat oranges by sucking them, or become a person with pronounced food likes and dislikes, the extent and importance of the weaning trauma, if it exists, will have to wait upon further study.

In some areas of the country, it is popularly believed that there is a certain definite time at which the child should be weaned, and that nothing should be allowed to upset this split-second time table.

In the rural South, there is a more easy-going attitude toward weaning, as toward most of the other problems of child-bearing. Mothers are likely to be more permissive, and to permit their babies more self-determination in the matter of when they shall be weaned as well as when they shall sleep or wake. This condition, as Dr. Ruth Benedict has suggested, tends to minimize the resentments which individuals have to work off in their adult life, as well as to increase the sense of security which the child may enjoy.[4]

One young mother, a white Farm Security client, has an unusually close association with her only child, a boy of two and a half. He runs up to her at any time during the day, climbs onto her lap and tries to nurse. When strangers are around, she abashedly tries to deflect him from his purpose, and says that she knows he's too old for that sort of thing, but that sometimes when he isn't feeling well, she lets him nurse just to comfort him.

Despite the lenient attitude toward weaning, compared with other areas of American culture, the rural Southern mother tries to wean her baby at about a year. This may be due partially to the fact that during her early married life babies come fast one upon the other. It may also be due to the fact that the mother herself, suffering from various degrees and kinds of malnutrition, may not have enough milk adequately to nourish a growing child. Because of the scarcity of milk in this region, weaning in many cases means being cut off entirely from milk—not just the mother's milk but *all* milk.

Overeating a favored food to the point of satiety is apparently a type of shock which can produce a temporary or permanent aversion. Finally, it is well known that the physical properties of certain foods are in themselves disturbing. You have to "acquire a taste for" olives or coffee. However, adults are inclined to forget that there are many other items, such as cabbage or ice cream, which at first are displeasing to children, who tend to prefer mild foods. Fortunately, some taste buds are so located in the pharynx that we can literally taste what we smell. Thus, as Renner suggests, children become accustomed to the physical properties of some foods by smelling them long before they are allowed to eat them.

Temperature

Miriam E. Lowenberg's studies of young children[5] indicate that a two-year-old likes food lukewarm. Thus a preference for hot soup and coffee and ice-cold water apparently has to be acquired. For confirmation of this, one has but to watch a baby getting his first formidable taste of ice cream—how he accepts a spoonful and then struggles to warm up his mouth with his thumb before venturing another spoonful.

Taste and Flavor[6]

While there are only four basic tastes—salt, sweet, sour, and bitter—perceptible to the taste buds of the mouth alone, a wide range of distinctive flavors can be recognized when taste is used in conjunction with smell. Undoubtedly some foods like bitter liver, and strong cabbage or turnip, tend to be rejected, particularly by children, on the basis of flavor alone, though later socio-cultural influences may secure acceptance and even preference. The rural Southern preference for buttermilk to sweet milk is an instance of this. Of course, with maturation, deterioration of the taste mechanism undoubtedly occurs, so that children may exchange their preferences for mild-flavored foods for a preference for strong-flavored foods when they become older.

Texture

The mouth is able to distinguish many qualities: solid, elastic, sharp, thick, dry, rough, soft, crisp, blunt, thin, moist, smooth, as well as minute gradations of pressure. Too little attention has been paid to these qualities, partially because they are usually not consciously verbalized.

Factors of texture have, however, great significance, especially when it is desirable to expand consumption. For example, cantaloupe experts in a State Department of Markets had developed a cantaloupe of high sweetness according to test. However, when samples were offered consumers, it was found that people preferred a yielding cantaloupe of 10 per cent sweetness to a much sweeter sample if it were hard. Furthermore, if the sweeter melon was mushy (evidently an unpleasant feature of texture), it was less favored.

In general, then, some of the factors of texture which are *disliked,* that is, serve as sources of food aversions, seem to be: dryness, mushiness, coarseness, toughness, stringiness, and hardness. Stale bread, mushy cantaloupe, stringy squash, sticky mashed potatoes, lumpy gelatin, and gummy tapioca are examples. Some children will accept moist fish loaf or fish soufflé but reject dry baked fish or meat when it is presented with a sauce.

Japanese informants living in Hawaii explained, "Our mouths are so sweet [meaning that they liked delicate foods] that we are not satisfied with coarse foods any more."[7]

Preferred factors of texture seem to be moistness, softness and crispness. An important adjunct is variety of texture. One reason for food linkages—those foods that are often preferred in pairs—like crackers and milk, ham and eggs, and liver and bacon—is the contrast in texture as well as flavor which is thus provided.

Appearance

How a food looks, either singly or in conjunction with other foods, conditions its acceptance. Baker and Ehlers, studying the acceptance of school lunch dishes, found that one of the chief factors affecting initial selection was appearance (mainly as a result of garnishing).[8] In a study by the Bureau of Agricultural Economics, "Rice Preferences among Household Consumers,"[9] brown rice was used by a minority (43 per cent), and the reason advanced by 37 per cent for its unpopularity was its appearance. Then, too, when a food is developed which differs from the accustomed article in color, such as yellow tomatoes or pink grapefruit, it is for a time rejected because of the unpleasant connotations evoked by the strange color. For example, rural Southern housewives felt that pink grapefruit looked as if it were streaked with blood. To many adults, a deep yellow shade in butter and orange juice connotes richness in the product. Examples will be given in more detail of the favor accorded light-colored foods in the rural South. A child, however, not having acquired unfavorable connotations for color, naturally enjoys such a bright-colored food as a raspberry gelatin dessert. As with texture, contrasts in color are a time-honored way of adding to the appetizing character of a menu. It seems possible that foods whose appearance gives an impression of trouble in preparation, such as radish curls, caterers' sandwiches, and lofty cakes, are more appetizing, though we are far from the molded birds of a Lucullan feast.

Market researchers have paid considerable attention to what various colors imply in packaging, with the result that a preponderance of white, yellow, and red is used. When consumers were asked what color they preferred in a food poster, the color red outscored all other choices.[10] It was also startling to marketing specialists that one of the big considerations that had kept housewives from buying potatoes was that they were unwashed! Simply cleaning the potatoes before offering them made them more salable.[11]

Thus briefly have been indicated some of the physical factors in foods and in the individual's perception of these factors that help to condition food attitudes. Research in this field has hardly touched the surface, although the findings will have tremendous implications for growers, marketers, and consumers alike. Once the facts are known it will obviously be a simple matter to develop food products that are as satisfactory as possible to the potential consumer. It is less easy to change attitudes arising from deep-set, long-established customs of the culture or attributes of the social system.

It seems convenient to call the specific elements connected with the individual's food activities his food habits, including in that term not only the diet itself but also individual habits of producing, purchasing, and preparing food, and attitudes, tastes, and habits of eating. Where possible, variations in consciousness or in sense of obligation may be indicated. These individual *food habits* are compared to the more general foodways, a useful term to apply to all those parallel elements of the food pattern which have considerably more than individual application. Where possible, the degree of application —whether to a social class, a community, or a region—will be indicated.

Conflict between food habits and foodways is minimized, and congruences are reinforced, according to the number and diversity of occasions on which the individual is exposed to different authorities. If the doctor recommends whole wheat bread, if the county agent recommends enriched white bread, and the school recommends a whole series of choices on the basis of nutritive value, and the neighbors may use all of these, it is obvious that a person may choose any bread version without having to adapt his habits to an implacable set of foodways. In such an unlikely case the foodways would be chaotic.

The point of view so far expressed of the close connection of individual *food habits* and the *foodways* may be summarized as follows: The relation is an interrelation in which no one-way influence may be discerned. To begin with, there is the individual's biological constitution, the peculiarities of the physical enjoyment he derives from these differences. Although the individual's biological constitution may influence his habits, although in some cases he may exert considerable influence on the general foodways, although his habits may coincide with the foodways without conflict, although he becomes himself a carrier of culture, *in general,* the foodways do determine what the individual's food habits are, and often they may exert a negative as well as positive influences upon him.

Evidence of Conflict: Discrepancy between Values and Practice

A difference between the individual's food habits and the foodways is usually an evidence of present conflict or a source of future conflict. Occasionally, the individual food habit may be added to the foodways, but the chances for this are slight.

Discrepancies may occur in various ways. There may be a difference between what the individual actually eats and what is actually eaten by the majority of people. There may also be a difference between what an individual actually eats and what an individual *thinks* should be eaten, or between what is eaten by the majority and what most of them *think* they should eat. The cultural idea of what should be eaten is not always integrated, for one group in a locality, e.g., the nutritionists, may conceive of a proper diet in an entirely different way from another group, e.g., the laymen. Examples of such differences will be given later.

Conflicts of Value: Nation and Region

If the individual were required to adjust to a single set of values which are internally consistent, some sources of conflict would be removed. This is not, however, the case.

The region under discussion here is first of all a *rural* society, while the culture of the larger American society may be characterized as tending to be predominantly *urban*. The values of a purely rural society in a state of isolation are based on the direct experience or knowledge of a relatively limited area.[12] Values thus evolved tend to be preserved,[13] while those of the city are rapidly changing. While the culture-complexes of both are mutually influenced, considerable conflict is felt in the course of time as the gap widens, because the rural dwellers are indirectly told by radio announcers and magazine writers that the urban culture's values are superior to their own.

The farmer tends to associate urban values with science, in contrast to his own "unscientific" ideas. This external science tells him to plough and plant and feed his stock in novel ways, with results often tangibly superior to older hit-or-miss methods. He admires the technological ingenuity of urban life and brings back labor-saving devices to the farm. He has been repeatedly told that progress is a prime value, and he finds in the mobility of the city a representation of progress. Finally, in school his children often find that the goal of education is more education which will take them spatially and intellectually farther from the farm. It is true that a rural society may believe in the superiority of its spiritual values. Nevertheless, to the farmer the foodways will share his respect for urban values in the physical sphere. Coexistent with an attitude of respect for the new are many traditional and conservative *practices.* Of course, these discrepancies are part of the total school scene.

Conflicts within the Region

Ordinarily, a rural value system is well defined in itself. The abundance of face-to-face relations favors an atmosphere of social solidarity in which religion, recreation, education, economic activities, ethics, and art are all interwoven, much as in primitive societies. The group is neither dense nor extended, so that the collective attention is concentrated. Casual visitors receive the impression that there is a strong in-group.

In the case of the rural South, this apparent cohesiveness is deceptive. There is no single yeoman class, as in rural New England and the Middle West, but a highly stratified society of classes and castes, including Whites and Negroes, owners, tenants, sharecroppers, and wage-laborers. Some of these groups find assimilation extremely difficult with the result that their differing aims are sources of conflict.

Those Who Leave

Whether the rural community sends its young people outside of its boundaries for higher education, or whether they leave it for better vocational opportunities, the fact remains that many leave, and never return to raise a family and take up their part in transmitting the cultural heritage. This emigration was evident in net population losses suffered by many communities studied. The ultimate result in respect to the foodways is difficult to predict.

Sanctions

In case of serious conflict, the individual may adjust his behavior to accord with the standards of the culture, or the cultural values may grow more similar to his own. If no adjustment occurs, the society may apply *sanctions*. A sanction is defined by A. R. Radcliffe-Brown as "a reaction on the part of society or of some considerable number of its members to a mode of behavior which is thereby approved or disapproved."[14] Such sanctions may protect the interests of society as a whole or the interests of individuals.

Like the personal-cultural relationship which they express, the sanctions are both positive and negative. They may be expressions of approval or of disapproval, of approval for behavior consonant with the ideal patterns, and of disapproval for deviant behavior. The expression of approval may vary all the way from a rising vote of thanks to a commemoratory monument, while the expression of disapproval may vary from mild ridicule to execution.

Now, it is not likely that either a monument or execution awaited the discoverer of oysters and tomatoes, nor are such extremes of sanctions applied in the realm of foodways in contemporary times. The relative mildness of food sanctions may be attributed to one of the following possibilities: 1. The foodways are so strong that they are absolutely followed and no deviations occur. (It is obvious, however, that variations *do* exist between the individual food habits and the food ways). 2. The foodways are so weak that any amount of deviation may occur without application of sanction. (Yet we *do* have expression of approval and disapproval for food habits as, for instance, when a parent deprives the child of dessert if it will not drink milk). 3. *The foodways are moderately strong, but they are considered subordinate to other values, hence deviations do not meet with the extremes of sanction.* This last probably represents the conditions under which food sanctions generally operate.[15]

Verbatim Case Material and the Foodways

In subsequent chapters, verbatim citations from field informants will be frequently used. In the light of what has been said, these citations should indicate: What are the general actual practices in connection with food? What are the *deviations in practice* among groups and individuals? What is *considered proper and improper to eat* by the society, groups, and individuals? To what extent are there discrepancies between *food ideals and practice?* What revealing clues are found in the *attitudes* toward food?

To be sure, informants' answers will tell us what they think and feel about food and the general value system much more than they will about what is actually practiced. Actual practice will be disclosed by supplementary observations (though the informants will tend not to be dishonest about food practices). What the informants tell us is what we are chiefly interested in here—*thought and feeling,* both about the *food pattern* and the *socio-cultural pattern.*

Summary

The basis of the food habits of the individual in normal circumstances lies not only in his biological needs but in the pleasurable and disagreeable sensations he comes to associate with specific qualities of food like temperature, taste, flavor, texture, and appearance. If no groups existed—an impossible assumption, for the family group is one of the strongest influences on food habits—these qualities would presumably be the sole conditioners of food choice.

The interrelation between individual food habits and the foodways corresponds to the interrelation between the individual and the culture. As, with important exceptions, the culture exerts an insistent influence upon the individual, so the foodways powerfully affect individual food habits.

Conflicts occur, in value and practice, between the individual food habits and the foodways. These are symptomatic of larger conflicts in the culture itself, e.g., between the nation and the region, and, within the region itself, between the different groups constituting the highly stratified society. The emigration of young people marks a period of change from the older value system to the new. A continual process of mutual adjustment in foodways as in other aspects of culture operates to integrate society.

Most behavior meets with sanctions of approval or disapproval which, in regard to food habits, are relatively mild because, it is suggested, the foodways are considered subordinate to other aspects of the value system.

The beliefs and attitudes of individual informants should afford important insights into the nature of the foodways, of the socio-cultural pattern, and of the relation between the two.

The question which next arises is: What is the nature of the social force which affects the individual's food choices, and how does it operate?

NOTES

1. Dr. Arnold Gesell, Director, Clinic of Child Development, New Haven Hospital, New Haven, Conn., as reported in the *Proceedings of the Conference with the Committee on Food Habits* (Washington: National Research Council, June 27, 28, 1941), p. 280.

2. Paul Thomas Young, "Food-Seeking Drive, Affective Process and Learning," *Psychological Review,* March, 1949, pp. 98-121.
3. H. D. Renner, *The Origin of Food Habits* (London: Faber & Faber, 1944), p. 33.
4. *Conference with the Committee on Food Habits* (Washington: National Research Council, May 23, 24, 1941), pp. 285-286.
5. Miriam E. Lowenberg, "Foods Children Like," *Hygeia,* November, 1948, p. 792.
6. Renner defines taste as "all perceptions transmitted by the specific buds of taste within the mouth and all that is perceived by the nose." *Op. cit.,* p. 16.
7. Jitsuich Masuoka, "Changing Food Habits of the Japanese in Hawaii," *American Sociological Review,* December, 1945, p. 761.
8. Dorothy W. Baker and Mabelle S. Ehlers, "Acceptance of School Lunch Dishes Studied," *Journal of Home Economics,* June, 1949, pp. 314-316.
9. U. S. Department of Agriculture, Washington, D. C., June, 1949.
10. Bureau of Agricultural Economics, U. S. Department of Agriculture, "Report on Consumer Reactions to Banner Buy Program," June, 1949, p. 25.
11. "Potato Preference Among Household Consumers," Bureau of Agricultural Economics, U. S. Department of Agriculture, Miscellaneous Publication No. 667.
12. *Cf.* Pitirim Sorokin and Carle C. Zimmerman, *Principles of Rural-Urban Sociology* (New York: Henry Holt and Company, 1929), Chapter XIII.
13. *Ibid.*
14. See detailed discussion by A. R. Radcliffe Brown in *Encyclopedia of Social Sciences*: "Sanction, Social"
15. Of course, it is possible that the foodways may temporarily assume much greater importance in the hierarchy of values, as in time of famine or war, in which case the sanctions might increase in power proportionately.

4

The Transmission of the Foodways: Social Factors

At this point let us take a closer look at the learning process involved in the case of the individual and the foodways. Here is an infant, ready for weaning. Theoretically he will behave like an experimental rat, freely selecting what he wants and likes from the well-stocked cafeteria which is the range of food items that can be produced in any region accessible to him. How does it happen, then, that an Australian aborigine esteems grubs while an American abhors them? Why does a gourmet at the Ritz pay a premium for putrid cheese while an Eskimo gourmet prefers rotten fish? For that matter, how does it come about that a child in a Westchester suburb enjoys as much milk as he can drink, while a child in a suburb of Thoms, Georgia, in the same country but a different region, learns to reject sweet milk?

Furthermore, adults' food habits must change—new products are introduced, old ones are served differently, and when we travel, as we Americans so often do, we are great ones for trying out the local "specialty of the house." So in peace, but under the forced draft of war, changes in food habits were more urgently induced than they had ever been before. Here we inquire into the ways and means by which the individual acquires the foodways of the rural South.

Adequacy of the Diet

The elements of the food supply and the daily menu with its

seasonal deviations have already been summarized in Tables I, X, II, and III.

It is difficult to state accurately how adequate the diet is, particularly without medical examinations which could ascertain the presence of malnutrition from blood analyses, and (as is most recently done) from the presence of vitamins within the muscles themselves. The Thoms County Nutrition Committee reported the diet as approximately 70 per cent adequate,[1] with deficiencies mainly in milk (calcium and phosphorous), lean meats (Vitamin B), citrus fruits (Vitamin C). Excessive use of unenriched white flour and white corn meal[2] for biscuits and bread, and of fat meat, without making up the resultant protein and Vitamin B complex deficiency, leads to pellagra. Since pellagra cases often do not go to the doctor but to the local druggists, and because several doctors in the area did not realize that pellagra is officially reportable, pellagra was considerably under-reported. Moreover, since pellagra is but one end result of many sub-clinical cases of malnutrition, some nutritional deficiency probably exists among persons of all classes with poor food habits.

Desirable elements in the diet are the extensive use of collards (kale) and sweet potatoes, which at certain seasons remedy the Vitamin B loss and are a bountiful source of Vitamin A, and the use of eggs and chickens (where these are not traded for cash). Thus briefly the diet may be characterized.

Adequacy of Nutritional Information

The folk beliefs that follow constitute the real tenets according to which people feed their families, in contrast to the instruction on food which is presented to children in school or to adults by nutritionists. Sometimes it is in accord with scientific food theory; more often, it is obscurely derived from individual or group experiences with food, doctors' advice and hearsay, all much changed in the process of transmission.

Meats, Fish

Remarks made in regard to meat include:

I don't think lean meat is necessary [Negro wage-laborer]. Babies shouldn't have meats because it ain't good for 'em coming up [Negro wage-laborer]. While a mother is still in the bed, give her soups and bread, coffee and no meat [Negro midwife]. Young people shouldn't eat hard fried ham [White owner]. Oysters often make people sick . . . you have to look out for them [White sharecropper]. Lot of people are prejudiced against onions, fish and oysters. [White owner.]

Mother didn't want us to eat hog meat for supper. She would say "You will dream about Latimer, the school teacher." [White owner.]

Milk and Other Beverages

Milk will fatten you up more than cake or candy. [White sharecropper.]

I can't drink milk—it don't set well on my stomach. [White sharecropper.]

My husband can't even eat a clabber biscuit. [White sharecropper.]

Orange juice, ginger ale and ice will cure bowel consumption. [White tenant.]

Bread, Biscuits, Cereal, Meal, etc.

Self-rising flour is bad for you. [White sharecropper.]

I used to eat so much biscuits like a pure hog until it got so I'd have indigestion and have to sit up straight in bed to catch my breath. [White sharecropper.]

Hot bread is better for you. [Several informants.]

I think babies should be fed something like grits and oatmeal, no solid food. [Negro wage-laborer.]

Yellow corn meal don't look so good as white. [Negro wage-laborer.]

Vegetables

Lettuce is good for the nerves. [White owner.]

Sweet potatoes give my baby the colic. [Negro wage-laborer.]

I don't like turnip greens unless they are cooked about two hours. [White sharecropper.]

Tomato seeds will give appendicitis. [White sharecropper.]

Strawberries and field peas aren't good in the summer. [Negro sharecropper.]

English peas make the baby sick. [White sharecropper.]

I just never would let my children have English peas. I was just afraid it would make them sick. [White sharecropper.]

Miscellaneous

If you are sick from your waist up, you can eat most anything, but if you are sick from your waist down, you have to be more careful. [White owner.]

If you eat chicken feed, it will make you pretty, and if you drink coffee you will be ugly and dark. [White owner.]

I like to eat oranges and grapefruit all the time when I first get up and just before I go to bed. They are as good as a physic. They're not fattening but they sure fill up the hungry spot. They're healthy, too. They're good for the heart, good for the kidneys, good for everything. I ain't aiming to die from heart trouble. [White owner.]

Foods Not To Be Eaten in Combination

Sweet milk and fish.
Buttermilk and cabbage.
Buttermilk and fish.

Crabs and sweets will sure do you bad if you eat them both at the same meal. [White sharecropper.]

In spite of the nutritional inaccuracy of some of these statements, we found that most people of this region are pretty well aware of what constituted *a balanced diet*, in general. There are some exceptions, as in Seaford, where the general idea is to have more of the same kinds of things—several starches at a meal, with milk conspicuously missing. Most other informants said a well-balanced diet would include: milk and butter, meat, vegetables, and fruit. Asked to prepare the most nutritious meal she knew, one White sharecropper had: fried chicken, stuffed eggs, potatoes, string beans, salad-greens (cooked mustard and turnip greens), pickled beets, onions, biscuit, corn bread, iced tea, sliced peaches, cake. This is not to say, of course, that people actually ate what they knew they should.

It is a different story when one asks about the refinements of nutritional information. Only one of the informants had any accurate idea of vitamins. This is not surprising, since several rural doctors in the communities studied were misinformed. We are reminded that in a nationwide survey (American Institute of Public Opinion, March 1940) only 15 per cent knew what food calories are and 9 per cent knew what vitamins are. A citrus survey in rural Nelson County, Kentucky (June, 1948), indicated that very few know what vitamins are to be found in what foods, nor is the nature of the physical effect of each vitamin known.

Back to the Land

The time may come when delivery boys will fly our order in from any fjord or pampas. With the world's great menu at our back doors, only then will food habits be freed from the context of local soil and climate. For a farmer, particularly, there are few supermarkets; he turns to his own acres—he grows what he can within the limitations of the climate.

The growing season is so long that the Southern farmer can grow nearly every vegetable. However, in summer the sun bakes the fields so severely that gardens turn brown and dry up. The effect is to shift the best growing season from the summer to the period between September to March (for vegetables like collards which can withstand possible frost), or from March to July for other vegetables. Summer is the very period of scarcity because few sharecroppers and wage-laborers who move frequently want to plant a garden that someone else may harvest. Also, the time when summer gardens dry up is the very time when the cash from last season's crop may be exhausted, while the next is yet to be received.

The extreme heat imposes a problem in refrigeration. Milk, for example, sours so quickly that either many people have a distaste for it on this account, or prefer it in the form of buttermilk or clabber in biscuits. Many White owners, especially those in sections where there are electric power lines, have refrigerators. The sharecroppers and wage-laborers ordinarily do not, though they may buy ice for ice boxes, a purchase which subtracts a large sum from their available cash for expenditures. The great value which is placed on refrigeration may be indicated by the repetitive and wistful nature of informants' remarks on this subject.

Yes'm, I would be glad to have a kerosene stove but people here can't have one. They don't keep 'em warm in the winter. It would be so much better if I could have a refrigerator. I one hundred times ruther have the refrigerator instead of the stove, 'cause the refrigerator would be better in the summer. I takes twenty-five cents' worth of ice every two days.

One of the features yet to be explained about the diet in relation to the climate is the high calorie content in the fatback and grease used for boiling vegetables, which are eaten with truly Eskimo enthusiasm.

Routine of the Day

At dawn, the housewife rises to get breakfast, typically on a wood-burning tin stove or, if she can afford both cooking and heating facilities, on a kerosene range. These types of stoves favor the frequent frying of food in grease on the top of the stove, and cooking a meal at noontime that can be served cold at supper. She gets the children ready for school, or, if they are grown, she works in her garden in the cool of the morning.

Soon after breakfast, a neighbor may drop in with some extra peaches or some honey, and she will stay for a chat. Household tasks take up a large share of the morning, particularly if cows are milked, butter is churned, soap is made, or vegetables are to be prepared for dinner. Cabbage is often put on early to cook with the fat-back or ham-hock. Corn bread or hot biscuits have to be prepared. Often the mother prepares several kinds of potatoes or hot bread to suit the preferences of her family.

Wage hands have only an hour for dinner, but the others rest on shady porches from the midday sun and watch the dust boil up behind the passing cars. Each member of the family watches for the grocery truck, and buys, if he can, cold drinks and candy. Now the farmer reads his newspaper or listens to the news on the radio, if he has one.

After a pause, work resumes in the cotton field: chopping, spraying, picking, or any of the numerous hand operations. Women and children have to help with this in the busy season.

At dusk they return to the house for a cold supper of whatever is left from the noon meal. The lack of electricity does not encourage reading, but there is much family banter before the hard day's work effects an early bedtime.

Social Relations which Alter the Foodways

It is the *group* which chiefly formulates the local foodways for the individual. Some social relations are *basic, long-lasting,* like those in the cotton and tobacco economies, with the social classes that accompany them, that of the family, of informal neighborly relations, and those concerned with the two races. Others are comets streaking across the social sky—*episodic* relations as with those occupying a certain occupational role, and rural-urban contacts.

Cash Crops and Store-bought Food

Southern farmers still grow mainly a cash crop—tobacco on the sandy coastal plain and cotton on the red clay hills of the Piedmont. As one consequence, they tend to buy at least half of their food. They buy flour, corn, meal, pork, lard, cow feed, mule feed, canned vegetables, and fresh meats.

There is considerable resistance to exchanging the staple crop for a cash food crop or diversified farming. Dairying, which seems most practical for this hilly country, involves a regularity of attention that is simply alien. Cotton and tobacco involve endless operations, but these are seasonal. The two periods of relaxation—the period between the last chopping and first picking ("laying-by time"), and the period between the last picking and the first preparation of the soil for the new crop—allow people to visit and to engage in social activities. It is an immemorial custom, also, to go to town Saturday afternoon, and to rest or visit on Sundays. A regular milk check could not make up for such relative freedom, even if the lower economic levels could afford to invest in cows. For fruit and vegetables it is difficult to find a market, and subsistence farming without cash crops also finds considerable resistance.

As the intermittent character of cotton production fulfills one cultural value, its speculative character fulfills another. One year eight-cent cotton and the boll weevil may mean that a sharecropper starves and is actually in debt for his year's work; another year, thirty-cent cotton may provide him with a car, a radio, a refrigerator, and ample meals.

Class Differences and the Food Pattern[3]

There is an apparent inconsistency between those descriptions of Southern food which speak of it as all fried chicken and hot biscuits and those which portray it as wholly molasses and hoecake. The fact is that there are two main levels of diet, the level of fried chicken, biscuits, sweet potatoes, beans, peaches and tea, and the simpler meal of corn bread and one vegetable and tea. The first level is that of the White owners and long-term sharecroppers and Negro owners, while the second level applies to the short-term White and Negro sharecroppers and wage-laborers. Furthermore, all these classes have a weekday and a Sunday level,[4] and a harvest and a scarcity level, all of which may be at great variance. Both plenty and scarcity are true of the South; but the occasions of plenty are fewer than the scarcity, which becomes the commonplace.

White Owners

At the top of the class and caste structure, the *White owners* eat more food in greater variety than the other classes, but often make food choices nutritionally in error according to present standards. It is this class which is most accessible to organizations, agents, and means of communication which may effect changes in food habits. Because of their supreme position in the social structure, the White owner's food habits are models for Whites and Negroes of lower social position.

White Sharecroppers, Negro Owners, and Sharecroppers

These classes have less food in amount and variety, and their diet seems definitely inadequate. Probably the *White sharecropper* is in the most disadvantageous position, because he does not join many organizations nor maintain community roots and has little chance to receive aid in fellowship, food, or food information from neighbors, professional workers, or organizations.

Wage-laborers

These are the most restricted in amount and variety of food and make the most uninformed food purchases. Their precarious position, with a long period of food scarcity, is bettered when they possess means of subsistence like a cow, hogs, or chickens.

In answer to the question as to whether nutritional adequacy is economically determined, informants indicate that lack of money is a major factor because of the cost of equipment, stock, seed, and canning jars, but also admit that it is not so important a factor as the presence or absence of initiative, resourcefulness, accessibility to means of bettering conditions, or desire to attain other values than better nutrition. Such values may be obtained at the expense of the food budget. The many rationalizations offered to obscure real issues suggest that money is not the only answer.

Family Relations and Food

Of all the social groups that affect the food pattern the family seems the most important. Indeed, Renner wonders why any food habit changes, "for there is a circle 'what one eats when young, that one likes and hands on to one's offspring,' which should rotate forever."[5] There is Macaulay's vivid picture of Samuel Johnson, who never forgot the deprivations of his early life:

> Whenever he was so fortunate as to have near him a hare that had been kept too long, or a meat pie made with rancid butter, he gorged himself with such violence that his veins swelled and the moisture broke out on his forehead.[6]

Bossard suggests that the meal is a forum, a place where social roles are created.[7]

Even more powerful is the influence of the Southern rural family, because the whole family cooperates in the production of cotton or tobacco, so that in work and recreation the family is closely knit.

To the *father* pertains all decisions concerned with securing and through the cash-crop system, of expending, money, and thus indirectly he is significantly concerned with the food supply, the planning of menus, including accession to his food preferences and avoidances, the distribution of food, and the order of serving. At the same time, he is less accessible than the mother to organizations dealing with the dissemination of food information.

The functions of the *mother* are also rather sharply delineated, since she assumes responsibility for the care of the garden, poultry, and perhaps the stock, for canning and preserving, for help in butchering, and for milking, churning, and butter-making, as well as for the choice and preparation of food for each meal.

The mother's direct control of the eating habits of her children—her technique of control—is of great importance. Whether or not she displays her own food dislikes to her children, for them to imitate, or forces herself to eat foods she doesn't like in order to set a good example; whether or not she commands or entices or fools her family into eating what she thinks is good for them, or caters to their prejudices and cajoles their appetites; whether or not she insists upon discipline at table; whether or not she uses food as reward or punishment —all of these matters are significant in the development of food habits. The process of *socialization*—the initiation into "the standards of expected performance"—both in regard to eating behavior and general behavior, which the child undergoes when growing up in a society, thus affects the child's experience with certain foods.

Lela, a Negro sharecropper, indicates some of the elements in the process:

I us'ally boss my chil'un. When they're little and don't do right I punish my chil'un. I sometimes have to whip 'em. After they git big, I don't think you ought to whip 'em all the while. I never deprive 'em of food. I always try to give 'em plenty to eat. A hongry child will jest steal. I don't think you ought to have to lock up your food from your chil'un. And if they takes food, I want my chil'un to tell me so if I asks 'em. Most people 'round here has to lock up their food from their chil'un. I sometimes punishes my chil'un by deprivin' 'em of candy, but then they don't get much candy nohow—I don't believe in givin' 'em many sweets. I don't want 'em to eat sweets even when they haven't done wrong. I has six girls and four boys. At the table I don't want 'em to quarrel, and I do think they ought not to reach all over the table and throw something across the table. My husband don't like fer 'em to talk 'cause he hard of hearing. If they jest git mad, I jest tell 'em to git up. I don't think they ought to talk about bad things or dead things at the table. I don't like them to sing or whistle at the table. Often I make 'em go wash their hands; then they say "I forget."

I expect my chil'un to do better than me, 'cause I teach 'em what I can.

More significant still are the *mother's attitudes* toward certain foods. As the chief culture carrier in regard to food, she may teach the child that certain foods are desirable, satisfying, delightful, good for him; or, negatively, that some are "heavy," not to be eaten at certain seasons of the year, not to be eaten with other foods, and so on.

Much of this teaching goes on verbally, but more goes on inarticulately as the child catches something of the mother's feeling from her example or some cue in her expression.

But it would be impossible to instruct verbally if every other sign the child was accustomed to catch gave different instruction. The food attitudes secured from the mother are suffused with such strong emotional overtones that they are enough to make a certain food like spareribs forever pleasing for the child, or to alienate him equally strongly from English peas. Thus the mother's favorite dishes carry over more frequently than the father's do.

The determination of food attitudes becomes almost exclusively the province of the parental generation. On the one hand, the younger generation of *children* is not yet allowed to determine menus and food preparations (though the mother caters to all her family). On the other hand, the older generation of *grandparents* or *kinfolk,* though in frequent visits sources of solace and sweetmeats, has abdicated from formally exercising its authority by force.

In the larger family of the rural community, the traditional neighborliness of the rural South is now undergoing adjustment to modern urban practices, though it persists in the White owner class. Here neighborliness provides crop-disaster and health insurance through the exchange of food and information. The sharecropper and wage-laborer groups have few food resources outside the family except by being adventitious to a White owner family. The Negroes' cohesiveness, in corresponding economic classes, insures some sharing of food and food attitudes, though technical information spreads by word of mouth. The degree of morale in a community affects attitudes toward varying food crops and the speed of changes in food habits. The civic pride in Westmore-Glen insures that relatively rapid food changes occur and that technical information is welcomed.

Informal Agencies for Transmitting the Foodways

One of the most important problems that can be discussed here is the relation between food and friendship. Southern hospitality is such a byword that it might be assumed that neighborliness is part of the process by which the foodways are diffused. However pervasive may be the influence of the family, we find some unexpected dams intercepting the free flow from neighbor to neighbor.

There is a great deal of evidence brought out here and elsewhere that while one may receive gifts of food from a friend, they must be in the class of the delicacies but may never be necessary food staples. One may receive information and advice about the choice and preparation of staple food from one's relatives and, recently, from the group of professional workers in food, but the *dissemination of ideas about staple foods seems not to occur where friends are concerned.*

Earl Koos conducted an experiment in the spreading of nutrition information through friendship patterns. Persons of different nationalities were chosen in Yorkville (N.Y.) who were to invite their friends to luncheons consisting of foods acceptable to each national group, and selected with the aid of nutritionists. The experiment failed since the housewives invited not their friends but acquaintances, some of whom they had not met in years.[8] It is a different story, reports Dorothy Dickins,[9] when it is a matter of trying out new recipes. The most important sources of such information for small town families in Mississippi were friends.

Therefore, there is considerable ground for believing that any formal attempt to change the foodways through friendship will fail. *The foodways are rarely changed through friendship explicitly; more often, implicitly.* Time and again, our informants stated that they considered it impolite to talk to others about what they should eat, and there was even some disinclination expressed by the White owners for talking to their sharecroppers on this topic.

One incident, which we directly observed, drove this lesson sharply home. In 1942, in the early stage of the war, there were embarrassing local surpluses of flour, milk, and cheese because of a shortage of ships for transporting them to other emergency areas. At the same time, block leaders had been used successfully to conduct air-raid drills, help salvage scrap, and sell war bonds. To move the glut of flour, cheese, and milk it seemed logical to use these block leaders to carry emergency messages, called food communiques, to, say, ten of their neighbors: "Eat more cheese," "Use more milk," and "Buy all the enriched flour you can use." We were sent by three government agencies as observers at the earliest try-out in Syracuse, New York. To the surprise of many, the food communique nearly broke up the ingenious block organization. The housewife message-carriers began to resign—partly because they felt messages about food didn't have the martial importance of their previous jobs, partly because they were exceedingly loath to tell their neighbors what to eat.

On certain levels, however, people may talk about food. Farmers may discuss methods of gardening. Their wives may plan party menus or exchange advice on the diet for illness or pregnancy. Club groups may talk over a projected community supper. But all of these are *extra*-routine occasions,[10] while food as a staple continues to be a tabooed subject.

There is also a level upon which nutritional attitudes and ideas about staple foods diffuse in informal relations (and this is probably the most important level of all), that of the most informal contacts. A food attitude is not best transmitted by pamphlet, poster, or even by a spoken comment, but by example and imitation. Duncker's study showed that when nursery school children were first permitted to choose the food they "liked best" from six different foods, there was a 26 per cent agreement when they chose individually; but when each had a later opportunity to choose immediately after another child whose choice he had observed, there was 81 per cent agreement.[11]

The *most informal contacts*—in the family, along the road, in town, in the country store—suffer least the limitations, either of implied *coercion, or the limitation of contact.* For instance, a sharecropper waits in the country store while a White owner orders a can of salmon, and perhaps without conscious imitation, the sharecropper buys salmon too. A child catches the minimal cue of his mother's slight expression of distaste as she eats English peas, and he pushes his peas away in spite of her explicit admonitions. Such contacts may not even rise to the level of what we ordinarily think of as informal contacts, and yet they constitute the most powerful propulsive forces of the culture.

Race Relations Affecting the Diet

A great deal of emphasis has been placed upon the rigid separation between the races in the South. It is true that in Westmore there is a taboo against eating together, inter-dining, and that among White attitudes toward Negroes is found the prevalent belief that Negroes do not need as much to eat or to live on as the Whites, and are less discriminating in their choice of food.

> Some niggers never think about anything but corn bread half-cooked, and syrup. Up there where we used to live, the niggers eat kidneys—Daddy said the niggers saved everything about a hog but the squeal. They eat fat-back three times a day and this ole poke salat. Sometimes we cook it in a big pot and feed it to the pig. They just don't keer; they don't have milk and butter. Them niggers don't have stuff like that.

But the strongest expression of race distinctions comes from the White sharecropper rather than the White owner, which indicates that social and economic *class* is of greater importance than color in the formulation of those distinctions that exist. That class is also the arbiter of friendly relations more than color is exemplified in the closer contact that exists between a Negro wage-laborer and a White wage-laborer (where there is no question of economic competition), than between a Negro wage-laborer and a Negro owner, thus exemplifying the fact that class is often more the arbiter of friendly relations than color.

Furthermore, in the rural setting, symbols of color distinction are somewhat relaxed. A Negro man may sometimes sit down around the stove in the country store with White men, or a Negro woman may hire a White dressmaker. These are privileges which, it is well understood, may be withdrawn. But in general the White owner is more lenient in his attitudes and aid than the White sharecropper. In an atmosphere of courtesy and paternalistic responsibility, the White owner seems to believe that relations are maintained as they are to each race's mutual satisfaction.

Racial differences in the diet follow the pattern of class differences, in that Whites generally eat more and in greater variety than Negroes, and owners of both races eat more than sharecroppers and wage-laborers. The position of "old-timey" Negroes is more nutritionally advantageous than that of some Whites, in that they eat more of undenatured foods, and make more complete use of the food resources available. While the Whites have been to some extent influenced by Negro food attitudes, the present tendency is for Negroes to emulate White standards in food, which are currently less nutritionally desirable in some respects.

Episodic Relations

Aside from these customary relations, there are many episodic relations with persons who in their occupational rôle may affect food habits.

Among these relations, those with Government representatives are of increasing importance, for many of these have the express function of interpreting the national foodways to local people. For example, the county agent may urge greater diversification of food crops upon the cotton plantation owners, while the home demonstration agent may bring modern methods of food preparation and preservation to this class.

Representatives of the *school* system who deal with food have the advantage that theoretically, at least, they reach all social classes.[12] Among these, the home economics and vocational teachers attack the problem of teaching food preparation.

Among the professional persons, the *doctor* occupies the most authoritative position. Although instances of the erroneousness of his advice were discovered, his dietary advice usually becomes part of the foodways. It is sometimes not directly accessible to the poorer Whites and Negroes, who often rely upon the advice of druggists.

Among relations with *tradespeople,* those with the country storekeeper are most important because of farmers' increasing dependence upon the extent and nature of his food stocks and because, in the store, caste and class barriers are temporarily crossed to afford opportunity for formulation of communal food attitudes.

In their occasional *contacts with village and urban residents,* neighborhood dwellers feel that the urban ways are superior to their own, and that urban canned, packaged, and imported foods are desirable and estimable, a feeling supported by "brand" advertising. In spite of a disinclination to experiment in food on the occasion of their infrequent excursions outside the neighborhood, Westmore people definitely feel that their home-grown food products are inferior. Urban food customs are found to spread generally from urban Whites to rural Whites to rural Negroes, and more infrequently from urban Whites to urban Negroes to their relatives in the country.

Influence of the Doctor

No professional person occupies a more authoritative position than the doctor. Even if his advice is erroneous, it becomes part of the foodways.

My doctor suggested grapefruit to me about ten years ago to build up a blood deficiency. They're good for blood cells.

We have made lard but the doctor told us not to eat the lard made from a hog, so we just stopped making it.

A hospital resident physician near Seaford, North Carolina, said that he would prescribe plenty of citrus fruit and Vitamin C for pellagra but he didn't suggest foods containing Vitamin B.

For pregnancy:

The doctor made me stop eating meats. When I was still in

bed, I ate milk, butter, and bread. They didn't give me any meat or eggs or fish, but some chicken.

In one rural Kentucky community, a rather widespread idea had developed among low-income groups of both races that citrus fruits should be avoided as being "too acid." There were two doctors in this community, one a young man, the other past seventy. When the young doctor was interviewed, it was evident that he had been passing on the orthodox nutritional views about citrus. When he was asked about the "acid" idea, he smiled and said that it was hard for the older man in the profession to "keep up" but that his fees were more within reach of the low-income groups.

For those who can't afford doctors' fees and dislike the stigma of the clinic, such sub-medical sources as the druggist, chiropractor, and midwife may also significantly change food habits. How this may occur is best illustrated by two incidents which concern the chiropractor and the druggist in a town eighteen miles from Seaford.

The chiropractor's office was part of his home, a well-kept-up white house on a pleasant shady street. Outside, there was often a patient's pick-up truck, dusted red from country roads. Inside, the waiting patient might be reassured by such signs as a long table with magazines, a card, "Doctor Is Out—Will Return at —— o'clock," and a calendar depicting a hero of medical science. When he had disposed of his other callers, the chiropractor was exceedingly cordial to us. He knew we were working for the Government, and (this being the early stages of the National Nutrition Program at the beginning of World War II) that we were interested in enriched food products and vitamins. In fact, he made a proposition:

"Why, there's no reason we can't work together on this thing. I'll send for a lot of vitamin samples from the big drug houses, and then I'll advertise a big clinic. We'll get 'em stretched out up on that examining table of mine, hitch a stethoscope on them fixed up to a loud-speaker, and when they hear that heart of theirs going, 'Ker-thump! Ker-thump! Ker-thump!' they'll be so scared they'll be ready to swallow all the vitamin pills they can hold."

However, we had a far better impression of the real services performed by the town druggist. It was a sparkling Saturday morning, with the streets already bustling with country people in town for the day. Outside the drug store, the voice of a loud-speaker detained a few loungers and ourselves. It came from the store window, where a patent medicine salesman was sitting at a table, holding up a knife and saying, "Now, if yuh got a pain that cuts yuh like a knife, try Gen-Seng, hit never fails." But this was a side issue, and we walked on into the little room at the rear of the store, where a circle of patients was already waiting for the druggist. Most were very poor—for a dollar they were getting advice on what to do for their symptoms, and medicine too. As to the advice, we joined the circle and listened as each told what ailed him. The "doctor" seemed to be a sincere man who confined himself to common sense hygienic measures in each case. The alternative, for most, would have been no professional aid at all. And far from objecting, the town physicians seemed to encourage the custom.

Country Storekeeper

News center, source of credit during the cash-cropper's period of food scarcity, cash outlet for butter, cream, and eggs—the country store plays a central role in neighborhood life. In a cash-crop system rural residents depend upon the stock carried by the neighborhood store for at least part of the food supply, while at the same time the credit system tends to put a brake upon outside purchases. Thus, in Seaford, North Carolina, you would find sufferers from pellagra who knew what they should eat but were unable to secure milk, lean meat, or whole grain breads and cereals from the country store. In addition to outright lacks, the grade of meats (with the exception of pork) and of fruits and vegetables is likely to be of shaky quality.

Summary

(1) The basic dietary is a composite of home-raised food and purchased food, so constituted that the home-raised food forms a much larger proportion than that of an urban basic dietary but a smaller proportion with respect to previous food habits.

(2) The basic food pattern is affected by:

- (a) the influence of the *mother* in the Southern authoritarian family through her *activities* in the care of the garden, livestock, preparation of meals and canning, her explicit *instruction* to the family and her implicit *attitudes,* as well as the *cultural concepts* about food which she holds and transmits;
- (b) the *father,* in his decisions regarding gardens, livestock, and a cash crop, his expenditures at the store and his food preferences supported by his patriarchal authority;
- (c) the *children,* to a small degree, in their introduction of learned food habits from school activities, and in their retention in the home as members of the production unit;
- (d) the *kinfolk* and *neighbors,* who prevent loss of food supplies in emergencies, and share surpluses, as well as transmit information and attitudes about food;
- (e) the paternalistic assistance of the *landlord* in his management of the crop, provision of equipment, and attitude toward sources of food like garden and livestock, items of "furnish" and his own food habits, and also indirectly, by regulating length of tenure and mobility of the *tenant;*
- (f) the interracial transmission of food habits by the association of Negro tenant families with White landlord families, as when the Negro woman serves as

cook in the White household, or helps in other ways, and also by the White belief in a racial differential in food needs, and by the inferior economic and social position of the Negro;

(g) the *doctor,* the *home economics* and *vocational agricultural teachers,* the *government representatives,* and *urban residents* who introduce changes in the basic dietary and affect the current ideas about food;

(h) the *country storekeeper* who significantly affects food habits through the kind and amount of foodstuffs carried in his store, and through the fact that the country store is an extremely important medium of credit, barter, and trade in the economic system, and of interaction in the social system of the rural South.

NOTES

1. Based on materials for nutritional analysis furnished by the Georgia State Nutrition Committee, 1942.
2. A survey conducted by Thoms County Nutrition Committee showed that 70 percent of people in Thoms County use white unenriched flour; 100 percent use white corn meal. "Enriched flour is white or near-white flour which contains not less than 1.6 or more than 2.5 milligrams of thiamin, not less than 6 or more than 24 milligrams of iron" (Definition of Enriched Flour, Food and Drug Administration). To counteract the over-refinement of flour and bread, the Middle-Western millers agreed to enrich their products according to the above formula. Enrichment by no means restored vitamins found in dark flour.
3. See Table IV.
4. See illustrations in Appendix.
5. Renner, *op. cit.,* p. 244.
6. E. Parmalee Prentice, *Hunger and History* (New York: Harper & Brothers, 1939), p. 68.
7. James H. S. Bossard, "Family Table Talk—An Area for Sociological Study," *American Sociological Review,* 1943, pp. 295-301.
8. Report of the Meeting of the Committee on Food Habits (June 16, 1942), Appendix II.
9. Dorothy Dickins, *Changing Pattern of Food Preparation of Small Town Families in Mississippi,* Bulletin of Mississippi Agricultural Experiment Station, No. 715, 1945, pp. 1-56.

10. The food served on these occasions is *extra*-routine like the occasion itself. At a church barbecue, cakes, fried chicken, potato salad, baked sweet potatoes, biscuits, corn bread, and pickles were served. At a women's club meeting, hot rolls, lime aspic, pecans, and iced tea were served, both of these in contradiction to the everyday menu. The use of these foods on such occasions tends to reinforce the prestige attached to them.
11. *Manual for the Study of Food Habits,* Bulletin of the National Research Council, No. 111 (Washington, D. C.: January, 1945), p. 86.
12. Actually, the lower economic classes' need of their children's labor, and their inability to provide equipment for school, materially cut down the attendance of poorer children.

5

The Transmission of the Foodways (continued): How Change Occurs

It is surely not enough to say that food changes occur under such and such conditions of soil or climate, or to describe the kinds of persons in a given society who hasten or hamper the process. We must also refer more directly to the conduits by which interchange of the foodways is effected. In a simple group like the family, the mechanisms are simple—one does not have to use a letter to communicate with one's son, aside from, say, a grocery list. Imitation, direct observation, facial expression, a word here and there—these most effectively suffice.

But just as in modern society we rarely exist from hand to mouth, our communication system is only in part by word of mouth. The more people, the larger the number of groups, the more artificial media are devised to convey ideas. That is, one learns at one's mother's knee, and one also learns from one's county nutrition committee.

Spreading the News

In this rural community, much is transmitted verbally through the telephone. Telephone subscribers are, it is true, chiefly White owners and long-term tenants, but local news is spread to other social classes through the lines of communication extending from White owners to their tenants. In Westmore there are from ten to twenty-four subscribers on the same telephone line.

'Twixt the Cup and the Lip

Listening in on any conversation is expected. Everyone knows the doctor's "ring" and hastens to find out who is ill. Sometimes the doctor has to request that listeners hang up when the current gets too weakened by these added listeners for him to hear the message. For those who can afford it, this grapevine is as efficient in broadcasting community announcements as an African tom-tom. Regarding this, a White owner says:

> If it was something that could go to the public, we would call up somebody. We would call our brother-in-law if it is about our relatives. If we heard of a new baby, we would call Cousin Anna. Cousin Anna's mother and our mother were sisters. If it was about some fancy dish, we would call Cousin Ruth Cone 'cause she likes fancy food. We wouldn't say anything about scandal—we would let them find that out for themselves.

Thus, the main lines extend to other White owners who are also relatives, but not to relatives who are of a lesser social class. The blood ties appear to be less important than the social barriers. This is borne out by the list of persons mentioned as the chief ones visited:

> We like to go see John Wall [an owner] and Mr. Marks [brother-in-law, owner], Cousin Susie and Mable [owners], Cousin Lloyd Thomas [Master Farmer, owner] and Cousin Anna [owner].

Similarly, the families mentioned as members of the Baptist church are the White owner families. Finally, there is this corroboration:

> Well, we visit all of our neighbors, mostly if they were sick or something like that, but we got to see those on our telephone line and members of our church.

Other Lines of Communication

The White sharecropper get news by different means. A long-term sharecropper like this informant may rise to prominence in the community organizations:

Now, we don't have a telephone but the news goes like a flash of lightning. Mrs. Don Gill [a relative, owner] can usually tell me more than anybody. She visits more than anybody in this community. She likes to go places but there is nobody but her and her husband. She don't miss a day but what she goes somewhere. You know if you hear anything of interest you have to tell your best friend, and they tell their best friend, and like that.

A Negro sharecropper says:

I would try to take the news to somebody like John and Bessie and then I talk with Jack and his people and Helen 'cause she natchully is my child and then Turners 'cause I'm interested in them and they are kinda backwards and I know I seem a little better than them, and they seem to want to know, and they don't get offended at what I say. Then Ella Tolley and Ola Johns, she is always talking about things.

Short-term White and Negro croppers and wage-laborers seem to be somewhat limited to members of their own class and race. They may intermingle at the country store, though not often in the more formal organizations like churches or clubs.

Aside from their ties with the rest of the plantation unit,[1] short-term White and Negro croppers and wage-laborers communicate most with members of their own class and race.

Periodicals

Many of the urban foodways are introduced ot the rural South through media like periodicals, radio, and motion pictures. It is well to consider the policy which actuates food advertisers in order to discover some of the underlying motivations.

A group of marketing specialists who dominate the food policies of the urban magazines stated before the Committee on Food Habits that "Emotional urge plus rationalism is the basis of all successful advertising."[2] As one result of such a policy, strong attitudes about food may be encouraged, even where they did not exist before. If the rural public, among others, is told that a vitamin-enriched food will not only prevent malnutrition, inefficiency, and borderline states of disease, but also is an aid to dieting, is economical, and is a means of winning the war, it is probable that the Southern esteem for foods especially prized will be greatly reinforced by this wider sanction.

It may be seriously questioned, however, whether periodicals reach as large a section of the rural populace as is supposed. It has been alleged that a well-rounded list of periodicals reaches seventy-five per cent of the population. The actual percentage of the population covered is much lower than this for the whole United States, and especially low for the Southern region.

Illiteracy itself is not the chief difficulty in Westmore-Glen. Rather, the community may be said to be *nonliterate,* that is, without a habit of reading or an interest in literature. The community learns by talking and visiting, seeing and doing, rather than at second-hand from reading. With one exception, none of the leaders in the three rural communities studied read more than the newspaper. One leader sat by the hour listening ot the conversation of newcomers to her boarding house; another attended all the public meetings she could; one landowner spent much time talking with others at the country store and the mill; another took trips to cities in the sate. A rural citizen who read extensively in these communities would be considered a little unsocial and eccentric.

Nor are the physical means for literary contact available. For Seaford residents, the nearest library was eighteen miles or more away, with a dollar deposit required for out-of-towners. The County Bookmobile offset this deficiency to some extent by its regular stops around the county. Similarly, German Flats people were sixteen miles from a library, and Westmore citizens were twelve miles away, with no Bookmobile available. Such is the situation for White rural residents; Negroes are limited to the few books available in local schools.

Not only is a low proportion of the population reached by periodicals, but also there is a class differential apparent here, in that the owners tend to make up by far the greatest proportion of those who do subscribe.[3] The custom of lending newspapers and magazines somewhat extends their influence.

Furthermore, the Southern farmer spends his spare cash on a magazine that can tell him how to raise more cotton and tobacco. The women's magazines do not perform a comparable utilitarian function for the Southern housewife because the electric stoves, aluminum utensils, and party menus there depicted are alien to her equipment and needs.

The informants show how periodicals reach them:

> I have read recipes in papers, but I don't take some, I jest get'm from different people; Mrs. Dan Norris (the landlord's wife) up here give me some *Southern Farmer* and *Southern Agriculturist*. About once a year I see the magazines. [Negro wage-laborer.]

> One good thing Mr. Norman did last year was he sent the *Progressive Farmer* to all his croppers. We have the *Country Gentleman* and the *Southern Agriculturist* and *Progressive Farmer, Ladies' Home Journal* and *House and Garden*. The menus are too fancy in the magazines. We just have to supplement something else.

If relatively few persons are contacted, how effective is this contact where food is concerned? Do the women actually read the women's page? Can they follow out recipes presented in the "canned" syndicated women's page prepared without respect to regional food habits and local surpluses? We must tentatively conclude that this happens only rarely, certainly much less frequently than over-optimistic food editors conclude.

Radio

As in the case of periodicals, the most obvious limitation to the influence of radio as a medium is the lack of radios. Though it is often claimed that there is a radio in nearly every American farm home, the case is very different in the South. As a matter of fact, about one farm home in three possessed a radio, and these again centered in the homes of the Whites and the owners.

It is true that electric power lines are being extended through the Rural Electrification program and commercial agencies, but some rural sections are entirely without electric power. Keeping a battery recharged is often too expensive for a sharecropper. Then too, battery radios and many others have a range of only about fifty miles, so that in Westmore one could listen to the Athens station, rarely to Atlanta. Finally, when a farm family listens to a program, they much more often choose a news broadcast than a Farm and Home Hour, and a radio comedian than a nutrition program.

Motion Pictures

Curiously, there was much less movie-going in Westmore and in German Flats than in Seaford. Though people could better afford to attend in these communities, they seemed more satisfied with sources of entertainment at hand (the movies were ten miles or more away), like calling on neighbors, club meetings, and church affairs. Then, too, very few of the professional pictures were close enough to the experience of farm families to affect them much, particularly where food was concerned. Scenes of cocktail parties, beautiful suburban kitchens, completely electrified, with perhaps a ruffled apron on the heroine as a concession to realism, even such a standard of living as that of the supposedly typical Hardy family series, were simply too remote from the Westmore world, even for aspiration.

While Westmore residents seldom attended professional movies, they did go to the occasional presentations of farm pictures which the county agent or the school superintendent showed at the elementary school three miles away. During the War, the Civilian Defense movie shown at Glen was a major event in the Negro community's year. This was a picture on fire bombs, describing their construction, illustrating how they could be extinguished and what preventive measures could be applied in attics. To begin with, no Negro in Glen had an attic or a stirrup-pump. Moreover, if a fire bomb should drop on a cabin, one Negro said he'd simply run out and let the shack burn down. None of our informants had seen a movie on nutrition, and as yet most such movies available still deal with the unfamiliar.

Studies in the Effectiveness of Techniques

Studies in other sections reveal the relative effectiveness of techniques used to change food choices.[4] How does a child learn about food? Is he to be coerced or cajoled into eating his spinach? Should he be allowed to choose what he wants? And as for adults—must they be lectured or will they learn best if they question what they are told?

In the South, children are made to work and obey but, like other members of the family, their preferences are catered to. There is much more free choice than cajoling, much more cajoling than coercion. There is little feeling that the nasty-tasting things are good for you, no Spartan reducing diets or use of food for punishment. If a food doesn't "set well on the stomach," it is simply omitted from the dietary. Thus, without planning, such families may provide exactly those conditions of watchful neglect, pleasing atmosphere, social conversation, and small portions recommended by G. M. Borgeson in her study of nursery school children.[5]

Where children are actively guided, they seem to learn most, at first, from the example of other members of the family. Food aversions of family members are associated with 35 per cent of children's food aversions.[6] Family authorities are replaced by outside sources as the child develops. Kurt Lewin says:

> The frequencies with which "mother" or "father" are mentioned as authorities in the "scold" question decrease steadily from the 5th to the 12th grade, while the frequency of a more impersonal authority such as "doctor" or "everyone," increases with age.[7]

By praise and scolding they influence the choices of children. Lewin found that they praised dairy products, vegetables, meat, potatoes, bread, and fruits, while they scolded children for eating candy, coffee, tea, cake, relishes, and alcoholic beverages.[8] That the sanction is effective at an early age is apparent from the children's own characterization of a "swell" meal as consisting mainly of praised foods and a "terrible" meal as consisting mainly of the scolded foods. Duncker has pointed out, as our data also indicate, that specific food items acquire connotations and that a food item will be rejected or accepted in accordance with its connotation.

Wilkins made an important contribution to the problem of changing children's food habits in his experiments with school lunches in North Carolina. Here he found that the consumption of evaporated milk could be increased daily by presenting the child with very small portions and lowering or increasing the quantity in accordance with his consumption. Indeed, repetition of food seems to overcome food dislikes, for Kurt Lewin found that "people like what they eat, rather than eat what they like."

Some studies of change in adults' food habits have been made. An experiment in the Merrill-Palmer School reported by Mary Sweeny disclosed that the reasons for change were, in order of importance: education, medical advice, change in environment, change in taste and ways of preparation, reducing, professional connection, and social reasons. The changes reported were higher among adults and private school parents than among students and W. P. A. parents.[9] Dorothy Dickins' study of small town families in Mississippi further indicates that high income and professional groups are most inclined to try new dishes.[10]

An experiment in adult education in new habits, *The Relative Effectiveness of a Lecture Method and a Method of Group Decision for Changing Food Habits,* was conducted by Kurt Lewin in Iowa. The attempt was made to induce groups of adults to eat the nutritious internal parts of animals like liver, kidney, and brains. Some of these groups were lectured to by a speaker while in others the project was open to question and discussion, in the course of which the nutritionist spoke briefly as if a member of the group. A check was made later upon actual consumption of the commended foods. Lewin concludes: "In other words, the lectures led to action in 10 per cent of the participants: the group decision led to action in 52 per cent.[11]

The effectiveness of such a technique may be contrasted with negative findings in regard to formal efforts by a nutrition committee and use of multiple media to change food habits in Charlottesville, Virginia, over a period of several years. When a nutritionist and a nurse work personally with families, Gillett and Rice found that the families ate more protective foods than when impersonal methods were used.

In a cafeteria study the consumption of soybean dishes was observed. When four appeals (nutritional value, American rather than Oriental food, good value for your money, variety) were used in four identical cafeterias, it was found that the use of the nutrition appeal seemed a poor one for introduction of such a new food—perhaps, it is suggested, because to Americans a food which "is good for you" is quite likely to be not "good to eat." Soybeans, incidentally, are an interesting instance of what happens to a war-fostered food product. Introduced with considerable publicity, as in Governor Dewey's soybean luncheon, they have now, reports Jeanette B. McCay, been generally forgotten except for a small steady demand for soy publications and such use as a stretcher for meat loaves.[12]

This review of the various studies on changing the food habits of children and adults must lead to the conclusion that our society induces changes by education rather than by coercion, and by informal education rather than formal. If we review the means of changing food habits and disseminating ideas about food demonstrated in Westmore and Glen, there, too, a vast process of education is going on, not one of coercion by economic circumstances, governmental programs, tyrannical landlords, or disapproving mothers.

To a certain extent, the informal agencies, except at the least formal level where feeling is not verbally expressed, are restricted by custom from exchanging food attitudes and information about the routine foods. There is some reason to believe that techniques involving personal decision and contact will be more successful in a rural setting than other techniques. One such device is the use of demonstration. The rural sections described here are not accustomed to the literary tools of academicians and advertisers. They are accustomed to the primary stuff of experience—whatever can be touched and seen and heard. Thus the formal agencies find their greatest success with model housekeeping apartments (used by the school in Seaford, N. C.), with demonstrations in cooking (used by the Home Demonstration Clubs in Seaford, German Flats and Westmore), and in soil conservation demonstration projects (used in all three places). That the commercial agencies find demonstration effective is shown by an informant's account:

> Now last year the Georgia Power Company had a trailer in Westmore and gave a beautiful demonstration. They invited one from each family of the people who had lights and the home service agent just had a regular luncheon for them and she cooked everything right there that day and baked a cake,

had potato salad, ham, apples and fixed it in such an attractive way. They had things that were nutritious, that showed a well-balanced meal. They demonstrated a washing machine and had a movie to show how to use all these things.

Thus the demonstrations stick in minds that soon forget what they had learned in textbooks and pamphlets. In the same way children learn how to make biscuits and corn bread and sausage from the informal demonstrations of their mothers and not from perusing written recipes.

The Dynamics of Food Habits

No part of the social structure in any area remains static. No system of food habits is ever fixed. We have, therefore, been dealing with a shifting food pattern, social relations and a culture in flux.

Since we are interested in trends and processes in the minor area of food, we must first consider what has been happening in the major area of culture in general. Within the present century, improved techniques of food production and distribution have made accessible to Westmore a range of food items hardly imaginable previously, while the twentieth-century nutrition research which has been disseminated through the improved techniques of communication has drastically changed attitudes toward food among certain groups in the most isolated sections.

Over and over, the larger society stresses the *validity of scientific knowledge*. Ancient science greatly concerned itself with the elements of the dietary: Pliny gives us twenty-seven uses of cabbage. But modern science has articulated and compiled its discoveries in the field of food comparatively recently.

Change through Outside Contacts

The process of change in food habits may be thus described: after a readiness for change has been established, the traditional dietary inculcated by the permanent relations of family and neighborhood, race and class undergoes substitution, addition, or subtraction through episodic relations which introduce first

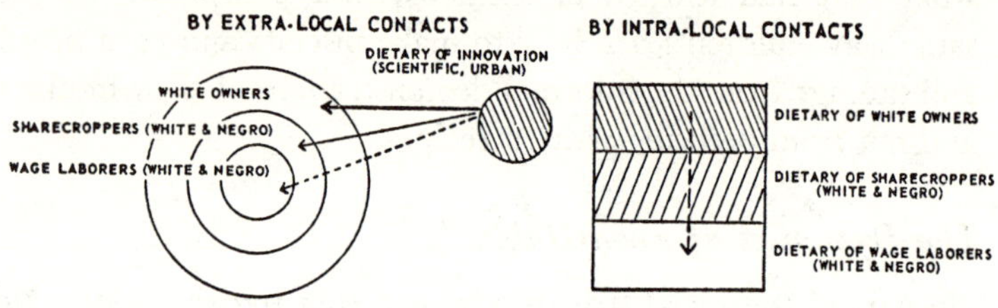

FIG 2. DYNAMICS OF FOOD HABIT DIFFUSION

the *idea* of scientific urban knowledge, and then its specific recommendations in the field of food. At any given time in a locality there is a changing area in the dietary which may be

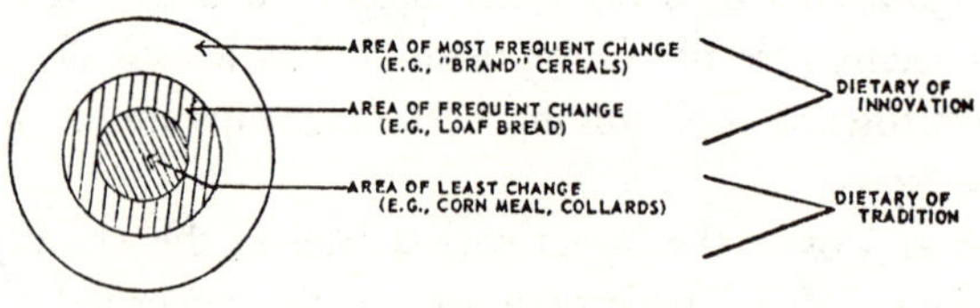

FIG. 1. DIAGRAM OF STRUCTURE OF BASIC DIETARY

called the dietary of innovation. Since food innovations are differentially adopted by various social classes, races, and individuals, the dietary of innovation is extremely varied in any locality. In the rural South, innovations in the food pattern seemed to be most quickly adopted by the Whites, particularly owners and long-term sharecroppers, who have more outside contacts.

Change through Local Contacts

Within each local area, a similar process of establishment of the dietary of innovation goes on. Foodways associated with the lower social classes tend to be eliminated, while the new foodways tend to be those associated with the higher classes. In the rural South, the trend is therefore toward the food habits of the White owner class, whose food habits, in turn, are participating in the world trend toward a scientifically sanctioned dietary. In the rural South as a whole, however, as in each local area, there are eddies in this current. The general process of diffusion of food habits is interrupted by the strength of Southern family relations, which puts the parent before the book or the nutritionist. It is also deflected by the high regard the South has on the one hand for tradition, and on the other, for the worth of individual tastes.

The Function of Individual Preferences in the Process of Change

Much research remains to be done on the psychogenetic causes of personal aversions and preferences. *Why* so many foods "do not agree with" Southerners we do not know. The South does not dispute much about tastes. There may be individuals who drink a pint of milk a day in Seaford, or Westmore women who eat meat in the post-partum diet. It would be enough for such individuals to say to their Southern neighbors that milk or meat agreed with them.

Nevertheless, what is significant about the individual preferences in the process of changing food habits is that individuals do *not* generally oppose the prevalent foodways, and that food deviations obtain in a considerable group, either throughout a locality or a social class, so that on closer inspection what appears to be an individual deviation turns out to be really the foodways of a particular group.

All foodways are in a certain sense magical acts. The dietary of innovation is usually selected in accordance with the approval of (1) one's group, specifically those of the dominant social group, and (2) the culture. Such a selection is followed by psychological satisfaction and improved digestion. Conversely, if an urban Northerner should eat only one meal a day or eat his meals at irregular times, he would feel both psychological and physical discomfort in contrast to the Southerner, who expects irregularity. *The strength of the psychological and physical reactions to foods is proportionate to the degree to which the individual becomes aware of the standards of his socio-cultural environment.* It is all one to an infant: he will *attempt* to eat pencils, insects, dirt, or raw potatoes, while an adult choosing food will abide by example and tutelage, as well as by experience. In the stratified social system of the South the Negro is tending to abandon his more undiscriminating consumption of the foods available to him in wild game and edible plants for the more discriminating standards of his superiors in the social structure.

Summary

The transmission of foodways is a dynamic process. Although the rate of change in food habits varies in accordance with disaster and prosperity, we are mainly concerned with how it takes place under normal conditions.

Interchange of food ideas and attitudes as such through the medium of most informal relations is considered proper only for unusual occasions, and for food items with high prestige value. It is not considered proper to discuss routine elements of the food pattern with an implication of teaching or coercion.

However, in the most informal relations, as within the family, the foodways are communicated by example and tacit expression of attitude. The use of demonstration appears to be the most successful means of introducing new foodways formally in a Southern rural setting.

Just as all parts of any culture are in the constant process of changing, so are food habits. The change may be so slow that it is almost imperceptible to the observer, limited by living in only one time and place. But signs of the changing pattern as well as the traditional stability may be seen. Science introduces new foods and provides means for distributing them. These changes are adopted by various individuals, then by groups, whose contacts outside their home communities have taught them new ways of doing things. In the rural South, changes in foodways appear to be most quickly adopted by the Whites, particularly owners and long-term sharecroppers, who have most outside contacts. Lower social classes in turn tend to look to the White owners as bearers of new methods and the standards worthy of imitation. Individuals tend to reflect the foodways of the group of which they are, or aspire to be, members, more than their own tastes in deciding whether or not to try new foods.

NOTES

1. This is defined as any farm with two or more tenant families. Westmore plantation units are small and not comparable to the plantations of the Mississippi Delta, for example.
2. Conference with Committee on Food Habits, National Research Council, June 27, 1941, p. 6.
3. In Seaford, magazine subscribers represented 40 percent of the Whites, but only 20 percent of the Negroes; and 44.6 percent of the owners but only 16.8 percent of the non-owners. Newspaper subscribers ranged from 32 percent in Seaford (40 percent of the Whites, 14 percent of the Negroes; 44.6 percent of the owners, 11.2 percent of the non-owners) to 65 percent in Westmore community and 15 percent in Glen.
4. This material is cited as summarized in the *Manual for the Study of Food Habits,* Bulletin of the National Research Council, No. 111, January, 1945, pp. 84 ff.
5. Gertrude M. Borgeson, *Techniques Used by the Teacher During the*

Nursery School Luncheon Period (New York: Bureau of Publications, Columbia University, 1938).

6. D. McCarthy, "Children's Feeding Problems in Relation to the Food Aversions in the Family," *Child Development,* 1935, No. 6, reported in the Conference of the Committee on Food Habits, June 28, 1941.
7. Kurt Lewin, *A Group Test for Determining the Anchorage Points of Food Habits,* Committee on Food Habits, National Research Council, p. 8.
8. *Ibid.,* p. 7.
9. Percentage of changes: Merrill-Palmer staff, 40 percent; Merrill-Palmer students, 36 percent; Merrill-Palmer parents, 94.5 percent (women, 50.5 percent; men, 44 percent); W.P.A. parents, 32.8 percent. Reported in Conference with Committee on Food Habits, June 28, 1941.
10. Dorothy Dickins, *op. cit.*
11. Kurt Lewin (director), *The Relative Effectiveness of a Lecture Method and a Method of Group Decision for Changing Food Habits* (Washington, D. C.: Committee on Food Habits, National Research Council, 1942), p. 4.
12. Jeanette B. McCay, "Soybeans Are Here to Stay," *Journal of Home Economics,* December, 1947, pp. 629-30.

6

Tradition in the Foodways

In any society certain prevailing values develop which are peculiarly characteristic of the culture. A great number of these values—for example, that we ought to be kind to animals, that everyone ought to earn his own living, that big boys don't cry—are brought home to the child in nursery rhymes and in Sunday School and in the behavior of persons he observes. They are the principles by which a given group of people lives. Since these values are often implicit, and in simple societies infrequently find their way into written statement, they are rather difficult to determine.

Recognizing this, we nevertheless find at least four configurations or prevailing values in Southern culture appear and reappear in the interview material often enough to justify special discussion. They are: respect for tradition, reverence for science, affability, and approval of social distinctions. These are by no means the only values, but they do appear to be major ones for the study of food habits. In this and the next three chapters we will see how the food patterns reflect these values.

Anglo-Saxon Heritage

It is often too comfortably assumed that the Southern heritage is represented by the mythical mint-julep sipper on a shaded verandah—a hangover from the Cavalier influence—while the Northern heritage is Puritan. But there are no simple stereotypes in any region. Not one of our informants could be termed a "typical" Southerner. For example, Lela Fouche, whose case interviews are cited at length in the Appendix, might be called a typical Puritan in her zeal for proselyting her neighbors, or a typical Yankee in her stress upon turning a penny to account. It is only by analysis of the more complex character of the culture that the real patterns appear.

Actually, the fifteen hundred Cavaliers reputed to have left the heritage of gaiety and laxity to the whole South were concentrated mainly in Virginia and Maryland, while fifty thousand colonists bearing other traditions came to the Southern states: Scotch-Irish Covenanters in the Piedmont, French Huguenots in the tidewater districts of South Carolina and Virginia, and English middle-class immigrants into Georgia. Aside from those who can legitimately claim descent from the aristocratic Cavaliers, many are descended from white immigrants who came or were deported as political prisoners for having committed offenses against the sometimes cruel laws, and from those who had been coerced or lured by agents getting a shilling a head for immigrants.[1]

It is obvious that the Southern heritage is not wholly aristocratic, gay, gallant, violent, and dissolute in the Cavalier tradition, nor wholly commoner, serious-minded, righteous, and zealot in the Puritan tradition. But two strains of influence appear dominant among the traditions to which Southern folk look back: the Anglo-Scotch-Irish ancestry, and religion.

There are many indications of English roots in this culture. The names of Westmore residents are the same as those found in any English village, while a foreign name immediately marks an outsider. Old English expressions persist, such as "holp" for "helped" and "rude" for "strong." In diction, the omission of the final "g" as in "goin' " was common in eighteenth-century England. The omission of the "r" in "pork" and "more" is common in East and South England. The pronunciation of "heard" as "heerd" resembles the Anglo-Saxon "hierde." The use of the "y" sound, "cyar" and "gyarden" for "car" and "garden" is found in North Derby, Leicester, Northwest Oxford and Hereford.[2] An historical study has stated that the

English tradition also had an important effect upon the cooking in this section:

The cooking was English. Large dinners, crowded teas, picnics, and fishing parties, and functions borrowed from the English, were popular.[3]

Religious Background

Closely associated with the Anglo-Scotch-Irish strain is the religious character of the heritage. This is overwhelmingly Protestant. Odum calls the South the stronghold of Protestantism in the United States, since only five per cent of the total church membership in this region is non-Protestant. The two main denominations are Baptist and Methodist.

In contrast to many urban sections, the rural South still places great importance both upon religious institutions and upon the less formal expressions of religious beliefs.[4] The conversation of people in Westmore is full of references to the Bible —quotations, anecdotes, and characters, as this excerpt from a White sharecropper's case history will serve to illustrate:

You know the Bible says the first shall be last and the last first. There was that Mr. Green up on the hill and he had one-half million dollars and you know that is a lot for the South. He had ten sons and you know all of 'em died beggars except one and that was 'cause he robbed the others, so that is why I say the Bible is true, that God printed it. Now there is some that don't believe there are a God but you know there are a God.

A lot of rich people in the South after the Civil War lost all they had 'cause the niggers was freed. The rich people didn't know how to do anything and it was those who hadn't anything and learned to work and knew the hardships to work—it was those who could keep going. That's why I say, the first shall be last and the last first.

And another thing the Bible say, is that at the end of time men shall fly with wings. When I was a child, I was looking to sprout wings. I remember the first airplane I ever saw. I was so thrilled and I remember what the Bible said about men would fly with wings.

Thus similarity in nationalistic and religious background is a unifying influence in the Southern heritage, in spite of the social distinctions that exist. Surely the solidarity of the South is more real than any of its divergencies.

Echoes of this cultural background common to almost all the social classes are to be found in the food pattern in the South. There is, for example, positive sanction for the complex of tradition, pride in the past, and suspicion of innovation in certain areas. In the food pattern, comparably, there is positive sanction for the stability of food habits, food attitudes, food production and preservation, and cooking.

The forces of tradition are very strong as well as very old in the rural South. Frederick Olmsted, writing in the 1850's, notes this quality even then: "They say this uneasiness—this passion for change—is a peculiarity of our diseased Northern nature. The Southern man finds Providence in all that is: Satan in all that might be."[5]

To begin with, the past is regarded as more glorious than the present and the future. To a farmer, glory may be measured in the possession of land. Many old families contrast huge acreages of the frontier past with the dwindling acreages of the present. Attached to the homestead where we stayed there had once been a thousand acres and a mill belonging to the present owner's grandfather. Now there are only sixty acres in all, partly cultivated, with no stock, and but one tenant family.

One reason for this stress on the past is the predominance of older age groups within the White community. A White sharecropper says:

Oh yes, we really are proud of our young people to get educated and come back and work with us. But well, I will tell you that we haven't had much experience because some of them that go off don't come back.

It is hard for us to get the young people interested in the League, some have dates and I tell you we don't have many young people right now in the community. We don't have many young married people right around here, either.

It is, therefore, natural that the older people remaining on the farms should find consolation in remembering the past, since three-quarters of Westmore residents have no prospect of their children's carrying on their farms after them. The Negro community as a whole is increasing, but its young people, also, often leave for job opportunities in other sections.

Another indication of respect for the guidance of tradition is seen in the use of proverbs, local and Biblical, which were frequently on the lips of local informants:

There is one thing I've learned—that right goes a long way and wrong don't go far.

But I say the first thing put in your children is the last thing to go out.

A person who will be faithful over a little will be faithful over a heap.

Somebody will help you if you try to help yourself.

Attitude toward Living-at-home Practices

The isolated frontier farmer was forced to provide for his needs without much dependence upon outside resources. Even from colonial times, however, he found it profitable to raise specialty crops for sale, like silk, indigo, cotton, and tobacco. Provision for home needs gradually lessened in importance, while the production of the specialty crop increased in importance in accordance with the trend of the division of labor in society.

Living-at-home, therefore, is a tradition of the frontier rather than of the immediate past. The tradition of the immediate past is to produce a cash crop first and foremost, and to subordinate provision for home needs to this end.

This may explain the difficulty agricultural authorities have had in attempting to secure a return to live-at-home practices.[6] The appeal is not to tradition but runs counter to present traditions. The advocates of self-sufficiency on the farm are in the position of carriers of a new and strange cultural value, as was Gandhi in advocating the return of the spinning wheel. Living-at-home is not even a value of our European-American culture, since for us, presumably, the principle of the division of labor is too well established for question.

Westmore admires the tradition of the frontier past but practices the traditions of the immediate past. The household arts that accompany living-at-home include the making of soap, bread, lye hominy, butter, and the curing of hams. Back of some houses, the big black kettle bubbles, 'trying out the fat.' Later the housewife will cut slices of pale yellow soap. These are not in general practice. The household arts of making bedspreads and quilts, reed brooms, caning chairs, spinning, carding cotton into bats for quilts, and crocheting elaborate spreads are still practiced. But these activities are no longer characteristics of many homes. One family may make its own lard; another may make soap or reed brooms. The mothers who are now fifty and sixty years old are probably the last ones to make elaborately crocheted bedspreads, one for each child, as a dowry.

Mother did some of that reseating chairs but we don't. We have one chair that mother did when Martin was a little boy. It was at the Thoms County Fair. He entered his chair and the one that had the best got a ton of guano and he got it. When you buy guano they ask you if you want white sacks; of course, you pay two or three cents more for it. Some make dresses or pillow cases out of guano sacks, and they last so long, they are real heavy. [White owner.]

Many of the traditional household arts are becoming semi-commercialized. A White owner says:

The handicrafts are popular, they are a sorta luxury and play-work. There are several people who bottom chairs and charge for it; of course they don't make a living at it but they make something.

Others make a part-time living by quilting and embroidering. In itself, such commercialization is an indication that handicrafts are disappearing from actual practice in home behavior patterns. Women who order all their bedspreads at $3.98 from Sears-Roebuck may crochet spreads for sale at twice the amount. Such sales are almost invariably to outsiders, however, and seldom to members of the community, who are also patrons of mail-order houses. Often, however, admiration for others' traditional skills is expressed:

> These Brown girls over here make quilts and they are just as pretty on the bottom as they are on the top. Their mother used to spin. I wish I had my grandmother's spinning wheel. I could polish it up and wouldn't it be pretty! [White sharecropper.]

Tradition in the Foodways

Accounts of earlier travelers like the Bartrams and Olmsted show that the diet in colonial times was much like that of the present.

In Olmsted's account of a meal with a White owner in the 1850's, we may note not only the almost identical items of the diet, but also three contemporary characteristics of *frying* the food, serving *hot* breads, and *duplicating food groups* in one meal:

> There was fried fowl, and fried ham and eggs, and cold ham; there were preserved peaches, and preserved quinces and grapes; there was hot wheaten biscuit, and hot short-cake, and hot corn cake, and hot griddle-cakes, soaked in butter; there was coffee, and there was milk, sour or sweet, whichever I preferred to drink.[7]

Vance[8] believes that the Southerner inherited the English common man's love of meat—not fresh but salted meat because of the lack of preservatives and the hot climate. For

Negroes, the slaves' weekly allowance of three pounds of pork, a peck of corn, a pint of salt, and molasses may be compared with the contemporary diet cited in Table V.

The theme of traditionalism in the foodways is stated by a White sharecropper:

> Some people are in a rut and you can't get 'em to cook anything except what they are ustah cooking and that is the same way about farming, they raise what they usually do.

A Negro sharecropper shows how difficult it is to persuade her husband to change from the customary crops to include any food crops:

> When my first husband and me marry, we don't raise anything but cotton, and I get 'um to raise some corn when we have one baby. And then we have two chil'un and I get 'um to raise some cane, but I don't get 'um off of that cotton.

A striking illustration of the persistence of the older food habits was given in the experience of one of our Negro wage-laborer informants. She had been a cook for a Jewish family on Long Island but said:

> No'm, after I learn it, I don't eat it no mo' after I come home. When I was up there, I cooked duck twice, and I jest don't like their taste.
>
> I ustah cook cabbage for these people for twenty minutes. Now I don't know how long I cook 'em, maybe two hours. I simply don't time myself. I jest cook 'em till they get done and always season 'em with fat meat.

Unlike the case in the urban or small-town culture, food purchasing in the rural South is often done by the men on the weekly trip to town, rather than by the women. In addition, husbands usually control the major part of food production on the farm, and their food preferences are considered in the planting of gardens by the women. The latter consideration reflects the general patriarchal family structure. All of these customs mean that changes in food habits, as well as the retention of long-used, conservative practices, are dependent on the man of a family. Women introduce changes through the use of new recipes, or, more frequently, by following recipes of oral tradition. A Negro sharecropper tells how this works out:

> A lot of people go and buy meat and bread and a big, long piece of fat-back. My husband just buy some lard and flour and black molasses and a great long piece of fat-back, which is old-timey.

Her landlord's sister adds:

> Lena was telling me that she had spinach for dinner one day and Uncle John, her husband, does not like it. He wasn't there when the rest of them ate. But when he ate, Lena asked him if he would have some poke. He said he would take some and then asked if anybody else didn't want the rest of it. 'No,' she said, 'you go ahead and eat it.' So he went ahead and ate the rest thinking it was poke.

Summary and Conclusions

The cultural attitudes common to all classes of persons in the South appear to have two principal sources: the Anglo-Scotch-Irish heritage (rather than the Cavalier tradition as is commonly claimed), and the religious, chiefly Protestant, belief and practice. The regional value system also absorbs the contributions of divergent individuals as well as the influences of larger European-American culture. The traditional attitudes shown in cultural values have their counterparts in the food pattern.

One such cultural value is the traditionalism which focuses on pride in the past (expressed by the old persons who form the largest population group in the community). The foodways also show resistance to change and new practices, exemplified by the similarity of the frontier dietary to the contemporary dietary, and the failure of new culture contacts to produce fundamental changes in food habits.

There is every reason to expect that food habits might have changed. The great technological expansion has freed isolated sections from reliance upon their own resources. The diversity in the taste discriminations of individuals would lead us to expect changes. Differences in social structure and in race might have produced greater divergences than merely the quantity of diet. That the food pattern has changed so little is a proof that in the local cultural pattern there is a major sanction for stability in food habits.

NOTES

1. J. Edward Kirbye, *Puritanism in the South* (Boston: The Pilgrim Press, 1908), pp. 7-8.
2. William Cabell Greet, "Southern Speech" in *Culture in the South,* W. T. Couch, ed. (Chapel Hill: The University of North Carolina Press, 1935), pp. 594-615.
3. Lee W. Ryan, *French Travelers in the Southeastern United States, 1775-1800* (Bloomington, Indiana: The Principia Press, Inc., 1939), p. 39.
4. The religious influence is powerful though not necessarily institutionalized, particularly for the lower classes. *Cf.* Margaret Jarman Hagood, *Mothers of the South* (Chapel Hill: The University of North Carolina Press, 1939), p. 172: "The church is still the chief organization in which rural people participate. And yet about three fourths of these tenant mothers do not attend regularly and only three go every Sunday, although almost all go occasionally, and to revival meetings in the summer."
5. Frederick Law Olmsted, *A Journey in the Seaboard Slave States in the Years 1853-1854* (New York: G. P. Putnam's Sons, 1904), Vol. 1, p. 2.
6. One of the criteria for the Georgia State Extension Department's selection of Master Farmers is the raising of a large proportion of food and feed. South Carolina issues a certificate signed by the Governor for those who raise 75 percent of food and feed requirements.
7. Olmsted, *op. cit.,* p. 88.
8. Rupert B. Vance, *Human Geography of the South* (Chapel Hill: The University of North Carolina Press, 1932).

7

Science Tells Us–

Once upon a time, science was an infant like Hercules, grappling in its cradle with the serpents of superstition and unquestioned authority. To some persons it seems as if the infant science, in growing up, turned into the very serpents it strangled, rather like the unfortunate baby in *Alice in Wonderland* that insisted on turning into a pig. To Occidentals, at least, the words "Science tells us—" stop all questions, and, when they are uttered, freeze the awkward attitudes that speculation finds us in. "Unscientific" becomes the new anathema.

This happens because scientists can point with justifiable pride to substantial things like electric eyes and aureomycin and the too, too solid mushroom cloud. From them science acquires enormous prestige.

The difficulty arises when rural Southerners, like members of other simple societies, cannot distinguish the penumbra from the sun, nor the hangers-on of science from the real contributors. For unfortunately, the ritual of the scientific method is sometimes repeated for its own sake. The collection of data is considered only the collection of figures and the pseudo-scientists are back there in the counting-house, murmuring "Hollerith be thy name."

Conflicts in Cultural Values: Tradition vs. Science

Southern love of tradition is a current running counter to the scientific trend in the culture of Europe and America. The latter has elements which are urban, scientific, eclectic, mobile, impersonal, and academic; while the local Southern culture at present is predominantly rural, traditional, stable, personal, and based on experience.

While the rural group as a whole continues to be oriented toward traditionalism, some groups, as for instance, the White owners and young people, have begun to adopt the values of the wider culture. The further use of gadgets for tele-communication may be expected to close up the gap between the local and the national culture. This gap is less one of space than of time, the standards of today contrasted with those of yesterday. Furthermore, the innovations of today are quite likely to become the traditions of tomorrow.

Thus, along with the major pattern of tradition in the folkways and in the foodways, there is a second pattern of innovations in the folkways and in the foodways. More specifically, the stress on science, progress, urban superiority, and education in the folkways is parallel to the stress on progressive methods of food production, scientific nutrition for men and animals, adoption of urban choices, preparation, and serving of food on occasion, and attitudes deprecating rural foods and foodways as unprogressive.

The impact of the conflict between the rural tradition and the urban innovation is exemplified in one Negro sharecropper family. The mother characterizes herself thus:

> I had two children and I went to Augusta and got a job cooking for a rich lady. She wanted an experienced maid. I told her I wasn't experienced, but that I was willing to learn and to do everything she told me—I'm like that—I'm not hard to learn. I can change my ways and do things like people tell me.

This informant differed with her conservative, tradition-loving husband over many questions. One example of the clash occurred over the question of securing electric lighting. She describes their conflicting attitudes on this question:

They is a whole lot of people in the country that do like the city folks 'cause the city people have brought it to the country. When we started to have lights, my husband say we ain't going to have lights. I say we is. He say they ain't no need to, we got along so far without it. I say no need to stay in the same rut all the time, so we get lights.

The conflict between the rural tradition and the newfangled science is stronger when the new ways are introduced without regard for adaptations required in the local situation. The representative of science may be inept, unable to make such adaptations, and may therefore arouse overt local opposition to his interpretation of the universal culture. This incident shows such a situation:

Our first home economics teacher didn't make a success of her job because of her personality, I suppose. It was her first year teaching, you could tell that. She wasn't interested in her work.

Now let me tell you what she done. She asked several ladies to cook cakes for this dinner. She asked this lady that didn't at the time have any eggs or milk or butter much, to bake a cake. She baked a real nice coconut cake, and just because it was square she had it throwed away. It just made the lady sick. She said, if the teacher had sent it back to her, she would have been glad to have it, but to throw out a nice cake like that! [White sharecropper.]

Such a person may, as Linton suggests,[1] introduce so few alternatives adapted to the local situation that the local people cannot easily make them their own. That is, a teacher may not present the whole system of values of the universal culture but only a part of them presented in the single form which she has learned. Her little learning may be a dangerous thing. She will tend to stress that version of the foodways presented in a single home economics textbook, and further she will stress the recommended *forms* rather than the spirit even of that single textbook. Thus an adult nutrition class studies etiquette and the form of a menu rather than the many alternates possible for foodways:

> We have meetings on nutrition. The school is supposed to have these classes to keep on the accredited list. We have about eighteen or twenty if it is a pretty night. We started about eight o'clock, about three weeks before Christmas and lasted till about three weeks after Christmas. Our teacher would teach us etiquette and she had us once to make out a menu.

Thus, in this area the majority may follow the older rural values common to the locality and distrust new urban values; while, at the same time, a growing minority may align themselves with the new urban values rather than the old rural traditions. When these two value systems are presented in sharp contrast to each other, considerable social disturbance is felt.

Accent on Formal Education

The schools sponsor the values of an alien way of life rather than those of the neighborhood. Most of the textbooks are the same as those used all over the United States. The teachers themselves are imbued with educational standards that have much in common with standards of teacher-training institutions all over the country, and in turn pass on to their students in the name of progress the values that they have so picked up.

There is much evidence that the school is in high favor. The county superintendent of schools says he wishes the school to be regarded as the center of community activities in each neighborhood. Actually, while the school shares this function with the church, the school is increasingly the center for secular activities. Here, formerly, Farm Security Administration loan applications were made out, and ration boards for sugar and gasoline met, while, now, home demonstration clubs and P.T.A. meetings are held, and recreational programs, visiting speakers and community organizations use the school's facilities.

Moreover, education has long been regarded as one of the

chief "goods" in the community. One White owner devoted an entire room to the various certificates and diplomas of his large family, some of whom had become doctors and teachers. In another family, three sisters were proud of having acted as secretaries to their brother (a dean of a Southern university) while he was completing his Ph. D. thesis. A Westmore farmer was one of the trustees of a Georgia college.

The Negroes in Glen made great use of the school facilities for many purposes. The school commencement exercises took weeks of preparation in May and were the main event of the year. The glow from the forges from adult classes at the school could often be seen until midnight, though the day in the fields would start at dawn. For many, education is regarded as an economic protection, as a Negro sharecropper shows:

> They gits a colored person who hadn't got much education and they git him just dipple-dapple along and he don't understand it. They take his money and tell him to trade it out at the store and then they don't put it down right. But he couldn't read so he don't know.

Rural Expression of Urban Superiority

The countryman in his Saturday visits to town is put at a disadvantage, for his dress, speech, and conduct are set in sharp contrast to those of city-dwellers. His children, also, meet with many jibes at the hands of town children in school, and, moreover, their individualisms are treated as deviants from the cultural norms to be eradicated as quickly as possible by the processes of formal education. Regarding this urban attitude, a White sharecropper says:

> I think some town people think that country people are a low class of people. The people who are educated realize more and don't look down on farmers like that. A person who rents in town and doesn't have anything still looks down on the farmer who has a whole lot more.

Rural Attitudes toward Urban Foodways: "Storebought" Foods

While some home-grown foods head the list of preferred items, the provision of most food needs on the farm, as has been said, is preached more than it is practiced. One White sharecropper informant began by saying, "I believe in home-grown foods," and by claiming to grow practically all of the food consumed, but when questioned further proved customarily to purchase: coffee, tea, chocolate, flour, sugar, canned vegetables, loaf bread, cheese, salmon, apples, oranges, Karo syrup, and fresh meat. A White owner said that she purchased most of the family's meats, fruits, and fish, besides occasional purchases of canned fruit, salt, sugar, and coffee. The 1940 census shows that, in general, as the income rises, the number who use their own farm products increases. Quite frequently, the lowest income farms do not use farm products, usually because they either do not grow foodstuffs as often or else sell them off.

Sale of Home-Grown Food Products

A striking aspect of the rural premium upon urban, purchased foods is the sale of home-grown food products, sometimes to purchase processed foods, sometimes to secure other than food products. Poultry, hogs, eggs, and (by owners) occasional calves are sold or bartered in this way, at the local country store, to the traveling grocery truck, or to village stores.

An important question involved here is whether the sale of food products represents a true *surplus* or not. It seems fair to assume that a family cannot sell food as a true surplus until it is consuming the minimum amount and kind of food necessary for adequate nutrition, as determined by local nutritional authorities. Since, as has been already stated, Westmore families are consuming roughly only 70 per cent of the amount and kind of food considered nutritionally adequate, sales of food do not represent true surpluses in most cases. It is true that it is important to know what food is sold as a surplus, since a family can scarcely be expected to live entirely off its own potatoes, for instance. But the products most commonly sold here are poultry, eggs, and dairy products, of which there is probably no true surplus, except in some White owner families. Also, the existence of a food-deficiency disease like pellagra testifies against the surplus character of many food sales.

Some food sales, then, are not a surplus but actually represent voluntary deprivation by a family in the area of food, particularly for the lower economic classes. This deprivation is undergone in order to obtain food with special meaning, as when a home-cured ham is sold to purchase boiled ham. Often families deprive themselves to secure other than food values, as, for example, to buy gasoline for an automobile, or a ticket to a movie. It is interesting to note that such a procedure has long been a part of custom. Olmsted speaks of Negro slaves on one plantation who saved from their food ration enough to send five bushels of meal to town to be sold for them. Eggs are still the chief source of petty income as they were then:[2]

> Lots of people don't use eggs, they sell 'em. My family could use 'em all, but sometime I do sell a few.
>
> At the school play it cost 25 cents for us all to go. They all want to go, but I say, 'Ah, you too little, you don't need to go so much.' One of my daughters said, 'Well, give me some eggs, and I will sell 'em and get my nickel.'

Qualities Attributed to Purchased Food

In view of the fact that the same or better sustenance could be afforded by home-grown foods as by purchased foods, it follows that the particular foods purchased have, to their purchasers, valuable attributive qualities. Aside from items which could not be produced on the farm, and for which reasonable substitutes cannot be made, like coffee and salt, the purchased foods comprise certain general groups, as for example: *processed foods* (flour, loaf bread, cheese, vegetable oil); *light-colored foods* (white syrup, white sugar, white rice, bleached flour); *costly foods* (salmon, beefsteak, bananas, shredded coconut); *packaged foods* (Post Toasties, corn flakes, Klim); and *canned fruits and vegetables* (blackberries, peaches, asparagus, beans, tomatoes). Obviously these are not exclusive categories, since white sugar, for example, is *processed, light-colored,* and *costly,* in contrast to brown sugar.

Also, for foods in each of these categories there are many lesser meanings. Processed and canned foods may be approved because of their artificial appearance; light-colored and packaged foods carry a connotation of purity, prestige, and science. Costly foods are also rare, and because they are rare, provide variety. The consumption of brand-name foods gives local consumers a small part in one level of the wider culture. These connotations will be more fully discussed in a later chapter.

The point is that all of these qualities attributed to the purchased foods seem urban, scientific, and progressive.

Negative Attitudes toward Rural Foodways

Negatively, many home-grown foods carry some stigma. Says a Negro wage-laborer:

> Yes'm, the country hams is de-li-cious, but they just don't feel up to the city folks'.

The following are linked together as "old timey," "country," or "nigger": *items of food,* like fat-back, lard, poke (the young tender leaves of the wild pokeberry bush), and molasses; *ways of cooking,* as with very much grease, in a skillet over an open fire; *ways of eating,* as sopping up molasses with bread, drinking pot liquor (the water vegetables are cooked in) or soaking bread in it; and specific *times of eating,* with the main meal at midday instead of at night or without a regular schedule.

When city relatives or the preacher are expected for dinner, rural people make an effort to provide foods which are different, not only from their own weekday meals but also from their best Sunday foods:

I remember when a lady from the city come to visit in the country, and we had ice cream every day, when we could have had apple pie because apples were laying on the ground. We like country ham for ourselves, but when we have company we feel like we ought to have something else. [White owner.]

Another informant shows how urban standards affect not only the food itself but the manner of its serving:

The preacher ate with us one time and we had chicken fried a golden brown and stuffed eggs and put them around the chicken and it did look mighty pretty if it *was* our table. When the preacher came, he ate and ate and ate.

Then we had ice cream and cake and got ready to serve it.

They said, 'Whoever heard of having ice cream and cake out here?'

I said, 'Why we have ice cream and cake twice a week, sometimes more.'

Even when there is no question of entertaining an urban visitor, Westmore people make an effort to provide an element of urban foodways for *local* guests on special occasions. The fact that not only the best of rural food is served to honor a guest, but also that many feel that some kind of purchased city food or some urbane way of serving is preferable, indicates the strength of this value. Therefore, canned asparagus or boiled ham or bananas may be served, and special efforts are made to serve the meal in accordance with the urban standards expounded in a magazine like the *Woman's Home Companion,* even though this may necessitate buying some items. In Seaford, urban standards became so incumbent upon members of the Social Reading Club as to limit the membership to those who could expend effort and money to provide special foods for entertainment, candles, candelabra, lunch cloths, flowers, napkins, and the like.

Summary

As has been said in the preceding chapters, the rural South is predominantly traditionalistic. In contrast, the European-American culture stresses the contributions of science. Conflicts between the two points of view are apparent locally.

Since certain groups in this area, such as the White owners and the young people, are leaders in the coming swing toward science, a minor sanction for science and schooling is apparent. This orientation (implying science, progress, urban superiority, and education) in the folkways is paralleled in the foodways by progressive methods of food production, the stress on purchased as opposed to home-raised foods, and the feeling that urban foodways are superior to rural foodways.

One evidence of the value placed on science is the local approval of formal education, expressed both verbally and in community activities centering in the school. But here again, the tendency of young people who have been formally educated to leave the rural community permanently is an indication of the conflict between locality and larger world. Also, there is the local feeling that the urban culture is superior and connotes scientific progress.

In the foodways, similarly, there is community approval for purchased foods as opposed to home-raised foods, even when many alternates for these purchased foods could be raised on the farm. To secure these foods, farmers sell off home-raised products, some of which are true surpluses and some of which, especially among low-income groups, represent a desire for other values than nutritive values, such as artificiality, cost, rarity, purity—all of which are compatible with the values of the urban, scientific, progressive culture.

Negatively, certain items of food and ways of cooking and of eating are deprecated as "old-timey," "country," and "nigger." Therefore, to urban guests farmers serve food different in character and in serving from their own best level of country fare. Even in entertaining one another, hostesses feel some social pressure to provide elements of the urban foodways.

In short, the major sanction for tradition and the minor sanction for innovation in the local folkways find counterparts in the older foodways now gradually invaded by newer, generally urban and scientific foodways.

NOTES

1. Ralph Linton, *The Study of Man* (New York: D. Appleton-Century Company, 1936).
2. *Cf.* Frederick Law Olmsted, *A Journey in the Seaboard Slave States in the Years 1853-1854* (New York: G. P. Putnam's Sons, 1904), Vol. 1, pp. 123-124.

8

The Catering Pattern

The third in the quartet of basic values found in the rural South is the catering pattern. "Southern hospitality" is a by-word. It is one aspect of a pervading *affability* with which is associated as well hedonism, humor, sociability expressed in a love of visiting, politeness, sentiment, and freedom from restrictions of time and duty.

In the foodways, this affability finds its comparable elements in *catering to the food preferences of members of the family, minimizing the trauma of weaning, dislike for using food deprivations to reinforce authority, eating between meals and eating at irregular times, and the existence of a notable number of emotional attitudes toward food.*

The Pleasant Paths

Human personality is important in the Southerner's philosophy of life. The Southerner is as much concerned with "doing unto others" as being done by. The amiable Southerner "aims to please." This general feeling has been well stated by one of them:

> An at-home-ness among others is implied; and a lack of suspicion—the most vulgar and humiliating of traits, I was taught by my elders—with regard to others and their intentions—it was better a thousand times, they said, to be deceived than to be common; a taste for the approval of others—how Southern! —derived from politeness, friendliness and vanity; the belief that one of our most natural impulses is the wish that the other person may be happy in our company.[1]

Many social relations are carried on in a context of humor. Whether humor is the White man's escape from present problems and the Negro's reaction to the irony of his fate, like the hangman's humor—or simply the good spirits which express satisfaction with the rural life—jokes, jocular comments and greetings are everyday expressions of the general affability. The love of laughter undoubtedly has no regional boundaries, but at least it can be said that this rural humor, unlike urbane wit, is in constant current usage. Indeed, it is likely that the common enjoyment of humor is a useful counterbalance to the system of social distinctions.

The pursuit of happiness is considered in itself a virtue, both others' happiness and one's own. And if each Southerner's happiness lies in making others happy, it follows that little effort need be wasted toward achieving such goals as wealth, or scientific or business distinction.

In religion, the stress is upon the positive humanism of the Golden Rule rather than upon the negative theism of the Ten Commandments. The chief denominations, Baptists and Methodists, strike a keynote of emotionalism, salvation by grace, and friendliness. Instances of this tenor of emotionalism are the perfervid pulpit oratory, the invitation period in the church service, the revival services held during the two weeks' "protracted meeting" during the late summer, the elaborate nature of rites like baptism and communion, and, particularly in Negro churches, the antiphonal responses made by the congregation to remarks of the preacher.

Affability in Social Relations

In accordance with these values, the social relations of man to man become extremely important. First of all, the strength of family and kinship ties is very evident. In Seaford, we visited a family that was subsisting on relief aid in the most extreme poverty in a very bare two-room house. The mother was rejoicing that her son, who had been employed in the Civilian

Conservation Corps, had run away to come home and share their poverty. Family affection is enhanced by the importance of the family in both the cotton and the tobacco economy, as members of all ages share in the common work. If large families are to get along at all under crowded conditions, at both work and play they learn early to pay attention to one another's preferences.

Visiting and Hospitality

"Visiting" engages much attention. The five or six large White owner families in the Westmore neighborhood live within walking distance of each other. Since they are interrelated, the neighborhood becomes an extension of the family and supplies aid and comfort to its members. Any visitor, relative or not, regardless of the pressure of the day's work, is urged to linger and chat. Especially, many formal and informal occasions are sought for entertaining the visitor. Often he is invited to a meal: "Guess you can stand it for one meal if we can stand it all the time." One informant said that it used to be the custom to bring back several guests from church to share Sunday dinner. Even now, Sunday is a day reserved by agreement for visitors and for visiting—no work must be planned then. The customs of shaking hands on greeting and leaving or of embracing kinfolk, the frequency with which some sort of refreshment is served, the use of "Uncle" or "Cousin" in addressing even distant relatives, and the parting "Come back and see us," all indicate the cordial atmosphere of social relations. Even though the visiting and hospitality may be largely restricted within the confines of race, class, or the plantation unit, affability as a cultural trait is characteristic of the whole rural community.

Sentiment is warmly expressed. Children grow up in large families where there is a great deal of open expression of affection among all members of the family, and particularly toward the younger children. Birthdays, holidays, and anniversaries are commemorated in some way, even on a small budget. One informant felt affronted because her city niece-in-law (whom she had never met) addressed her in a letter as "Dear," and concluded "Sincerely yours."

Freedom from Restrictions of Work and Time

Not only is the Southerner affable toward others; he has also a sense of relaxation where he himself is concerned. He is bound by many absolutes—for example, by the duties he owes to his family, his kinfolk, the stranger, those who are dependent upon him in the social system. He can thus never really be selfish. But these duties are attributes of personal relationships. Over and beyond them, he is not bound by a stern code of work, self-discipline, asceticism, or the acquisition of wealth or status for their own sake.

Because work for its own sake is not considered a chief value, the Southerner is sometimes accused of being lazy. Actually, the raising of cotton and tobacco involves the hardest kind of manual labor for all members of sharecropper and wage-laborer families and attention to much administrative detail by the White owners. However, this work is intermittent, and all classes stop work without feeling twinges of a Calvinistic conscience during the periods of relaxation: week-ends, "laying-by" time (the period between the last chopping and the picking), the period between harvest and spring planting, and on rainy days. There is often much aversion to the introduction of types of farm work which demand regular, exacting work, even though this work may mean more income. In Seaford and in Thomswell, there was a hope often expressed that the hard work would be only for a few years, exemplified by the old Negro who said, "The only time I'm going to say 'Git up' to a mule again is when he comes and sits in my lap." In Seaford, there was a folk-saying that if one worked hard for five years, he could relax and enjoy himself the rest of his life.

There is also a feeling that time is made for man's use, not man for time. That is, as in most rural communities, individual families follow the larger temporal rhythms of the sun and the seasons and do not constrain themselves to regularity by the clock. This attitude is carried over even into formal social gatherings, which usually start somewhat after the appointed time. The superintendent of the Baptist Sunday School attempted to revolt against the local custom by stating that he would start the service whether anybody was there or not. The rate of tardiness and truancy is high for schools, nor is there any truant officer provided.

The sense of freedom from impersonal duty as it is expressed in the restrictions of work and time is highest among Negroes. A community teacherage (residence for teachers) had been started in Glen, but the Whites used to laugh about the months that would elapse before the community would do any more work on it. Negro schools in Seaford and in Glen started anywhere from a half-hour to an hour late, while pupils were seen straggling along the honeysuckle-fragrant lane toward the school long after even that time. Church and social affairs were conducted with similar irregularity.

On the other hand, a question of personal devotion may occasion exactly opposite behavior, as in the case of the Negro wagehand on the next farm who insisted on staying up night after night with his landlord who had broken his hip and in attending him as a personal servant. The same landlord protected *him* from the law when he got involved in a local "cutting" affair, signed his bond, and secured his ultimate release. In both instances, personal relationships take precedence over the demands of an impersonal duty.

One question that arises is whether affability pervades the *content* of the culture or is only a form. How, it might be asked, would it be possible to combine business practices with friendship? Or how can a stratified society exist in a region where there is undiscriminating geniality?

The Catering Pattern

Affability Always

The rural Southerner believes that business can be mixed with pleasure. When he goes to the country store or buys gas, he exchanges jocular comment with the storekeeper. When he buys an insurance policy, he stops to inquire about the salesman's family. It is considered uncouth, either for a customer to concern himself solely with his wants, or for the storekeeper to concern himself solely with a person as if he had no other role than that of the customer, even if he is a stranger. Thus, personalities are customarily exchanged with postmen, waitresses, hairdressers, bank tellers, and the like; and the forms of such interchange extend even to larger cities like Columbia, Athens, and Atlanta.

Nor, in spite of the number of social distinctions, is there much variation in geniality in accordance with social class or race. There are distinctions in *forms,* as when a Negro visitor is addressed by her first name when she comes to the back door for a call, but she is as cordially invited in to sit down for a visit as a White caller would be. White visitors to a Negro gathering are usually invited to say a few words. Whites and Negroes exchange greetings in passing on the road, and gossip around the country store.

But it must be noted that the very universal character of affability is one guarantee of the existing social distinctions. If it were not so thoroughly a part of custom, like the use of "Dear" to begin a letter, its expression might be construed as a license for overstepping social boundaries. Therefore, while it is often a real part of the social *content,* in that personal regard is usually felt, it is also by its universality accepted as a *form.* This may explain how a customer, in spite of his politeness, can insist on the right change; or how a sharecropper knows that the landlord who calls him "Cousin" today will expect a return of a loan with interest at the proper time.

We see this affability accepted as a form in the words of a White owner:

Our tenants are always glad when we come with our brother and they come out to the car. We'll go to see their garden but we don't go in and sit down. Then we say, 'Now, get your spring cleaning done, we want to come to see you,' but we never do go.

Here, then, is a pattern universally applicable to this social structure, though with reservations which are real if not always so stated.

Catering to Family Food Preferences

There is a great contrast between how parents act toward children's food habits in a rural Southern family and the attitude in some Northern families. The Northern mother may apply a discipline that begins with sudden, possibly traumatic, weaning, and proceeds with feeding on a regular schedule regardless of the child's wants, disapproval of eating between meals, deprivation of playtime or food as punishment, insistence upon strict ideals of tidiness and punctuality, administration of unpleasant medicines, insistence upon eating what is good for one rather than what is preferred, and in general consulting standards that are often unconnected with the child's preferences.

In contrast, weaning is not a painful experience for the Southern child. Babies are nursed along as among groups like the Bemba, Arapesh, Balinese, and Atimelangers, where a long nursing period is expected, and nursing is resorted to, not only to satisfy hunger, but also to relieve feelings of insecurity. A White sharecropper mother says:

My baby went to talking when he was five months old and walked when he was seven months. I weaned him when he was about two years old. He still thinks he ought to have it. I ought to have weaned him before, but he got sick.

He likes meats of all kinds but he don't like bacon much. He'll eat it sometime, but he wants beef or something like that.

He likes to eat candy. I guess he eats too much of it 'cause he eats it every day, about a nickel's worth.

This same three-year-old boy, though he was occasionally nursing, was importantly influencing the family menu, so that the mother avoided serving English peas, sweet potatoes, and bacon which he disliked, and secured beef and coconut pudding which he liked. In another family, the catering pattern was slightly limited by the cost involved, for the mother said, "I always cook what the family likes without going to expense."[2]

Some attempt is made to induce children to eat preferred foods, more particularly among the upper social classes, where the ideals of child training are somewhat more strictly defined. Even here few negative sanctions are applied:

I persuade 'em through kindness, but I never have taught my boy to eat turnip greens and carrots. Not even carrot soup. My son would say, 'Mama, this would have been good soup if you hadn't put carrots in it.' [White sharecropper.]

A Negro sharecropper agrees with this attitude:

I never deprive 'em of food. I always try to give 'em plenty to eat. I don't think you ought to have to lock up your food from your children.

One informant recalled that her mother would tell the children that they would have bad dreams if they didn't eat the right things. It is evident, however, that most of the direction is positive and that punishment and threats are infrequently applied and relatively mild. Families are permissive rather than harsh in control.

An interesting instance of how the native catering pattern may come in conflict with an alien value-system is related by a White owner:

I don't think my parents punished us for not eating certain

foods, but I remember our brother, James, was there for dinner and we had company. James wanted to start with the blackberry pie and the guest said, 'Aunt Lucille, don't give James blackberry pie first: make him eat something else.'

In order to please the whole family, the mother may serve a great many similar food groups, such as corn bread and white biscuits; rice, sweet potatoes, white potatoes, and grits; and a variety of vegetables, all at the same meal. This happens the more often because of the prevalence, not only of positive likings for certain foods, but also of food aversions.

I don't hardly ever cook meat, but I don't think it agrees with me unless it is boiled or something. Yes'm, I like lean meat better than fat meat. My husband likes it, too, but it disagrees with him. [Negro wage-laborer.]

A mother in even a poor family will make an effort to avoid serving a food like English peas or sweet milk and to secure a favorite food like canned salmon. Keeping the family happy is often regarded as a value more important than the money involved.

The food preferences of the husband are often consulted. When he says, "I am going to have salmon if it costs fifty cents a can," he can satisfy this preference, since he controls purchases of food. Yet wives also frequently mention catering in serving the husband first, cooking in a certain way, and giving husbands choice selections of certain delicacies.

Fried chicken is so often served on Sundays and special occasions that the family preferences for certain parts of the chicken become almost institutionalized. One White sharecropper wife shows how she has come to accede to others' preferences in such cases, especially in a situation of possible conflict:

My husband has always liked the back, my daughter likes the breast, and my boy likes the leg. I did eat the breast and the leg, but now I've drifted off to the wing.

The Catering Pattern

Sunday Dinner

An informant who had once lived for a short time in Washington started to talk about Sunday dinners. In her accounts one is not only struck by the general contrasts in regional points of view, but also by such recurrent themes as the worth of guests, the stress on the food itself and the chance for choice, the feeling that meals are a family affair including the children, and the religious flavor lent by the blessing:

There was one thing I was sure glad to get back to when I come back from my cousin Lila's that year in Washington, and that was our Sunday dinners. They had Sunday dinners up there too, but it wasn't the food people come for, no sir. I couldn't even see that they come to see each other. That old Washington crowd just sat around and talked about things that didn't really concern none of them, books and the like.

I was sort of looking after her children for her—she thought she had a lot of gadding around to do with her husband, who was a sort of big shot in the government then. Well, every time she'd have company she'd pack them off by themselves, and me too if she could. Sure was a far cry from the Sunday dinners I was used to down here. Why, she never had but one kind of meat—and that usually cold, and I thought not quite enough of it. And one vegetable—string beans, just boiled in water, no seasonin'—I don't think she ever cooked a mess of them done—and big chunks of cold bread with thick crust. Sometimes a fancy molded salad, and a boughten dessert, cake or pie. And she never passed anything twice—if people didn't get what they wanted, they just did without. She used to say, 'If they don't like what we got, they can live till they get home.'

Sure was a far cry from what I was used to, and what Cousin Lila grew up on, for that matter. The dinners we used to have in our family and still do! At them dinners, everybody comes—children and all. And they come to eat and to see each other. And there's plenty of food for everybody's likes—fried chicken and ham, cream potatoes and sweet potatoes, string beans and corn and peas, sliced tomatoes and cucumbers and home canned pickles and onions, hot biscuits and corn bread and iced tea and apple pie for dessert, or cake if anybody don't like the pie. Yes, sir, nobody ever left my Aunt Zoie's table without being filled up. And Aunt Zoie knew there waren't no talk too sacred to bust into to see that folks got seconds on cream potatoes or biscuits while the steam was still coming out. And another thing we always had was grace. I admit there wasn't as much to be thankful for at one of Cousin Lila's lukewarm Washington dinners, but I still think no matter what you got, you oughtta thank the Lord for it. We always had either one of the Uncles or one of the children who had just learned a grace to say it before we ate. Yessir, them dinners really made your family like friends and your friends like family. Sometimes Aunt Zoie would make you eat more than you really wanted, but nobody ever left hungry.

Irregular times for meals are sanctioned, as is lack of punctuality at other gatherings. The times of Sunday dinner and the evening meal, particularly, are likely to vary. Regularity seems to vary with social class, being strictest among White owners and least strict among wage-laborers and Negroes.[3] Children eat a great deal between meals without parental reproof, usually candy in or just after harvest time, but often, especially in Negro families, cold sweet potatoes. Older adults often satisfy a between-meal craving with snuff.

Informants of all classes agreed that changes in food habits could be more successfully induced through persuasion and example than force, even in the form of instruction. A White owner says she will not tell anybody what to do, merely that *she* is trying to have a good garden. She notes, also, that it is an effective appeal to ask mothers to serve food which is good for their children, rather than to eat for an impersonal or a purely selfish reason.

Summary

The pattern of *affability* is seen in the *folkways,* accompanied by love of pleasure, humor, applied religion, sociability, hospitality, politeness, and freedom from bonds of work and time; and in the *foodways* in catering to the food preferences of members of the family, minimizing the possibility of trauma in weaning, application of only mild negative measures for nutritional education, and in the irregularity of mealtimes and a permissive attitude toward between-meal eating.

Great emphasis is placed on humor, and the happiness of others and one's self. The local version of religion stresses the Golden Rule and salvation by grace.

Family ties are extremely important in an economy which stresses the family unit in almost every phase of life. In the family, coöperation and yielding to mutual preferences are culturally approved.

Expression of affability is found in frequent visiting, generally between related families of like social class, though exceptions occur. Entertainment for relatives, friends, and even strangers is an intrinsic part of the culture, both at the present time and by long tradition.

Since the custom of affability binds the Southerner only to the primacy of his duty toward God and man and not to a multitude of extraneous goals, he finds relaxation in the intermittent nature of his work. The lack of a sense of the insistency of time is also seen as an index of the general pattern, but again the need of a neighbor may take precedence over any occasion of personal enjoyment.

The spirit of affability pervades the folkways so universally that it enters into business relations and is applied without regard to social class or race. Precisely because it is so universal, it has attained the diffuseness of a form, and, though generally sincere, is regarded as merely a gracious form on some occasions.

The corresponding *foodways* appear in the attempt by parents to satisfy the food preferences of children, first in prolonging the nursing period in accordance with the child's preferences and then in avoiding his aversions. Only mild means are applied for nutritional education, and the menu is usually varied enough to avert dissatisfaction.

Other instances of the catering pattern in the foodways are seen in the attention paid to the dietary and cooking preferences of the father, in the irregularity of mealtimes, in the sanction for between-meal eating, and in the disinclination to use force to change food habits.

NOTES

1. Twelve Southerners, *I'll Take My Stand* (New York: Harper and Brothers, 1930), p. 345.
2. Audrey I. Richards, in *Land, Labour and Diet in Northern Rhodesia* (Oxford University Press, 1939), contrasts such treatment of children with the Bembas' practice of feeding children on refuse and forcing them to eat millet. She infers that children will survive almost any maternal treatment.
3. According to a survey in a Negro high school, 42 percent reported no regular meal hours.

9

Social Distinctions in the Foodways

So far the close association of folkways with the foodways, and of the general foodways with individual food habits, has been stressed. Tradition, science, and affability seem values basic to the whole region, and in a rural community, as most individuals share in the common folkways, so they tend to consume the same bill of fare. However, the South is peculiarly distinguished for a fourth principle underlying society and the foodways—that of *differentiation.*

In such a society men may have been created equal, but they quickly assume positions of superiority and inferiority relative to one another. It has been called a highly stratified society not only because of the owner, sharecropper, and wage-laborer economic classes in each of the two races, but also because of a number of other factors helping to fix one's social position, such as whether one is a long-term or short-term tenant, one's blood ties, education, money, degree of color if Negro, personal qualities, occupation, and the like. "One's place" is thus a point in rather delicate adjustment in social space, since so many social forces may affect it. And "knowing one's place," for White as well as Negro, owner as well as wage-laborer, is no small achievement.

Social stratification here historically antedates the equalitarian tenets of the Constitution. The very colonists themselves comprised a number of social classes, as slaves, poor whites, or aristocrats. But these three classes were also early colonists of New York State, where the social structure developed very differently.

One then notes that in the South all three classes engaged in the same occupation. If you lived in an industrial region like New England where the brick mills began to rise beside the rushing streams, or got your quarter section early homesteading in the West, you could ride the social escalator quite freely. It was to the cities that most of the forty million immigrants came, and their jostling about at the bottom pushed their predecessors higher. At the same time, when a number of occupations with rather vague demands for capital or training were open, it was more possible for a poor boy to become president or merchant prince.

In the cotton or tobacco South, it is also possible to perform Horatio Alger feats, but it is rarely done. The land itself as a basis of wealth does not frequently change hands. It is extremely difficult for a wage-laborer on a daily wage of $2.00 to save up enough to buy the land, and extremely difficult for a Negro who is without White influence. The customary 10 per cent a month credit rate for food, equipment, seed, and fertilizer is also economic sanction for the *status quo*. This is experience of a typical White sharecropper:

> We have lived here 29 years and rented from Mr. Howell. We have tried to buy it, but he won't sell. I don't suppose we will ever have a home now of our own because my husband is 61 and I am 50. For the last few years it has been hard to make a living but we have tried to do good.

Under these conditions, the extremely high tenancy rate (71.3 per cent) is not to be wondered at.

Since there is little opportunity for rising in station within the locality, the only hope for ambitious young people lies in going away. Their departure tends to leave unchallenged the existing social distinctions, since pressure for equal status is removed.

As has been suggested, an intricate set of "thou musts" and "thou must-nots" tends to support every individual in his position. Nor does social superiority emancipate the White owners. On the contrary, there is a pressure upon them also to maintain their distinctions, a sense of *noblesse oblige*. The rules are well understood. Only rarely are they articulated as in a church sermon:

I think sometimes if the Negroes are going to copy us, we ought to try to live the best we can.

A preacher was preaching about smoking and dancing, and he said:

If any of you that do smoke could have seen this big fat Negro in the rumble seat of a car just sitting all rared back and puffing away, it would have disgusted you.

Without such a sense of distinction, any person, whatever his origin, becomes a despicable object, a social mongrel. He may be like one who has put himself beyond the local law of gravitation and now floats helplessly in space. A poor person who knows and abides by the etiquette may be poor, but he has a place; a poor person who doesn't is "white trash." The first says of himself righteously:

You know there is some people who are just trash, "white trash," I guess. I know we are poor but I know right from wrong.

"White trash," then, are, in part, so defined because they have no distinct appreciation of their place in the social system. The White owner snubs them and the Negro despises them. They may attempt to participate in the activities of White owners but the practical difficulties to their taking a full part are so great that they soon drop out. Even their church attendance may be limited to the time of the "protracted meeting" to which they go for a time and then drop out as they feel themselves not needed. Some join small evangelistic sects which help to satisfy their social needs. Therefore, it is significant that the criterion of both a well-reared White owner and a Negro sharecropper is their recognition of the intricate and subtle ways in which the status of the one is distinguished from that of the other. It is undoubtedly true that each takes a certain pride in this recognition as do both the officers and men in a well-disciplined army.

The distinctions based upon race and class are profound. There are the separate schools, churches, doctors, organizations and public accommodations for the two races. There are also rights and duties incumbent upon members of different classes. The lines of communication are usually separate, in that White owners visit, entertain, and engage in formal activities chiefly with other White owners; White sharecroppers with other White sharecroppers; and wage-laborers chiefly with people of like status. It is true that length of residence in a community may foster cross-class communication.

Besides those attendant upon class and race, there is another set of distinctions less frequently noted. These are the relations which unite the White owner and his White and Negro sharecroppers or wage-hands in one farm unit in distinction from those of other farms. A White sharecropper who would not think of visiting another White owner may be allowed a certain friendliness with the owner of the farm on which he works, though here, too, the limitations are carefully set. A Negro sharecropper may talk freely to and visit with his White landlord when he would not visit the neighboring White owner. In this way, not only are there horizontal lines of social intercourse between members of the same class, but also vertical lines of communication, duty, and obligation, so that the whole rural society is exceedingly complex.

Distinctions in the Foodways (Appendix E, Tables IV & V)

Certain items of food: fat-back, poke salat, and pot liquor are associated with Negroes and lower economic classes, and are also called "country" and "old timey."[1] A White sharecropper stresses her distinction from the Negroes by pointing out that she feeds the pot liquor to the pigs while the Negroes eat fat-back three times a day and don't have "stuff like milk and butter." Similarly, a White owner will stress the fact that she knows pot liquor is "uncouth," that she serves meals regularly, that she purchases much food: all of these in contradistinction to the practices of the subordinate classes.

Consuming all the available food without exercising a nice discrimination is also considered *déclassé*. A White sharecropper says:

> The niggers eat kidneys. They eat everything about a hog. I don't eat the feet. There is not many [Whites] that fix the hog head, they just lay 'em around and let 'em ruin.

This same scorn for lack of discrimination is shown by another White sharecropper:

> I find that if Negroes have fat-back and bread they get along all right, and a lot of them don't have anything but dry bread. Some of 'em sell everything they can get their hands on and just do without something to eat.
>
> Poke salat is not fit for anything but for the pigs. Well, the pigs get most of the pot liquor here; we just don't care for it.

On some occasions there are surpluses of food which may be given away. It is interesting to see what distinctions regulate the disposal of this food:

> Oh yes, neighbors swap when they have surplus fruits and vegetables 'cause they have no market for them; if they did have a market for it they would sell it.
>
> Well, we would give our surplus to shiftless people, but we would rather give some to those who try and don't have enough. We don't have any preferences much about giving to the colored or White. But I guess we give it to the White quicker.

These distinctions also apply when food gifts are sent by a sharecropper to his landlord. In such a case, the items which are considered particular *delicacies* are given to the landlord, such as the brain and tenderloin of a recently butchered hog. Of course, such gifts do not put the landlord under obligation to reciprocate in kind.

White owners recognize that differences exist in the amount and variety of food eaten by those of the lower economic classes, but they sometimes attribute these differences to the improvident persons' substitution of other values, or laziness:

If they would leave off some of these other things like gasoline, they would soon have enough to buy a pig. They could do a lot more, just a lot more if they would. They would have to be willing to sacrifice something. You can't go off and leave your cows and chickens and come back and your cows and chickens be doing all right.

Besides discrimination in food gifts among recipients, there is discrimination in some of the semi-commercial activities within the rural areas. The hog-killing procedures provide an example, with the Negro assistants being given what Whites regard as an undesirable part of the hog, the intestines or chitterlings:

When we have a hog killin', some others come in and help us, so we pay in meat. Sometime we will go one day and help her and the next day we will all go help somebody else. When the niggers help us, we give 'em the chit'lin's.

Summary

This chapter has shown the force of the sanction for *individual variations* in the foodways. The principle of differentiation is further discussed here in relation to *society* and the *foodways.*

In the rural South, the retarded rate of social change contributes to the persistence of fixed social position in a stratified system, and change of status is lessened, principally by the similarity of occupation which enormously minimizes the opportunities for advancement. The falling birth rate and emigration of ambitious young people, and the amount of capital required for advancement in the economy are additional factors.

A sense of variation in one's duties, obligations, and privileges exists among members of all classes, and those who are the least conscious of these variations meet with social disapproval. There is class variation also in participation in social activities and in lines of communication.

Besides the horizontal lines of social intercourse, there are vertical, quasi-familial, social relations consisting of the White owner and his White and Negro sharecroppers or wage-hands, so that distinctions in many circumstances are evident in the social structure.

In the foodways, the sense of social distinction operates to deprecate certain items of food, ways and times of cooking and eating, and too complete and undiscriminating consumption of food as "low class." Members of both upper and lower classes express discrimination in the type of food gifts in relation to their recipients.

Thus, in the four basic values referred to, tradition operates to maintain the individual and social differences already established through the influence of affability and stratification, while science operates to introduce ever new foodways from outside.

NOTES

1. *Cf.* John W. Bennett in "Food and Social Status in a Rural Society," *American Sociological Review,* 1943, pp. 561-569. In Southern Illinois high prestige items were: fresh fruit, candy, hamburger, oysters, and foods prepared by urban recipes, whereas low prestige (out-group) items were "nigger food": muskrats, yellow corn bread, wild game, and greens, and German foods: blood pudding and the excessive use of white bread.

10

The Preaching and the Practice

As we consider how foodways are related to the basic values of the region, it is necessary to recognize that the foodways are a composite of (1) actual behavior, and (2) expected behavior.[1] That is, while the consensus of local opinion may approve living-at-home as the ideal, most local residents may actually buy most of what they need. Similarly, while the eating of sweets may be disapproved in theory, in practice a large majority may actually choose and consume sweets.

It is possible that the consumption of forbidden fruit, from that in the Garden of Eden down, is attended by especial satisfaction, particularly if what one *should* eat has been formulated. Often, where the ideal foodways go unarticulated, preaching tends to coincide with practice.[2] As a matter of fact, as might be expected in a tradition-loving society, food theory and practice tend to agree, and this congruence is backed by the very tacitness of the standards in respect to food. Routine foodways have immemorially been pursued in deep unawareness, while it is only the extra-routine foodways for special occasions that are made explicit.

There is a certain amount of pressure in the local area toward conformity. The fewer the persons, and the more frequent the first-hand contacts, the more this pressure is likely to be exerted. But the pressure toward conformity is not only related to the fact that a rural area is under discussion, but also to the degree with which the region approves conformity. A rural mother in the North, for example, may insist that her children wait until home-baked bread cools before eating it, on the ground that hot bread is indigestible. A rural mother in the South, where hot breads are favored, may urge her children to eat the biscuit while it is hot, but will not employ harsh measures to enforce conformity. Non-conformity and catering, as has been said, are themselves values of the region.

To be sure, we will expect more censure for deviants in some areas than in others, according to the position occupied in the hierarchy of values. Eyebrows will be raised at a drunkard if the society highly values sobriety. An informant describes such a deviant:

> People don't have much confidence in Dr. Ed Mohlton. He is on the Governor's staff and people around here don't like him much, especially since Talmadge has done the schools like he has.
>
> Dr. Mohlton gets drunk lots here lately. Somebody said if they would make Dr. Mohlton superintendent of our Sunday School, it wouldn't be any time before we would have a lot more members. He has a lot of White people on his place, and if each went to church he would run that school bus and there would be a church full. But I said I wouldn't come, in fact I would be tempted to move my membership. He needs somebody to work on him, instead of him working on us.
>
> Dr. Mohlton may have all the money he wants and his wife too, but I wouldn't be in her shoes for anything. Dr. Mohlton gets on these big hullabaloos and calls up people on the phone and cusses 'em out. Lots of times when her children were younger and he would get drunk, she would take her children to a hotel and charge it up to him. He's a cutter, I tell you.

But we do not find an informant similarly censuring a deviant for not eating in accordance with the foodways. A cold bread eater or a person who sips his Coca-Cola through a straw is hardly whispered about at Ladies' Aid meetings. The influence of food deviants is not dangerous to the young, as are deviants in the fields of marriage or religion. Also, the standards in respect to food are less definite.

Standards for Food

It is difficult to get people to say what food items are necessary, both on ordinary and extraordinary occasions, but particularly on ordinary occasions. Informants in Seaford could scarcely conceive of an interest in a daily menu but were eager to tell about food for illness. In German Flats, there was considerable interest in the traditional German dishes which were beginning to be regarded as extraordinary foods. Also, techniques such as those of cooking and canning, though not difficult to explain, do not rate much interest in informants' eyes. Finally, attitudes about food, while pronounced, are difficult for informants to analyze and interpret.

Nevertheless, the standards for food as far as people voiced them have been presented in Tables VII and VIII. They include those ideas of the proper food pattern which the majority within the region accept as proper. It must always be remembered that considerable swerving from these standards is expected.

But the nutritionists may have another idea of what is proper food, an ideal by no means necessarily identical with the local ideal. Milk, lean meats, and citrus fruits may be designated by nutritionists as essential foods, yet rural Southerners not only believe them nonessential, but in some cases actually harmful. This other ideal embodies the nutritional value of the national, scientific, urban culture, and is an ideal as yet only of certain receptive individuals, a few members of the professional and White owner classes, themselves a minority.

Since standards are constantly in flux, it is extremely likely that the nutritionists' ideal may some day become the local ideal, and also that the people will in practice more often eat what science tells them to. Meanwhile, there is a great deal of discrepancy between the various theories of what food should be eaten (folk and scientific beliefs) and actual behavior. Furthermore, to explain these discrepancies where they are recognized, a number of rationalizations has appeared.

In turning now to examples of those discrepancies, it must be remembered that we know only part of the facts. We have abstracted from the informants an expression of what they as representatives of the region believe. But to a very great extent, of course, the words of informants imperfectly express what happens. Therefore, even what is designated as a practice in the foodways is only the informants' version of what the foodways actually are, though, in many cases, supplemented by direct observation.

Nutritional Know-How

As has been suggested, the White owner and long-term sharecropper classes have considerable *knowledge* in a general way of what is currently considered the true nutritional gospel. One White owner distinguishes as essentials: proteins, calcium, fats, minerals, and carbohydrates. Milk, butter, eggs, and vegetables are mentioned as protective foods by both a White owner and long-term sharecropper. A Negro sharecropper said:

> Well, I think ev'vybody should have plenty eggs, milk—about a pint a day, butter, some lean meat like liver, plenty vegetables and fruits and whole wheat bread.

Sweet potatoes, pot liquor, and fruit juice were recognized by members of these classes as protective.

There is, however, less mention of fruits, nor is enriched flour or bread mentioned, but rather, "brim," "dark" or whole wheat bread.

Among members of all classes there is very little accurate knowledge of vitamins or minerals. The term itself has an "open sesame" quality. Vitamins are thought to step up the dietary, but people are vague as to just how or why. While a White owner may say:

> Oranges and cabbage are rich in Vitamin C. I wondered how people ever discovered those vitamins. We have been hearing all along about Vitamin C in citron and fruits. . . .

a White short-term sharecropper is more typical:

> I don't know what is a good balanced meal, but we studied it in school. Yes'm, we had to make that chart about vitamins in school. I don't know what vitamins are in different foods. I don't know much about proteins and minerals. We studied it, though.

Disregarding the Nutritional Ideal

The path of history is strewn with the bodies of reformers who collapsed waiting for the pagans to mend their ways. Nevertheless, it is still glibly assumed in many circles that knowledge is all. Is the dietary at fault? Do the poor people get pellagra because they're not eating the right foods? Well, that's easy. Give them the good word. Trouble is they don't *know* any better. If they only know better, they'll eat better. And pellagra will plummet to the bottom of the ranked list of diseases causing death in the South.

Observation suggests that once you have caught the hapless consumer by his lapel and prodded and wheedled him into *knowing* what he should eat, you'll get two sorts of reactions. The "I want to do what's right" type of person presumably will eat better, but the "It's my life, isn't it?" person may spurn milk and take a pull at a coke with new relish. One reason for not becoming dogmatic about good nutrition is the possibility that, for some persons, committing nutritional sin may be a new and tempting avenue of transgression.

More often, of course, people are simply too accustomed to their bad food habits to want to change. Pellagra patients who had been advised by doctors what to eat would fail to carry out the advice, even when remedial foods were given them for nothing. (Incidentally, pellagra—beri-beri's second cousin—is no prerogative of the poor. One of the town leaders in Seaford, a woman with the means to purchase any food desired, periodically went to the Duke University Hospital for nicotinic acid injections—to apply by the needle at $5.00 a shot what she was unwilling to get in proper food.) Another woman in embarrassment hastened to cover her arm (showing the telltale pellagra patches) with a towel when a welfare worker arrived. "I know I did wrong," she said abashedly, "but I just couldn't eat right the way they told me."

On the other hand, not eating "the way they told me" sometimes pays off. This is true, not for the high-income, White owner class whose nutritional information is more or less scientific, but for the Negro wage-laborer who is not scientifically well-informed. For her, the stereotype of a good dietary is likely to be actually a very poor one—the highly refined, artificial, denatured foods that are actually eaten by the upper classes and constantly pictured in food advertisements. One wage laborer says an approved dinner is "one raw vegetable and a cooked one, one potato and some kind of meats," but her actual diet includes the milk, fruit, and eggs omitted in her ideal pattern. The consumption of highly nutritious foods with low prestige value—the internal organs of animals, poke, collards, dark bread, pot liquor, sweet potatoes, yellow corn, and molasses—are other instances of the superiority of the practices of subordinate classes as contrasted with their food ideals.

In general, however, the practice coincided with the ideal pattern, as indicated by nutritional studies, roughly about 70 per cent in Westmore, lower than that in Seaford, and higher in German Flats. As has been indicated, the general knowledge of what should be eaten, scientifically speaking, is much lower than this coincidence might indicate. Where tradition favors foods now scientifically approved, this has far greater influence than any conscious adoption of nutritional standards.

Rationalizations of Dietary Deficiencies

When an informant becomes aware that there is a discrepancy between what he ought to eat and what he does eat, he usually advances an alibi. A sharecropper may dismiss the matter by saying, "We just not able to, that's all." A landlord, attributing discrepancies to laziness, may say, "It is just like all people who are lazy, they are not going to be thrifty in anything. They all reason themselves out of things and find excuses for not doing things." The true explanations are difficult to find. The ones cited here show what the people say about areas where discrepancy occurs.

Lack of Gardens and Garden Failures

Chief lack of gardens existed among wage-laborers and short-term tenants. It is noteworthy that none of these complained that the landlord wouldn't allow them land or time to make a garden; indeed, the landlords often tried without effect to induce their hands to grow gardens. Lack of equipment, however, was a common explanation, including lack of a mule to plough the garden, lack of seed for planting,[3] lack of fence material to keep the chickens and cattle out of the gardens, lack of sprayers and poison to keep bugs from destroying the crop. Short-term tenants often felt that planting a winter garden or planting an orchard was useless since, after they moved, someone else would harvest their crops.

Many of these explanations are legitimate. Although agencies do exist for supplying those "jes' not able to do" with seed and fences, and although no one of these explanations might be the real one, the combination of them all may be, in addition to not knowing where to turn for help. Where the way is once made clear, as in Westmore, the rule is to plant and maintain a good garden.

Most of those who lack cows (wage-laborers and sharecroppers) say they are not able to buy them. More prosperous tenants say, "Some folks don't want to fool with taking care of milk and butter." They probably have in mind the confinement that daily milking represents to a people fond of visiting and of more companionable agricultural tasks like chopping cotton and tying tobacco. Also, there is a dearth of sanitary equipment and refrigerating facilities, inability to afford the investment in time and money which a dairy herd represents, and (in Seaford) a lack of pasture.

The reasons given for not drinking milk seem pretty far-fetched. Sweet milk particularly is said not to "set well on the stomach." It "makes my blood go up" or "makes me bilious." Some say they "can't drink buttermilk 'cause it will just swell 'em up like a frog." It is probable that sweet milk is in disfavor because it is hard to keep successfully cooled; at any rate buttermilk and clabber find more favor.

Wheat

Not much explanation was found for the lack of wheat production and its consumption as whole wheat. Although many said "Wheat don't produce so well here," we found that those families who raised the crop were well satisfied with yields, after learning how to grow it.

Canning

Both White and Negro sharecroppers and wage-laborers said they lacked cans and pressure cookers. Short-term croppers said it was too hard to transport a year's supply of canned goods from one place to another when they moved. Upper classes often said it was cheaper to buy canned goods than to can them, although on the whole, people who could afford equipment tried to can both fruits and vegetables.

The very number of rationalizations given, regardless of how well founded on facts they may be, indicates: (1) that the people have little accurate conception of scientific nutritional standards; (2) that there is a great deal of prestige attached to science as final authority for an ideal standard; (3) that consequently many explanations are offered for non-conformity to scientific recommendations; and (4) that non-conformity is not always the result where scientific ideal patterns are not understood, since behavior may be closer to the scientific ideal than to any other ideal consciously recognized.

Health

Although Thoms County has an ordinance on the books requiring blood tests for cooks, it is not enforced, since there is no active county medical officer nor any provision for treatment. The Negro school principal opposed enforcement of this ordinance on the ground that many Negroes who are found to have venereal disease will lose their jobs. There is no inspection for soda fountains, bakeries, restaurants, and other places where food is handled, nor is there much public feeling that there should be such inspection. Fortunately perhaps, food and disease are not associated in the public mind.

The patent medicines most frequently bought here are:

For malaria
- Quinine (in bulk)
- Grove's chill tonic
- 666
- Vinotone

For colds
- Vicks Vatronol
- 4-Way pills
- Mustarole

For indigestion
- Black Draught
- Feenamint
- Simmon's Liver Regulator
- Bi-Sodol
- C.R.C.

For blood tonic
- S.S.S.
- Iodized yeast
- Sarsaparilla compound
- Peruna

For Pellagra
- Iodized yeast
- Nicotinic Acid

Other Patent Medicines
- Dr. W. S. Caldwell's Syrup of Pepsin
- Laxated King of Herb Tonic
- Grover Syrup for Roundworms
- Dr. Dewitts' Eclectic Remedy

Folk beliefs about food contrast strikingly with the nutritional ideal. Old men shake their heads stubbornly about them, nor do they think it worthwhile to justify them, except in the form of an occasional personal experience. This we would expect, for the foodways, once accepted as such, do not have to be proved. The fact that so many food items, as, for example, meat, are surcharged with emotional attitudes, is another attribute of accepted foodways.

We have seen that the nutritional ideal and practice are different. To what extent do the folk beliefs and actual food patterns coincide? This is difficult to ascertain, but it is safe to say that *there is no exact correspondence between the two.* A number of factors intervene: physical factors, like the inaccessibility of an approved food, or a peculiar allergy to it; economic factors, like its cost; and, perhaps in most cases, a simple individual preference which may contradict the foodway. Certainly, *there is more correspondence between the folk belief and behavior than between the teaching of scientific nutritionists and behavior,* for nothing, for example, would induce an informant who believed that oysters were injurious to eat them, or to eat yellow corn meal when she had been taught all her life that white corn meal was preferable.

Summary

Looking more closely at the foodways, we find that they include both actual food practices, and ideas of what food should be eaten. There is no exact correspondence between these two.

While there is a certain amount of special pressure upon food practices to conform to the ideal, in contrast to many rural areas, non-conformity is less censured in the rural South because latitude in food choices is a value of the region, a "specialty of the house," and because the foodways occupy a subordinated position in the hierarchy of values. To a lesser degree one conforms because one is not challenged by a formally stated ideal menu.

There are at least two types of ideal food patterns: the food pattern presented by local agencies of scientific information (at present only incompletely incorporated into the foodways), and the folk beliefs about food accepted by the majority.

The scientific ideas about food are accepted mainly by the

White owner, long-term sharecropper groups, but are imperfectly understood. While some knowledge of the general food groups is observable, specific accurate knowledge of the constituency of food is scarcely ever found. This knowledge of the nutritional ideal is much less than the good food practices themselves, which often correspond more nearly to the scientific ideal. The number of rationalizations advanced for the discrepancy between reading and practice indicates the prestige attached to science.

The folk beliefs exemplify the unreasoned element of tradition. Though a number of factors operate to prevent an exact correspondence between the ideal and behavior in food, there seems to be much more correspondence between folk beliefs and food behavior than between the scientific alternatives and food behavior, a correspondence that may be expected to change if the nutritional values of the nation are accepted by the region.

NOTES

1. Most of the concepts used in this chapter are derived from definitions advanced by Clyde Kluckhohn, "Patterning in Navaho Culture," *Language, Culture, and Personality* (Menasha, Wisconsin: Sapir Memorial Publication Fund, 1941), pp. 109-130; an unpublished dissertation by Florence R. Kluckhohn, *Los Atarquenos, A Study of Patterns and Configurations in a New Mexico Village,* Radcliffe College, 1941; an unpublished article "Toward a Common Language for the Area of Social Science;" and more indirectly, concepts developed by Talcott Parsons, Edward Sapir, Ralph Linton, Ruth Benedict and A. A. Goldenweiser.
2. This premise has important implications for nutritional policies and programs which, by their very formulation, may induce lack of conformity between ideal and behavioral patterns.
3. Lack of seed was mentioned by several informants, even in such a prosperous community as Westmore. A family seed packet secured by the F.S.A. cost around $5. There was great need of a $1 seed packet, and this was sponsored by the Thoms County Nutrition Committee in 1942.

11

Foods Which Seem Emotion-Centered

We enter here, with due caution, an exceedingly obscured area. As our eyes get accustomed to the darkness, we can distinguish vague forms without yet seeing their interrelation. For lack of fuller evidence and further verification, they can only be reported at this stage, and reported as question marks.

Here are areas of abnormal activity, groupings of cells, so to speak—knots in the regular pattern of the grain, a massing of clouds in the blue empyrean. A cluster of attitudes appears about a certain item of food. When an informant in Kentucky, an observation in North Carolina, an incident in Georgia, and a nation-wide survey in Great Britain show a common element, one says: "There's something queer going on: what does it mean?"

Now in both the preaching and the practice one sees constant evidence that food is not a matter to be settled rationally between one's head and one's stomach; the heart has a good deal to do with it. It has been amply shown that people often turn to eating as an unfailing source of satisfaction when they are frustrated. Like Solomon, sick of love, they have been stayed with flagons and comforted with apples. Obese persons and drunkards have learned to react in this way repeatedly. In her studies of obese persons, Hilde Bruch has pointed out that food comes to stand for the satisfaction and security denied by their relations to people around them.[1] It is possible, therefore, that if our society provides increasing tensions in some areas, or if there is less concern with spiritual matters and more monotony, people will become increasingly concerned with what they eat and how they eat it. In a sensate era[2] food will share with sex a larger and larger place. New social inventions like the drive-in theatre will be successful when they can combine automobiles and movies with smooching and snack bars.

In some instances, the reasons for emotional attitudes seem well-founded. In others, the logical sources have been long since lost sight of, but what is interesting here is the fact that such strong emotional reactions to food exist. These complex attitudes have but slight connection with the four fundamental tastes of salt, sweet, sour, and bitter. Strong preferences and aversions exist which cannot be explained on a physiological basis alone.

The South sanctions the maintenance of these preferences and aversions. We find informants frankly expressing them and accepting their existence as perfectly natural phenomena. There is little effort to repress food aversions or to inhibit the satisfaction of food preferences, as might be the case in an urban culture. Therefore, whatever physiological, economic, or social bases there actually are for emotional attributes to food are reinforced by the community's approval.

Anxiety and Digestion

Further, in the larger American culture we find that for many people the process of digestion itself, as well as many specific food items, becomes a source of anxiety. Unlike the accused who is assumed innocent until proven guilty, the American digestive system is considered faulty unless artificially succored. Its colon is lazy; it has gas on its stomach. It needs six-way action, priming with laxatives, roughage, or mineral oil from above, internal bathing, high colonic irrigation, and suppositories from below, and constant exploration of the dark continent in the middle to find the source of the Bile.

If a boy doesn't eat Wheaties, he won't grow up to be a major league ball player; if the young man doesn't keep regular he will miss out on promotion; he has to look out "after forty," and success will bring him at once more bathrooms and more ulcers.

Echoes of this theme are heard in the rural South. That a food is said to have laxative qualities is more likely to secure acceptance for it than if it is considered an aphrodisiac. Asked about the food values of lemons and fresh oranges, one informant said:

> They must have some because I know they are given to sick people and to babies. [Do you happen to know why?] I believe they help cure colds. You know they help keep your bowels open. [She added this last in a whisper.]

One mother was a scandal to her relatives because she didn't become unduly concerned when her baby "missed a day" and refused to give it an enema or milk of magnesia or Castoria. Some mothers gave laxatives to their children, whether they were constipated or not, as a regular weekly routine. The general store is more likely to carry a full stock of patent medicines than of groceries. Many of them, like Black Draught, Feenamint, and Simmon's Liver Regulator are particularly known as laxatives. In the study of Seaford, where a random sample of the entire township was interviewed, discarded gallon glass jars once containing mineral oil were frequently seen when one went around to the back door.

In the rural South, many aversions and preferences also appear to be founded upon a given item's possible hazard or help to the blood. This concern is similarly found in many primitive societies. Some food items "make the blood thick" or "thin the blood," "clear the blood" if you have "bad blood," make your "blood go up" and give you "high blood."

Anxiety about digestion is further shown in respect to general food groups that are considered "too gaseous," like onions, cabbage and beans. In a nationwide survey by the American Institute of Public Opinion, in 1947, 29 per cent of persons interviewed in the United States—a very sizable proportion even for a hypochondriacal country—said "they found they had to avoid certain foods," and 4 per cent of these mentioned *gas-*

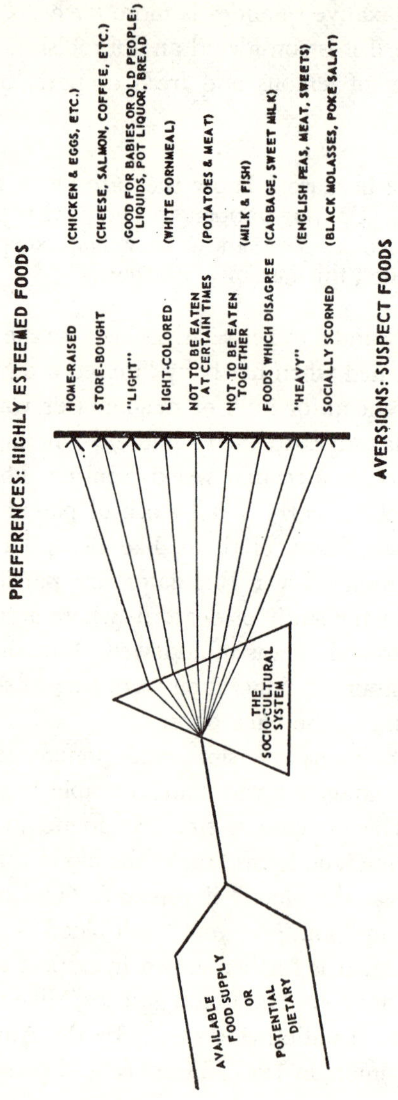

FIG. 3. THE FOOD SPECTRUM: RURAL SOUTH

eous vegetables, 3 per cent mentioned avoiding *acid* foods.[8] In the citrus survey in Kentucky, while oranges, grapefruit, and lemons were valued by many for special uses, they also fell under suspicion (sometimes by doctors' orders) as being too acid, and therefore causing stomach trouble, heartburn, and the like.

We now consider two aspects of the emotional connotations of foods: the *specific items* in which strong feeling centers in the South, and *kinds of qualities* which appear to call forth particular emotional reactions.

Foods with Special Powers

Certain items of food have acquired a special sentiment, generally through a long process of community approval of the foods, so that even after the reasons, the occasions, and the expression of the sentiment have been discontinued, the special power attributed to the food remains.

A good example of foods about which special attributes cluster is citrus—oranges, lemons, and grapefruit. When people were asked why they did or did not use citrus, the very range of their answers seemed significant: they had too much acid, they would stop rheumatic pains; a train caller felt they would restore one's voice; they would purify the drinking water; they don't stick to one's ribs; they make the blood thick; they must have calcium because the speaker's nails don't break off like they used to; they'll keep you from having heart trouble "and I ain't aiming to die with that"; they're good for reducing; they will give you an appetite; and so on and on. It is not necessary to discover the sources of these attitudes—their very number (as contrasted with those held for bread or potatoes) indicates something which we cannot fully explain.

All foods fall in somewhere along a general spectrum or scale, ranging from those that are highly esteemed and sought after to those that are scorned and tabooed. The place a given food item takes along this scale is a function of the social values of a given group and of individual taste. In the first place there is the available food supply or potential dietary, including all the food that can be made available under existing conditions of climate, soil, transportation, etc. This is always more comprehensive than the actual dietary. It is subjected to the society as to a prism, which on various grounds (texture, flavor, rarity, cost, association) begins to assign a status to one food, relative to another, much as is done in respect to persons in a society. Some foods are highly prized, some commonly accepted, others rejected. Of course, food items maintain no hard and fast position, since technological changes are always affecting the dietary. The individual, because of some experience or taste, might have an entirely different ranking system, but, by and large, fairly permanent attitudes center around a given food. Some elaboration of what these classifications include may here be noted:

Highly Esteemed Foods		*Less Highly Esteemed Foods*
Home-Raised Foods	*Purchased Foods and Those Infrequently Secured*	
chicken and eggs	beefsteak	dark flour
corn bread	fish	yellow corn meal
white flour	ice cream	black molasses
vegetables	oranges	brown sugar
peaches	celery	internal organs of animals, except brains
pecans	cauliflower	rabbit and 'possum
honey	strawberries	poke salat
	apples	English peas
	cheese	sweet milk
	bananas	
	dates	
	pineapple	
	salmon	
	boiled ham	

"Such as Have Need of Milk, and not of Strong Meat"

Milk is one of the chief food items with which an emotional reaction is associated. Among the various peoples of the world, aversion to milk is the rule rather than the exception. It is occasionally regarded as "an animal secretion" to be equated psychologically with other animal secretions we ourselves would not accept as food. But the pattern in this region is the more striking in that, while milk is strongly endorsed by our scientists today, it is one of the food items frequently omitted from the Southern dietary. Even though milk is often *called* a protective food, the same persons may not only fail to drink it but express a strong aversion. To begin with, the aversion seems based on the fact that there is little milk available. The deficiency in dairy production and milk-drinking in the South has often been noted. Far fewer farms than in other regions have cows, and the average production per animal is about half what it is elsewhere. In Seaford, North Carolina, a school lunchroom serving over 200 students used only 10 pints of milk daily.

In addition, sweet milk does not long remain sweet in so hot a climate, and where most people lack refrigerators. An informant describes what happens:

> Some people try to keep milk from one meal to another, now like they milk that morning, but by supper it is soured. Last August we had a spring to set the milk in and it would keep good and cool. But if you haven't got any to keep the milk cool, it sho' ain't good. I have a receipt for cottage cheese but I jest never have made any.
>
> A refrigerator would mean all to the milk and butter. It is a whole lot disconvenient not to have ice. But we jest have to cook in the kitchen and eat there when it is so hot right after I finish cooking dinner, it is so uncomfortable. But with the flies and the milk hot, you can't rest while you are trying to rest to go back to the field. [Negro sharecropper.]

When milk is consumed, it is often preferred in the form of

buttermilk, clabber, or sour milk. This taste has evidently been culturally acquired, in part because of the conditions of the climate, but is now so firmly a part of the foodways that even persons possessing refrigerators prefer buttermilk or sour milk to sweet milk. An aversion for sweet milk appears:

> Yes'm, I drink buttermilk. I don't like sweet milk much, seem like it make my blood go up. Maybe I be bilious at the time. I take it to be the milk, I don't know. [Negro wage-laborer.]

The remark "Sweet milk just don't set well on my stomach" was heard so often as to rule out the possibility that this aversion might be actually individual allergy to milk.

A further evidence that milk is a suspect item in the foodways is its repeated appearance among *foods which, according to folk belief, should not be eaten in combination,* as for example, sweet milk and fish, buttermilk and cabbage, buttermilk and fish, ice cream and oysters.

The attitude toward milk appears to be closely connected with changing its constituency or appearance; that is, milk in its natural state is suspect, while milk in some changed form meets with tolerance and even approval. In Seaford, a mother would often proudly say, "I raised my baby on Carnation Milk." A wage-laborer mother complained at the high cost of Klim, a powdered milk product, but was willing to make sacrifices in order to secure it for her baby. As sour or buttermilk is more acceptable to adults, butter is a dairy product that is preferred to milk in any form. Clabber biscuits are liked, and cream gravies are used. Thus while the aversion to milk in any form is marked, both by repute and in practice, this aversion is lessened by the transformation of the natural product.

One Man's Meat . . .

Meat is an item to which both marked aversions and preferences accrue. In a 1949 survey in Great Britain, it ranked next to fats as a food which people felt they had to be careful about. Locally, we have to consider a difference in idiom. Ordinarily, "meat" means pork, while "lean meat" means beef. A Negro wage-laborer said:

For dinner, I have milk, corn bread, and eggs. I don't hardly ever cook meat, but I don't think it agrees with me unless it is boiled or something.

This same informant says children shouldn't have meats " 'cause it ain't good for 'em coming up." She added:

Now, I heard lean meat is good and then again I heard it ain't. I really don't know for myself.

It is significant that fat meat is frequently eaten by the low income groups while at the same time many believe fat meat is harmful, especially that it produces high blood pressure. It is possible that the high calorie content of fat meat may produce a physical reaction easily confused with high blood pressure.

Not only is meat thought to be harmful to children but it is often forbidden to people in precarious states of health, as during pregnancy, post-partum, convalescence, or in advanced age. Often the connotation here is that meat is too strong a food—too virile for children, "will make the mother's milk come too fast, too 'heavy.' " This attribution of especially powerful magic to meat reminds us of the general attitude already cited, that meat is regarded as a dangerous food, as Westermarck suggests, because of man's guilty feeling at having to kill a fellow animal to secure it.

But meat also has special *positive* properties. The poorest informants in the South, when asked which foods they would feel are most essential purchases, would answer, "I buy my meat first." This type of meat thus regarded as essential is usually fat-back or fat butts, used not only itself as food but as a means of flavoring vegetables like collards and cabbage. In many cases, meat is part of the perfect meal, as in many folk societies.[4] A nationwide survey in 1949 showed that meat, fowl, and fish outranked all others in answer to the query, "If you had more money, what foods would you spend it on."[5]

For extra-routine occasions, as on Sundays, or when guests are expected, lean meat, particularly steak, is preferred. A wage-laborer informant bought beefsteak even when it cost fifty cents a pound, though the daily wage itself amounted to only $1.50. The *pièce de résistance* for most *extra*-routine occasions is fried chicken, to which, moreover, no taboos were found to apply. Chicken was never forbidden to children or persons in precarious health, nor did those who took care of the poultry appear to suffer a disinclination to consume their charges.

Meat is, of course, usually changed in its appearance by the cooking process, particularly the fat-back, hams, and sausage which are most often eaten, and the fried chickens are dissected. Certain kinds of meat, however, are presented in forms very close to their originals, as, for example, the hog head or jowl, a traditional New Year's dish, and pigs' feet. Brains, on the other hand, considered a delicacy, are scrambled with eggs.

Sweets

Children and Negroes were two groups which expressed especial craving for sweets. In Seaford, the school lunch cost five cents a plate, but so many children preferred to buy a candy bar instead of lunch that the situation was proving a considerable problem. In Thomswell, the sale of candy by the home economics department, to provide equipment for the department, helped along the candy purchases. The traveling grocery truck found many customers for candy and soft drinks among both children and adults. Many Negroes said that they craved sweets, not only in the form of candy, but as molasses, syrup, or sugar. A favorite between-meal food in Negro families is the cold sweet potato. Wartime deprivation in countries like England and Hungary made candy disappear from the shelves as fast as it was offered when rationing was relaxed. It is probable that the hunger for sweets in the South is closely associated with deprivation.

Strangely enough, sweets are not spoken of as foods one ought to eat, although sweets are so often eaten. Perhaps because of this the attitude toward sweets is somewhat shamefaced. A mother will say, "I know the baby shouldn't eat so many sweets, but he craves them so," or she will deplore her own liking for candy. It is probably true, also, that particular satisfaction, as well as some guilt, adheres to sweets for the very reason that they are not positively sanctioned. The sense of guilt, probably attended by an aversion to sweets, would probably be stronger if the cultural disapproval were more strongly or explicitly stated, as in the case, for example, of Jewish dietary laws.

The attitude toward sweets provides an interesting example of a discrepancy between the physiological taste for sweets and the cultural disapproval of sweets. It is often claimed that children eat more sweets than adults because they are satisfying a physiological need for more calories, but it is also possible that the cultural disapproval of sweets is, in adults, overwhelming a natural craving. We see a similar discrepancy in the South in the other direction between the unpleasant taste of sour milk and the acquired taste for it in the culture. The catering pattern, however, holds true even in the case of such discrepancies, for there is more inclination to follow the natural than the acquired taste.

A Food Carrying a Particular Aversion: English Peas

The pronounced aversion to English peas in Thoms County, Georgia, seems to be a local attitude and did not appear in other parts of the South. The only explanation given by informants was that peas "do not agree with them," but no credible explanation appears for this aversion. The fact that it is so pronounced in the neighborhoods of Westmore and Glen, though uncharacteristic of other parts of the region, shows how regions themselves may comprise a variety of smaller segments at variance with the regional foodways.

"Light" and "Heavy" Foods

Aside from particular food items with which many emotions are associated, there is a group of foods to which the adjective "light" is applied and another often characterized as "heavy":

Heavy (in order of frequency of mention)	*Light (in order of frequency of mention)*
meat (fat meat and lean meat)	"liquids"
beans	milk
English peas	pot liquor
cabbage	hot bread
potatoes	corn bread
eggs	bread
cake	blackberry wine
	butter
	grits
	oatmeal

One of the chief clues as to the status of a food on this basis is its place in the dietary of a pregnant or parturient woman. There is, for example, marked suspicion of meat for anyone in the state of pregnancy. Dr. I. H. Moore found the typical post-partum diet in Hancock County, Georgia, to be: ". . . Rice, grits, light bread from the store, and butter. Coffee is usually given to increase the milk. Milk is thought to be harmful to the baby. Vegetables, fresh meat, eggs, and fish are considered highly dangerous. They are resumed gradually after the sixth week."[6] When we asked about the dietary, an old Negro mid-wife advised:

Childbirth foods is butter and bread, drink a little coffee, rice and grits, toast and eggs. Eat lightly, not cabbage, meat, canned meats, fish, or potatoes—potatoes is heavy, don't digest so well.

Foods are called *heavy* if they are thought "not suitable for certain seasons of the year" or "not for children, sick people, or old people," "hard to digest," or "to be used sparingly," as opposed to connotations of vigor, healthfulness, "good for workingmen," and "rib-sticking."

The light foods are regarded as "food for children, the sick and the old," "easily digestible," "delectable." A good many of the "light" foods seem liquid or bland in texture, while several of the "heavy" foods seem hard in texture or of the kind requiring long cooking or frying. Aside from this distinction, there seems, as with so many such characterizations, little rational explanation for this concept.

Urban, Refined, Packaged, and Purchased Foods

The sanction of science reinforces preferences for foods in this class. The trends in food choices (Table IX) also indicate that such foods are valued.

There is a parallel aversion for foods considered rural, unrefined, raw and home-raised. For example, a Negro informant dislikes rabbit and 'possum because they represent foods in the natural state with which she has been forced to deal at firsthand:

There is rabbits and 'possums that make me sick. I like squirrel and birds. I just clean the rabbits and 'possums so much. I think that is what made me sick.

Many of the refined foods are light-colored while the natural foods are often dark-colored. This light-colored quality of refined foods is often transferred to natural foods also. Thus, children are told, "Choose the white corn for your bread corn." When meal or flour is home-produced, there is much preference for refinement which will lighten the color of the product. A Negro wage-laborer says,

Yes'm, we raise our own grain. We did have our flour ground over here into white flour mostly. I don't like the dark as good as the white. The family don't like it much neither.

Also the informant who says, "I like the black molasses better than the cane syrup," nevertheless mentions Karo syrup—a refined, lighter product—as the proper food for children, an indication that in this region, despite the adult's personal preference, light-colored syrup is felt to be more easily digestible.

Summary

The region sanctions the formation of strong feelings about food and digestion, especially preferences and aversions for certain foods based on other than their simple taste characteristics.

Long after the original reasons for such emotions have disappeared, certain items of food have strong emotional connotations. The consensus of feeling places these items of the dietary at different positions along a scale ranging from those in high esteem, through those somewhat suspect, to, finally, those wholly tabooed.

For instance, the emotions regarding milk are significant, for little milk is produced or consumed in the South, although elsewhere it is regarded as an essential food. When consumed, it is preferred in a changed form, as sour or buttermilk. This is an instance where a taste, originally conditioned in part by the climate, may be culturally maintained in spite of the directive, by science or taste, toward this food in another form.

Although fat meat and meat in general are considered suspect, in practice meat is generally liked and valued. Chicken meets with only a positive approval and is not restricted to persons in good health as meat often is.

While sweets are not considered an ideal food, a strong craving for sweets often exists, especially among children and Negroes.

Little reason can be offered for classifying one group of foods as "light" and another as "heavy."

Urban, refined, packaged, purchased, light-colored, and relatively expensive foods are liked, while in general foods which are rural, home-raised, "old-timey," unrefined, and dark-colored are disliked.

One of the most significant of attitudes found is the preference for food in a transformed state and the aversion for food, like meat and flour, which too closely resembles its original form. Often, various ways of preparing food are used by the mother to accede to the family's food preferences.

In general, the strength of the emotions associated with food and the number of food items toward which pronounced emotional attitudes are held are a striking characteristic of the regional foodways. The frequency with which aversions are stated, when informants say particular foods do not agree with them, suggests that there is a possibility of vicious circles operating here. Poor nutrition may entail poor digestion; poor digestion may lead to attempts to diagnose the cause; false diagnosis may lead to narrowing the number of foods eaten; while narrowing the number of foods eaten may lead to even poorer nutrition, and so on.

The existence of pronounced attitudes toward foods in this region is logically inevitable, even though the attitudes themselves may be non-logical. Since several of the regional values positively approve such expression of collective sentiment, their appearance in the foodways is documentation of the validity of the folkway-foodway relation.

NOTES

1. Hilde Bruch, "Psychological Aspects of Obesity," *Psychiatry,* November, 1947, pp. 373-381. Hilde Bruck and Grace Touraine, Obesity in Child-

hood V "The Family Frame of Obese Children," *Psychosomatic Medicine* (1940) 2: 141-206.
2. Pitirim Sorokin, *Social and Cultural Dynamics,* 4 vols. (New York: American Book Company, 1941).
3. American Institute of Public Opinion Survey, April, 1947.
4. According to A. I. Richards, *Land, Labour and Diet in Northern Rhodesia* (London: Oxford University Press, 1939), "To the Bemba each meal, to be satisfactory, must be composed of two constituents: a thick porridge (*ubwali*) made of millet and the relish (*umunani*) of vegetables, meat, or fish, which is eaten with it" (p. 46), and, "In his own country it is no exaggeration to say that a native would give anything he possessed or do anything he was asked simply in order to get a piece of meat" (p. 57).
5. American Institute of Public Opinion, December 5, 1949.
6. Report to the *Conference with the Committee on Food Habits* (Washington: National Research Council, May 23, 24, 1941), pp. 95-96.

12

Implications for Food Policy

From out of the South

The original material here presented seems to lead to some general conclusions.

The potential food pattern of a region undergoes modification by individual taste, by social relations, and by the cultural values held by those around us. The actual food pattern here is a composite of home-raised food and purchased food—more home-raised than in an urban society, but less so than in the past.

This actuality has been chiefly influenced by members of the family, less so by kinfolk, neighbors, and the landlord group, least of all by formal professional workers. Even in a region where changes are relatively few, the food pattern is changing. The dietary of innovation is scientific and urban, reaching the White owners first. Foodways adopted by the lower social classes tend to be those associated with the higher classes. In the rural South, the trend is therefore toward the food habits of the White owner class, whose food habits in turn, as already described, are sharing in the world food-habits trend toward a "scientific" dietary. Thus a vast process of de-differentiation may be seen as the international, national, regional, and community foodways slowly tend to lose their local flavor. In the rural South as a whole, however, as in each local area, there are eddies in this current as the general process of diffusion of food habits is interrupted by the strength of Southern family relations, which give precedence to parental recommendations over scientific recommendations, and by the region's stress on tradition and the validity of individual preferences.

That is to say, what happens when a Southern sharecropper finds a new packaged breakfast cereal in the country store is that he tends not to ask himself, "Will it nourish me?" and "How much does it cost?" but rather, provided the answers to these questions are reasonably satisfactory, he notices the posted advertisements (which, incidentally, suggest other reasons than these for his purchase), sees that it is conveniently and attractively packaged, observes that it claims to be enriched with the new vitamins of which he has vaguely heard, and perhaps is mainly influenced by the example of a landlord. All of this occurs in the framework of a culture which stresses tradition, expects social distinctions, is inclined to cater to individual tastes, and is constantly bombarded by the recommendations of the men in white coats.

In the course of time, attitudes about foods grow up which are exceedingly non-logical. The power attributed to a food may be originated by an individual. It may extend no further than part of the region, as in the local aversion for English peas, or it may become an integral part of the culture. Many food prejudices are initiated or reinforced by food advertisements. Others appear as the result of incomplete scientific investigation or inaccurate nutritional education. One of the paradoxes of present-day civilization is the boost which "Science says—" has given to nonscientific prejudices in this field.

By this time it would be hard to find a person who has not, during World War II and in the interim period, had his habits shaken if not changed by some large-scale food program. But the planners are shaken too. In the reports of the Food Stamp Program, the Army Quartermaster Corps, Office of Price Administration, United Nations Relief and Rehabilitation Administration, and the Food and Agriculture Organization appears a note of petulance out of key with the even tenor of official papers. Food by fiat, eating by edict, was not so easy as it looked.

There was the question of rice, for instance, so important to millions of the world's population. Said the Philippine Committee in 1947:

> Our health authorities are at a loss to find a remedy to check the production and distribution of polished rice. It is very difficult to persuade people who are now consuming polished rice to replace it with brown rice.
>
> The practical solution of this problem does not lie in the hands of the nutrition experts alone. If milling were merely a bad habit from the nutritional standpoint, the matter would be simple enough, but in reality the question is more complex. Under-milled rice, stored under ordinary conditions, deteriorates more rapidly than polished rice. Moreover, its white color gives it a much more pleasing appearance than rice which has been merely husked, which is usually yellowish or brown or red, and whose use denotes a kind of low social standing, since the more prosperous people eat only white rice.[1]

In India, where there was so severe a Vitamin A deficiency as to threaten people's eyesight, the people would not switch to protective foods which could remedy the deficiency simply. Instead, in some cases, large doses of Vitamin A had to be administered subcutaneously to save eyesight.[2]

But let us look nearer—at the civilized consumers of Europe. It is the Secretary-General speaking—he has a report for the fourth meeting of the International Emergency Food Council.[3] It appears that, during the War, Europeans thought rice important for the treatment of diarrhea in infants and young children. However, doctors thought that rice was not essential, even harmful for this purpose. Nevertheless, since rice was universally regarded as a household remedy, sentiment seemed to necessitate importing the regular annual quota of 1,200,000 tons of rice. *Sentiment,* gentlemen? Sentiment sits easier at the dinner table than at an august conference table. One million tons of sentiment when shipping space is so short?

Alas, nothing but sentiment. Wherever one looked, planning programs were riddled by the force of unreason.

Switzerland: when grain supplies were *cut* by a third, people ate *more* bread.[4] Germany, after World War I: supplies of corn sent to starving Germans go scorned because in Germany corn is regarded as a food fit only for pigs. But since foreigners may be unstable characters, let us return to America, God's reasonable country.

United States, World War I: to push potatoes, the planners are forced to weave children's stories about how the Little Brown Prince after long years of neglect was finally recognized by the King of Vegetables and placed by the side of Prince Wheat and Prince Corn.[5] (Uneasy the head which wears a princely crown, one adds, for potato consumption has steadily fallen during the succeeding years.[6])

United States, "the Great Depression": graham flour on the list for which food stamps could be offered, nutritious graham flour, and estimable dried prunes. Unfortunately, hungry families wouldn't eat the items that cost the fewest stamps. But when pork was added to the list, demand for it shot upward—well, past all reason.[7]

World War II and rationing: what in the world had got into people, thought the planners, looking at their sheaves of statistics on pre-rationing consumption patterns. Had all the non-coffee drinkers suddenly taken to gulping coffee? They raised the points on condiments, pineapples or peaches—up, up, and *still* people saved up and swept the shelves bare of them, while good, sensible, low-point foods stayed unloved, uncherished, and unsought. Even the soldiers, in a most unmartial manner, were reporting that the identical beverage tasted different according to the container used.

Shifts in Consumption

In spite of the difficulties, many changes in food habits were effected by emergency programs of one kind or another. In many cases, nutritionally speaking, the changes were all to the good. Citizens of countries consuming 3,000 calories and up in 1935-1939 (United States, United Kingdom, Canada, Australia, Denmark, Argentina, New Zealand) were forced to eat less, a condition which within limits is advantageous.[8]

In addition, the quality of this restricted diet seemed improved when people had to eat less fats, sugars, and highly processed white flour, and more foods in their natural state. It was hoped that these advantages would be maintained after restrictions were lifted. There is already evidence, however, that consumers are doing a great deal of backsliding by reverting to their long-time dietary practices.

According to John D. Black, we are now eating about 17 per cent more calories than in 1935-1939, and a menu providing a larger assortment of items. We are eating more meat, butter, eggs, fruits, and vegetables. We have increased our consumption of carrots 745 per cent; of lettuce, 475 per cent; spinach, 590 per cent; asparagus, 300 per cent; kale, 290 per cent; and green peas, 196 per cent.[9] We have become, above all, a nation of meat-eaters, insisting on meat for the main meal.

A great deal of attention is being paid by international organizations to food targets for the countries of the world. While these targets are mainly aimed at upping the calories for low-calorie countries, it is quite likely that once that has been attained, we shall see the same shifts in consumption we have had in the United States: more foods in quantity, a wider assortment, and a stress on highly processed foods.

Foods for New Types of Families

As women continue to take jobs outside of their homes, the chore of preparing meals becomes shortened. Marketing seems easier in self-service stores. All kinds of foods are pre-packaged, including meats. Every day adds to the number of powdered, dehydrated, frozen, and prepared foods. Why shell peas or squeeze oranges, asks the housewife in increasing numbers, when prepared frozen peas, orange juice—practically anything you can name—are so readily available? Cook Boston baked beans for six hours when you can buy a can for fifteen cents?

At the same time the size of the family is decreasing. Grandparents and aunts and cousins join the family table only on holiday occasions. It doesn't seem worth while to heat up the kitchen for roasting or baking for just three people who would be all week working their way through the Sunday ham. So the housewife doesn't buy a whole watermelon, she gets a cantaloupe instead. She doesn't buy by the bushel or bagful, but by the pint or small-sized can. Just as the heavy damask tablecloth and the one hundred-piece dinner set disappears, out of the kitchen go the coffee-grinder, the rolling-pin, and the ice-cream freezer.

Foods for an Aging Population

Many of the trends mentioned are fostered by the fact that our population is an aging one. Old people, too, welcome the convenience of packaged foods. Eating alone on reduced incomes, they tend to buy in minimal quantities. We shall probably see less steak and corn-on-the-cob, and more soft-textured foods, easier for false teeth to manage. Some of the maladies of old age have psychosomatic elements which pose serious questions for the geriatrician. For example, will a patient with congestive heart failure fare on the whole better or worse on a salt-free diet, if he is greatly disturbed by the deprivation?

SOME QUESTIONABLE ASSUMPTIONS IN FOOD POLICY

It seems useful to comment on certain claims that have made a respected place for themselves. This and other studies puts them in question.

That all you have to do for low-income groups is to devise a cheap nourishing diet, and people will eat it.

According to the Stigler diet, costing only $40 in 1939, one could live a year adequately nourished on: 370 pounds of wheat flour, 57 cans of evaporated milk, 111 pounds of cabbage, 23 pounds of spinach, and 285 pounds of dried beans.[10] It is conceivable that war and famine may lead those in desperate circumstances to eat this diet. In less stringent straits, the Southern sharecropper, poor as he is, insists on buying occasionally a non-essential like ice cream or Coca-Cola or snuff. Furthermore, as new knowledge of the importance of trace minerals is acquired, one suspects that the definitive diet has yet to be developed. Quite possibly it would have to be diversified. One likely suggestion that has been made is that a basic world diet built around the foods the world can produce could be formulated, together with a choice of adaptive recipes.[11]

That you can devise a consistent price scale for food such that, if you reduce a 15-cent item by 5 cents, people will buy a third more.

It is constantly suggested that one way to relieve the agricultural surplus and at the same time improve nutrition is to reduce the price of protective foods. This again, providing times are "normal," assumes an economic determinism with respect to foods which many studies have refuted. High and middle income people will not buy more of what they don't like, merely because the price is reduced. It is true that low income groups (who tend to follow the lead of upper income groups) are more affected by price, notably in regard to preferred foods which they buy anyway, and would buy more of if the price were reduced. Undoubtedly in critical times the cost of staple foods has been important in the past and may be in the future. Currently, practical and material factors seem to be overemphasized, which is not to rule out the possibility that sometime they may be neglected. Certainly no *consistent* scale can be formulated for foods other than staples. You can eat just so much garlic or pepper or watermelon.

That you can discourage consumption of foods in nutritional disfavor by pricing them prohibitively.

Aside from the slightly undemocratic flavor of planning on such a scale, the practical difficulty arises of what is "prohibitive" pricing. The sharecropper who will buy salmon if it costs fifty cents a can has his counterpart in the suburbanite who might insist on white sugar if it cost $100 a pound.

Indeed, there is plenty of reason to believe that cheapness has a negative implication in America and that expense adds to prestige. If we believed in economic determinism, which we don't—maybe what we should do is not lower prices of protective foods but raise them. One remembers that even in the inflation period of 1948, even for the thrifty Pennsylvania Dutch, there was no run on the Banner Buy foods. Was it the mission schools abroad that learned to add prestige to their wares by charging tuition?

That you can get people to eat more of a given food by the same educational program and to the same degree that you can get them to eat more of another given food.

Is getting rid of a potato or wheat surplus essentially the same problem as getting rid of a cantaloupe or citrus surplus, aside from the price factor? It seems that the answer is *no.* Every social group develops certain foods which it regards as staples, regardless of their nutritional qualities, from the Negro sharecropper who says, "I buy my meat and my meal first," to the Habersham Road hostess who starts out by buying a shelf full of potted meats and fancy groceries, in case an unexpected guest should drop in. In our culture generally, bread, meat, and potatoes have become staples.

From this very fact, the consumption of staples has more nearly approached the potential demand than the consumption of special food items. We have pointed out how great a range of attributes is assigned, for instance, to oranges and grapefruit.

When an item can tap a *great many* important springs of action in a society—it is good as a laxative, good for reducing, good for babies and old persons, something which is a sign of prestige, doctors include it on special diets, and so on—the consumption can skyrocket far more than for an item which is simply presumed to be a filling staple.

That high income automatically means adequate nutrition.

Simply giving people more money, food coupons, and the like will not necessarily insure better nutrition. In Canada and elsewhere, where adequacy of diet has been measured on a nationwide scale, a high proportion of the well-to-do was found to eat inadequately. Such families tend to overeat and overdrink, to eat too many foods like eggs, butter, sugar, and meats, and too few whole grain cereals, beans and peas, milk, tomatoes, green and yellow vegetables, and fruits.[12]

That having many pronounced food preferences and aversions is normal for an adult American.

While it's all right to be choosey about one's food in the rural South, in America as a whole this quality is likely to be symptomatic of personality disturbance. Our society often says to a child, whatever his initial reaction, "Eat your spinach," "Clean your plate," "Eat all of the blue plate special—Daddy has to pay for it." When this happens, only neurotics are likely to retain a great number of food dislikes.[13]

On the other hand, maybe the rural South handles hunger best. It is possible that hunger satisfied in a framework of good interpersonal relations in an atmosphere easy-going, generous, cordial, catering to food preferences, and without tension, has a contribution to make to a disturbed world.

That better nutrition will make people happy.

When attention is centered about any one need—better housing, medical care, old-age pensions—enthusiasts are likely to assume that once this single need is met all other problems will be solved. Not so; Southern sharecroppers could learn to eat faultlessly and in the process lose other, more desirable advantages. Is the physical monotony of an Oriental rice diet worse than a Westchester suburbanite's spiritual monotony? Not that good nutrition and spiritual excellence can't go together. But let us recognize the *entire* situation involving any given problem in our action programs.

*That "educating" rural people, especially low-income groups, will make them see nutritional light and eat more **wisely.***

We have underscored the point that, in general, informing people is not the same as securing different behavior. Even as a preliminary step, perhaps we should not use the same methods of education with either these groups or the high-income group that we use for the great middle-class.

Who attends home demonstration classes? Who goes to nutrition classes? Who listens to lectures? Who reads government pamphlets? Certainly not the very people "who need it most." Indeed, reaching them is one of the major problems in research and action programs. The big research projects and mass surveys are increasingly directed from skyscraper offices and green university campuses by persons who know better what to do with a card catalogue than with a dog that comes barking from the front door of a tenant house. We tend to hire interviewers instead of going to have a look ourselves. We organize from our own point of view, use teachers, social workers, and interviewers like ourselves, posters and radio programs *we* enjoy, demonstrations that make use of kitchen equipment found in *our* kitchens, and appeal to motivations that make *us* act.

To certain groups in America—the transients, the migrants, the persons of little or no education, and the low-income rural population—we are worse than second cousins once removed.

They are less the forgotten than the never-known. They are hard to reach—so hard to reach, that it is safe to say that no research or action program knows much, if anything, about them. It seems a pity that only a caricaturing novelist, a Huey Long, or a rural representative for Watkins products takes the trouble to know them.

That food habits rarely change—that food habits change quickly in time of need.

Either is an extremist position. One should neither cry, "What's the use—you can't change people," nor believe that a food czar or campaign will be very quickly effective. There are plenty of instances, in Puerto Rico, Hawaii, Alaska, even high on the mesas of Arizona, where food habits have greatly changed. They change, but they change slowly.

The new Malthusians have been looking at their watches. "High noon: time for dinner: millions clamoring to be fed today. Millions more coming to dinner tomorrow, and less and less in the larder."

The Earth has so far set a good table. Perhaps tomorrow's guests will be dining on delicacies imported from far flocks and vineyards. Or perhaps we shall be ingesting algae or plankton. In any case, some of the factors that intervene between the cup and the lip have been indicated here. If they learn to understand and apply these factors well, the guests themselves may concoct of almost any fare their own good cheer.

NOTES

1. *Special Report of the Philippine Committee,* Food and Agriculture Organization, 1947, p. 34.
2. John D. Black, *Future Food and Agricultural Policy* (New York: McGraw Hill, 1948), p. 50.
3. Food and Agriculture Organization, Washington, July, 1947.

4. J. Rosen, *Wartime Food Developments in Switzerland* (Food Research Institute, Stanford University, California, 1947), War-Peace Pamphlets No. 9.
5. M. R. Dickson. *The Food Front in World War I* (Washington, D. C., American Council on Public Affairs, 1944).
6. *Potato Preferences among Household Consumers,* Miscellaneous Publication No. 667, United States Department of Agriculture (Washington, D. C., U. S. Government Printing Office, August, 1948).
7. Norman L. Gold, A. C. Hoffman and Frederick V. Waugh, *Economic Anaylsis of the Food Stamp Plan.* A Special Report by the Bureau of Agricultural Economics and the Surplus Marketing Administration, U. S. Department of Agriculture (Washington, D. C., U. S. Government Printing Office, 1940).
8. Black, *op. cit.,* p. 42.
9. *Ibid.*
10. *Ibid.,* p. 115.
11. David Cort, "Food: Angel of Peace," *United Nations World,* April, 1950, pp. 34-38.
12. *Ibid.,* p. 117.
13. H. G. Gough, "An Additional Study of Food Aversions," *Journal of Abnormal and Social Psychology,* 41, 1946, pp. 86-88.

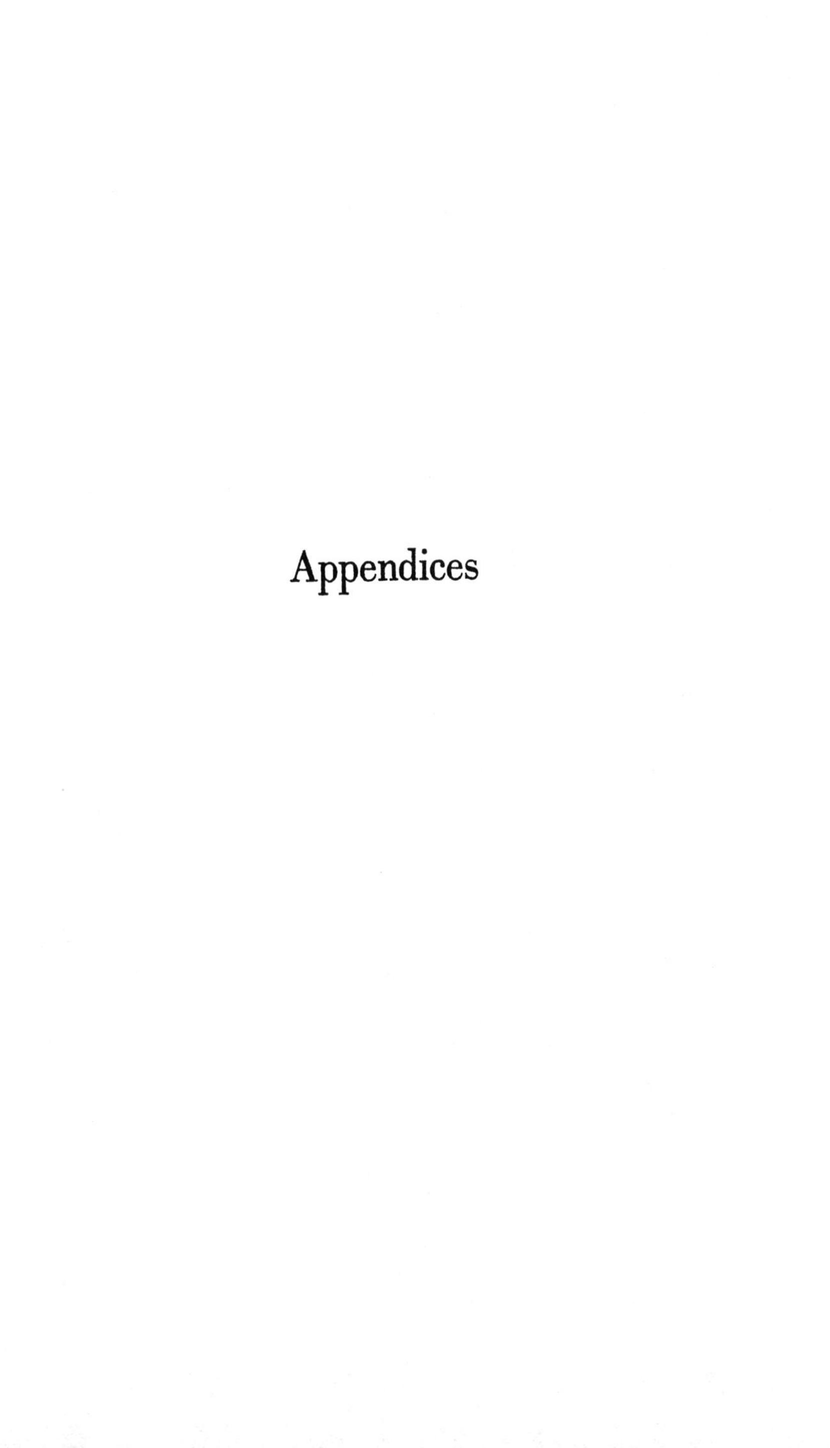

Appendices

Appendix A

DOCUMENTARY PHOTOGRAPHS AND MAP

CUSSLER

1. Piedmont Plateau cotton land . . . contour plowing is necessary even on ground that is not steep but gently undulating, and is already widely adopted in many counties.

CUSSLER

2. When farmers no longer raise the food they need, they must buy it from the "rolling store" . . . but often cigarettes, snuff, soft drinks, candy or kerosene come out of the budget

DE GIVE

3. A 400 lb. hog is a welcome addition to a family's food supply, providing valuable B vitamins in all the lean cuts and organ meats which will be eaten.

4. There is much work to converting all the hog into edible form. Some people "eat ever'thing about a hog but the squeal."

DE GIVE

CUSSLER

5. Many farmers don't have barns. Livestock, and hay to feed them, spell the difference between good nutrition and "hidden hunger."

6. Tobacco beds have to be prepared in mid-winter, and the seeds sown under muslin . . . long before you start to think about a garden.

CUSSLER

CUSSLER

7. A Farm Security Administration client has met her "quota" of canned goods for the year, and is congratulated by her supervisor.

8. A winter garden of collards and turnips provides vitamins all winter long to a family industrious enough to grow one.

DE GIVE

CUSSLER

9. Crocheting is a disappearing handicraft, along with spinning and weaving, bottoming of chairs, quilting, and making soap.

10. A sharecropper sweeps off her doorstep with a homemade sedgebroom.

DE GIVE

CUSSLER

11. A once common live-at-home practice, followed now by only a few of the old people—carding batts to spin into cotton thread.

12. Like their pioneer forebears, most Southern women still know how to make soap out of fats and lye.

CUSSLER

CUSSLER

13. Much out of little. Conjuring up a hot school lunch with such poor equipment is a daily triumph.

14. The school lunch in the Negro school provides many needed calories and vitamins, even if it's only prunes, cornbread and mashed turnips.

CUSSLER

CUSSLER

15. New additions to the family mean new additions to the house. Often, it's the diet that suffers while "improvements" are being made.

16. "I buys my flour and my fatback first of ever'thing". Some White people feel there's a racial differential where food needs are concerned.

CUSSLER

CUSSLER

17. As poor as Tobacco Road, but with a self-respect that allows her to pride herself on leaving the shack clean and neat for the next tenant.

18. Moving-day for a sharecropper—the old house . . .

CUSSLER

CUSSLER

19. . . . and the new. Many sharecroppers move so often that they do not try to raise gardens. This family has moved four times in five years.

20. In the new house, the first chore is to put up the tin drum-stove. It is used both to heat the house and to cook on.

CUSSLER

AGRICO
THE G. F. HARVEY CO.
PHARMACEUTICAL MFG'S
SARATOGA SPRINGS, N.Y.

CUSSLER

22. The final test of politicians and nutrition campaigns is the country store. The climate of opinion is formed here on everything from elections to diet.

CUSSLER

23. The annual Church Picnic, where plates of fried chicken and biscuits, baked yams, cakes and pies, make the long "tables" (of chicken-wire stretched between wooden horses) sag dangerously. Here are all the "prestige" foods on parade.

24. "Praise God from Whom all blessings flow"—grace at Home Demonstration Club Banquet for husbands. An important occasion for diffusion of new food ideas.

CUSSLER

CUSSLER

25. "Cornelia and her jewels"—except that Cornelia has pellagra and her children rickets on white flour and fatback.

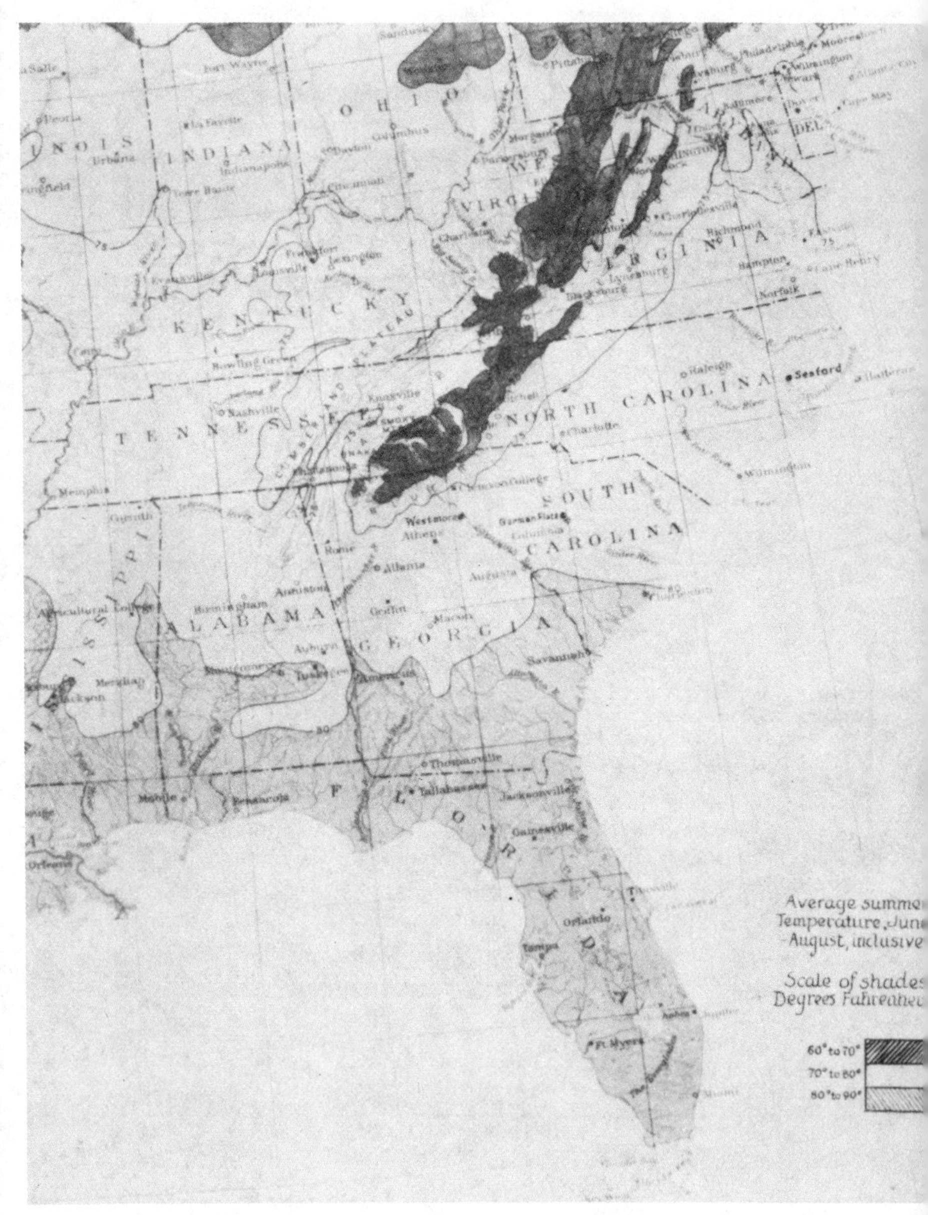

CUSSI

26. Map of the Southeast showing the location of the three communities studi (Seaford, N. C., German Flats, S. C., and Westmore, Ga.) within the region temperature zones.

Appendix B

OUTLINE FOR INTENSIVE INTERVIEWS ON FOOD HABITS

(Conversation with the informants usually centered about one topic each day, although informants were encouraged to make discursive comments.)

I. *Food Practices per se*

Dietaries, methods of cooking, saving, gardening, storing, grinding, marketing. Amounts of food eaten: milk, lean meats, eggs, butter, whole wheat or enriched flour, vegetables, fruits, cold drinks, "sweets," etc.

II. *Character and extent of nutritional knowledge*

A. *Correct nutritional ideas*

For example, what is known about the "protective foods"? What are the attitudes toward these? What is known about a balanced diet? Do people think they have an adequate diet? What is known about the special dietary needs of different members of the family (babies, young children, adolescents, pregnant women and nursing mothers, working men, old people, the sick)? What is known about certain nutritional substances: vitamins, minerals, proteins, fats, carbohydrates? What is known about the effect of horticulture and cooking upon these substances? What are thought to be essential foods? What are considered luxury foods? What is thought about "sweets"? What is thought about whole wheat flour, yellow corn meal, and hot breads? What is known and thought about Government programs to improve nutrition: Food Stamp Plan, School Lunch, Home Demonstration and County Agent Activities, Surplus Commodities, Farm Credit, Home Economics Classes, Agricultural Council?

B. *Folk beliefs, superstitions, prejudices, fads about food*

For example, what foods should not be eaten at certain seasons of the year? What foods are "bad" for you, and how? What foods are "good" for you, and why? What foods should not be eaten by persons of certain ages and conditions—the very young, the very old, the menstruating woman, the pregnant woman, the sick and convalescent? What foods should not be eaten in combination with other foods? What foods "go against nature," i.e., produce impotence? What foods are valued for certain purposes, for instance, "building up the blood," "building resistance to colds or other illnesses," "spring tonics," building energy or strength, curing specific ailments, making for strong teeth, helping the digestion, relieving fatigue, soothing the nerves, reducing weight? What drugs and patent medicines are used, and for what purposes? What food practices are considered in accordance with moral virtues, religious doctrines, common sense, scientific knowledge?

III. *Sources of knowledge and superstitions about food*

Tradition, early training, neighbors, clubs (Home Demonstration, Women's, P.T.A., etc.), children attending school (Home Economics classes or school lunch), meetings or adult classes, doctor, dentist, druggist, public health nurse, Farm Security Home Supervisor, Georgia Power Company Home Service Agent, County Agent, minister, movies, radio, magazines, newspapers, etc.

IV. *Susceptibility to education, advertising and propaganda about foods*

What information has been heard about foods recently, and through what channels, that has caused a change in food habits? How much effect have Government efforts to improve nutrition had upon individual families? Which appeals have been most successful: patriotism, large-group or small-group well-being, personal interest, praise, fear, duty, desire for beauty, popularity, etc.?

V. *Attitudes toward sources of nutrition information*

What do people think of "the Government"? Is it in good repute—do they listen to its food recommendations? What do they think of food advertisers? What do they think of salesmen? What is their attitude toward strangers, toward technical workers from the outside, toward women food or agricultural technicians? Will they take advice from young people or from an older woman, from a married or unmarried woman? What Government agent enjoys the greatest favor among them? What citizen, or citizens, is most influential? Do they listen to their own young people who have left the community and come back educated? Do the lower classes and "inferior" groups ape the higher-ups, and how much? Would they resent a member of the higher caste or class interfering with their food habits? What words, phrases, references to food habits would lower-caste or class persons object to if used by nutrition workers? What do they think about listening to nutrition programs over the radio, reading nutrition articles in newspapers and magazines, trying out recipes, etc.?

VI. *The influence of the social structure upon food habits*

What foods are considered "White folks' " food? What foods are considered "niggers' " food? What foods are considered "fit only for pigs"? What foods are considered "country" foods, "town" foods (to designate one's rise in status from rural to urban life) ? What attitudes toward such diets are held by the respective groups? Are certain foods eaten by the respective groups out of a sense of obligation to their status? Is there shame attached to certain foods and practices, for instance, fat meat, communal use of the dipper in the water bucket?

Is pride felt about certain other foods and practices?

For instance, does the farmer consider his food habits healthier? Is he proud of his "country hams," home-grown wheat, etc.?

What is the status pattern within the family? Who gets served first, and who gets choice pieces of food–father, children, youngest child, oldest son, etc.?

How much and what kind of neighborliness is practiced with regard to foods and feeding activities?

Do neighbors help with the plowing, harvesting, planting and caring for a garden, preserving of foods, hog-killings, syrup making, getting the grain to the mill, etc.? Do they lend machinery for these activities willingly? Is there much borrowing of foodstuffs, and are they lent willingly? Do neighbors give away or swap surpluses often? What recipients are preferred by them—White, Negro, hard-working, shiftless, destitute, widows, etc.?

What is the landlord's attitude toward his tenant's food habits and nutritional status? Is he concerned, does he try to help, is he indifferent, does he actively oppose better nutrition for them?

VII. *Chief lines of communication in the community through which nutritional information may be disseminated*

What is the usual route a rumor travels in the community? What are its eventual boundaries? Who are the leaders of the community? What are the patterns of neighborhood visiting? What groups are reached by different channels of communication, such as: the radio, various magazines, newspapers, the different churches and schools, Home Demonstration clubs, Vocational Home Economics and Agriculture teachers, P.T.A., Farm Security and other Government agencies, etc.?

VIII. *The extent to which food habits are conditioned by economic conditions, either actually or imaginatively*

What changes in food habits are economically possible? Can sharecroppers manage to have a cow, pig, chickens, garden? Are they convinced that they cannot eat better than they do? Are they dissatisfied with their present diets and do they wish that they could eat better? Do they believe that recommended dietary improvements are "too expensive"? Do they feel that they should be "satisfied with their lot"? Do they known about sources of credit for food production? Do they feel that shortage of equipment is a problem? Would they do better if they had better refrigeration, stoves, cooking utensils, pressure cooker, canning jars?

IX. *Attitudes toward "live-at-home" practices advocated by the Government*

Extent of family self-sufficiency in nutrition and other domestic needs. How much are the family food needs satisfied at home? What handicrafts are still practiced? Are these practices considered virtuous? Are they considered "backward" by younger members of the family? Are they kept up as a point of pride? Are they practiced just because economic conditions make them necessary? Would they be abandoned as soon as it was economically possible to do so? Is agricultural specialization considered a higher type of farming?

X. *Rationalizations of dietary deficiencies*

Reasons for a poor garden or no garden, for no cow or

milk, for not drinking milk, for not growing one's own wheat, for not having an orchard, for not canning, etc.

XI. *The extent to which food habits have been conditioned by personal experience, both individual and social*
Experiences in childhood, in sickness, with former changes of diet, with farming, with landlord-tenant relationships, with other cultural areas. In childhood, were certain foods or a meal used as reward or punishment? Was a child sent from the table if bad? What were the methods used to get children to eat certain foods? Was the child taught cleanliness in all things pertaining to food? Was he taught that too many "sweets" are bad? Was he taught to eat certain unpleasant foods that were good for him?

XII. *The effects of culture contact, cultural diffusion, and cultural change upon food habits in this locality*
Changes in food habits between generations still living. Changes from earlier times. Vestiges of old food habits not now generally held. Diffusion of new food habits. What groups or persons introduce them? What groups accept them? What are the conditions of their acceptance?

XIII. *Food practices which are apt to be affected by war*
Habits of buying (in bulk, for a week at a time, marketing done by a child, attention paid to economy). Deliveries, particularly milk. Transportation of milk and dairy products to market. Marketing, if traveling grocery stores can no longer get tires. Preservation of food if there is a shortage of cans. Methods of cooking if there is rationing of electric power. Adjustment of diets and menus to fit reductions in sugar, fats, and whatever else becomes scarce, and to fit rises in food prices.

Appendix C

EXAMPLE OF CASE MATERIAL SECURED BY INTENSIVE INTERVIEWS WITH ONE INFORMANT USING OUTLINE IN APPENDIX B

Lela Fouche (Negro) April 16 - 21, 1942

"I Want To Do What's Right"

(First interviews included general preliminary material without verbatim record.)

John and Lela Fouche are tenants on the farm of Martin Norman, the most outstanding farmer in this section. Mr. Norman was chosen a master farmer in 1937. He represents the most enlightened practices in landlord-tenant relationships. John and Lela Fouche came from nearby Lincoln County, and have been married only six years, though John is over 70 and Lela is in her fifties. John is her second husband, and she has raised ten children. Both of them are unusual for people of their class, both intelligent and both with pleasant personalities. Both are of a light-brown color, and Lela looks as if she could have Indian blood—her features are sharp and her profile like that of the Indian on the nickel. Lela is anxious to learn, and is smart and enterprising. John has rheumatism and hadn't ploughed for 50 years, because he's always had sons at home to do it, until the other day when there was an extra mule in Mr. Norman's barn, and he wanted to help out, so he tried to plough again. It laid him up. Lela has ten children; one daughter here (Helen Johnson—Jo Johnson's wife) twenty-four years old, has five boys, lives near by. She feeds them what her mother tells her to. Lela says when she "come along" she didn't "know what folks know now, because people can read books and all." In this house eight live in all the time. The girl in Thomswell school boards for 30 cents a week rent, but she takes food to her every weekend, and furnishes her linen and wood. She can't get milk, and the milk brought from home has to be kept a week; in winter, a gallon at a time will keep all week but now where there is no refrigerator, it's hard. Two teachers board there. There are several girls in a room and thirteen girls in the house. Doris Fouche (wife of one of John Fouche's sons) lives on other road—eight children. "She have children every year. She have 'em too fast. It doesn't give her any time to work or ketch her strength. She go on and work and leave 'em in de bed." "I had a good time, because with my first children some of my sisters would come and stay with me or my grandmother. I never did take any of mine to the field. One time I wanted to pick cotton and had to take my baby to the field in a box but the baby screamed and screamed till my husband said, 'Take dat baby, take her to the house and never bring her back.' So I never took my babies to the field after that. That's the reason I keep two of my grandchildren from Augusta here. Their mother has to leave 'em from seven in the morning 'til seven at night. And you can't raise children that way. I tried it after my first husband died. I had two children, and I went to Augusta and got a job cooking for a rich lady. She wanted an expeerenced maid; I told her I wasn't expeerenced, but that I was willing to learn and to do everything she told me—I'm like that—I'm not hard to learn. I can change my ways and do things like people tell me. So I made $9 a week cooking, and some little extra. She would give me her dresses to dry-clean and would pay me same as the cleaner, and instead of paying somebody else 25 cents a pair to have her curtains washed, she'd let me do them, and she'd let me make the uniforms for her maid and pay me for that. So I made good money. But money's not all you need to make you happy. Your children run in street in all rags and dirt, hongry half the time, steal fruit off the fruit wagon—I don't want my children raised up that way. I took those children back to country, can teach 'em how to chop cotton, help me in the field and so on; won't earn so much, but be happier. (She worked in Augusta for a rich lady, who wanted her to leave her children to go to the Island but she couldn't leave them.) I learned 'em church and Sunday School. My oldest girl will finish Junior High School this year. That'll mean a white gradchation dress and a white petticoat and shoes. I'll have to pay for that out of my own money, and my other daughter in school won't be gradchating, but she'll want a new dress 'cause she hasn't had one all year. All that'll have to come out of my own money. I didn't marry till my oldest girl got grown and married because you never know what kind of man you're going to get. Might marry someone without principles for your children. I married this old man I'd been knowing a long time, he's a good man, to help me raise my boys because boys need a man. My oldest boy's working at Camp Gordon making 33 cents an hour. He helps me keep my girls in school. I have a girl and boy big enough to do the chopping. Oldest boy offered to come home but money was more useful. My other older boy works in the hospital at Augusta. I usually boss my chil'un. When they're little and don't do right I punish my chil'un; I sometimes have to whip (switch) 'em. After they get big, I don't think you ought to whip 'em all the while. I never deprive 'em of food. I always try to give 'em plenty to eat. A hongry child will just steal. I don't think you ought to have to lock up your food from your chil'un. And if they takes any food, I want my chil'un to tell me so if I asks them. Most people 'round here has to lock up their food from their chil'un. [?] I sometimes punishes my children by depriving them of candy, but then they don't get much candy nohow—I don't believe in givin' 'em many sweets. I don't want 'em to eat sweets even when they haven't done wrong. ["Where did you learn all these things and get all these ideas about how things should be done?"] I didn't learn 'em from my mother, 'cause she died when I was a baby, and so did my father, and I was taken and brought up by white people. I didn't have much schoolin', never got beyond the fourth grade, but after I had learned to read and write, then I read all the books and literature I could find and learned myself that way. They learned me to sew and crochet, and I've learned to knit just lately, and I learned the white children their lessons and learned some more myself doin' that. When I was fifteen I married, and I wouldn't have done it if I had had somebody to really take care of me, somebody I could have turned to and worked along with." ["Does your husband have the same ideas about bringing up children as you do?"] "Just about, but John isn't particular as I am. That's why his chil'un hasn't turned out as well as mine has." If she tried to "wear the pants" she'd do better, but doesn't want to get her husband thinking she's doing the farm part. She believes it best to take out a Government loan, to buy rather than to rent. "I clothes my chil'un out of eggs and chickens. Out of my little money, I bought a extra room and furnished it and screened the house, bought a Government bond at $18.50. Fouche handles $1000 but doesn't ever save anything. I tell him: 'I give you all of my time on the farm but I take my money to clothe the chil'un. You say we eat it up. But we don't have the food we need.' I don't like for 'em to have a whole lot of candy. My oldest girl always wins the high-jump. This year with the pitcher-show [the fire-bomb] they cut out the jumping. Her teacher don't like for her to eat a lot of candy, think it makes her short-winded. When insurance man come he give her a nickel every time he come and she would spend it right off for candy." ["Where do you get your books?"] "White people give me some, but not able to get even a dictionary for the chil'un. I never had a father, neither mother. I never reached over the fourth grade in school, but still I can come up with my chil'un that's nearly finished because I learned so much from White people. I married when I was fifteen. I'm now fifty. I learned most from other people. I help the White children with their lessons. What I see other people do I figure I can learn, too. Lots of people go around with their eyes shut." Her gums are bad. "I let 'em get so bad before I do anything. I use Vince's mouth-wash. I'd rather have 'em took out in the spring. My teeth jus' get loose." They have a cow, pigs, chickens, garden.

Summer Garden: She takes great pride in her garden. She grows all the customary summer vegetables, with several plantings. She even replanted beans and squash in late summer, when everybody said the frost would surely get them, and in October she was able to exhibit them at the Negro Fair at Glen and to give some to her landlord's sister, Miss Quillie, to show at the Thomswell Fair.

Winter Garden: She grows collards, turnips, mustard, rape, kale, carrots, onions, beets.

Canning: "I can lots of peaches and tomatoes. All my crowd just loves tomatoes."

Cooking: "Cooking for eleven takes you the best part of the mawning. Chil'un helps you wash dishes."

Garden: "I have beans, lettuce and squash, cabbage. Volunteer lettuce would just come up. Salad's all gone to weed now."

Meals: Summertime: "I don't cook but twice a day, have enough left over from dinner. Most people don't cook but twice."

Winter: "So cold, better to have 3 warm meals. Right now we don't have much to eat. A month from now we will have plenty to eat. Have to buy some now. Today cooked salad, and I put it in icebox." Today's dinner: salad, dessert, milk, cornbread. Sunday dinner: peaches, cabbage and white potatoes. Supper: cornbread, milk, sometimes meat. "I know yellow meal is 'stronger.' My chil'un don't think it looks good." Hot bread in the morning: either "shorts," muffins, batter-cake, or biscuits—each about once a week. Cold biscuits toasted make toast-biscuits, which are dipped in milk (milk-toast). Butter beans now, white peas. "Chil'un don't like much breakfast but eat a big supper." Eggs for breakfast. Apples bought at Christmas time last quite a time. They are given pecans; Miss Quillie gives them a lot. She knew more about what constitutes a balanced diet than anyone I've spoken to so far. To the question: "What foods are good for you?" she reeled off the items of a perfect diet: "Well, I think ev'ybody should have plenty eggs, milk—about a pint a day—butter, some lean meat—like liver—plenty vegetables and fruits, and whole wheat bread. We grows our own wheat and has it ground at the mill. 'Brim bread,' we calls it—it has the brown in it. It's good for you." We found out later in the conversation that she had been to the Westmore store the day before and had seen the nutrition exhibit recently placed there showing the daily minimum requirements for the individual. She had evidently memorized it—though we may be able to determine later just how much she knew before she had seen it. She is an extremely intelligent woman, with a quick mind and a pride in her knowledge and accomplishments. She knew all about us before we got there, having been told who we were and what we were doing in the community by Miss Quillie. She says that she has always worked for intelligent people and has tried to learn from them. She has also attended Home Demonstration meetings and canning demonstrations in the past at the Glen school. She says: "There's some who won't try, and wouldn't plant a garden if you put the seeds in their hands, but I'm not one of them—I've always tried hard to learn the best way of doing a thing." She is also very proud of her soap which she makes herself. It's whiter than most, and she showed it to us proudly. It's not too strong for washing the body, because she tests the amount of lye she puts in by sticking a feather into the solution, and if it is eaten up she adds more water until it does not eat the feather.

"Too much fat meat is bad for you. More vegetables and fruits should be eaten–they're good for you. Eggs butter and milk are good for you, also lean meats." She believes "babies should be started on a little bacon (fat meat with a streak of lean) when they are weaned." She raised ten children that way and prescribes it for other children. She wouldn't eat fish and buttermilk together.

Medicine: "I don't use any medicine at all, only what Dr. Harper says. I jest send the chil'un regular to see him and he jest send a bill, $5 or $6 in fall of the year. He come to make a local operation when I had that bad flow and he only charged $15 then. I take some liver and yeast last year when my blood was so low for vitamin C and B and it helped me 'bout the best. We've been wonderfully blest—we haven't had a doctor's bill here in a good long time. I went to the field in my change and picked 300 pounds a week."

May 11 - 14 1942

Sources of Knowledge and Superstitions about Food (III)

"At the barbecue we have our county agent usually talks. Mr. Norman [the landlord] have a chart and says 'Now this is what I want you to do this year, I want each one to have so many green things.' He talks about what each man made, how much he increased, how many pounds of cotton gained each year. Year before last we had 28 acres and 28 bales. I think it do help to go around and see the other fellow's property. When I could get about I like to go. [?] John did plow a little bit Friday evening, and he felt pretty dull the next morning. I had 26 vegetables already planted and most of them was up. I was the best he had then. Just the men go on tours of the farms. I always wanted to do what other people do. He gen'ally have two meetings a year, first thing is about the garden—he say if we couldn't get the things we need to let him know. [?] The Government forgot us but maybe they will think of us when they get ready. Yes'm they gonna get it [allotment money] and just a lot of other people have gotten theirs. Some of 'em couldn't write their name. [?] None of my sons have been sent over. They just work right over their job, have finished at Camp Gordon. They don't much want to go to Virginia where they will have to go. [?] He have told them when they didn't have a cow, why, he would let them have one for 50 cents a month. Maybe this fellow right here don't have a cow. He does get plenty milk. He went to sign up for a cow on this Government plan but he say he going to get one so he gets plenty of milk. [?] He [Mr. Norman] even has hands he don't know. Some live way down on the river. He has about forty families. He have one way back over there, one way down on the river, and one way above Thomswell. [?] I went up once and saw the exhibit and I already knowed it though. I read a lot, they had one up at our school. I use to cook up at Glen school. [?] Yes'm, they all take Home Economics and she take it for four years at Glen. They had a salad over there, I like to learn everything. I couldn't tell what was in the salad, it was carrots and a whole lot of things they has the children to make. A lot of people looked at it. The Home Economics teacher looks after it. [?] Well, not so much from my neighbors but especially young people. [?] I don't have much trouble. I fed my baby on cow milk, karo syrup, puff wheat and oatmeal. Started him eating before weaned him. [?] Home Demonstration Agent ustuh visit pretty regular but they don't have it now. They have uh vocational teacher there. Robinson certainly have learned the boys lot. They fixed pots and pans and just fix them good. [?] I learned about food because I ustuh work with white folks. The very best rich people in Augusta; hear a lot about it over the radio. [?] I don't have any special magazines and got some through white people but I don't take any. I think it is good to know about it [fancy food]. We took the farm magazine for five years. He [Mr. Norman] gives it to all his hands (the *Southern Agriculturist* and *Progressive Farmer*). [?] The Doctor gave me some medicine today. But I'm not going to take it until tonight so I can go to the school house. [?] I don't like to sew. This other lady us'ally does most of my sewing. She made Winnebelle a dress and pleated the skirt. I tole her to turn the pleats this way but she turned them under; if she had turned them like I tole her they would'da been fixed more. I try to get things nice. [?] Yes'm, she will be over there Friday night. She is in both of the programs. She is just finished grammar school. [?] Then we lived way down on the river, nine miles from a doctor. I didn't even see a doctor unless some one was real sick and people didn't know as much then like they do now. Down in the country, we had a very good school. We had sometimes ninety to one teacher. [?] No'm, I had my baby at home. We live just twenty miles on the other side of Washington, Georgia, not as large as Thomswell. When we lived in Lincoln my boy ate some watermelon and got a seed in his windpipe. The Doctor said it was a cold. But he tole me where to carry him and I took him right on down there. [?] I think they put $10,000 in it [surgical instrument] and he was the first one they used it on. The people who I worked for were real nice but they were not even at home. They had a taxi to take us right on up there. They transferred him to Macon. Those doctors wired them that we were coming. They brought him back on the stretcher. He just wake right up and call 'Mama' and next day at twelve o'clock they give him a discharge. [?] No'm I never did have a dentist. I have one boy that had a bad tooth. It had a black spot on the tooth and when he shed it the other tooth had a black spot on it. It is right in front. [?] No county nurse. Now, one last week was supposed to come but didn't; that was week before last. [?] The land is fine in Lincoln and wood, more wood. When we came up here it look funny, and we live right on the river on the forks. We had a little creek right over there. We had these great big springs and keep our milk cool. On this side of the creek we have corn, five or six ears to the stalk and my husband would make five or six bales of cotton. The finest I most ever saw. The man wanted that place so they sold it. We all caught malaria fever and we had to leave it. My husband died there with it. They gave me some quinine and I take it six weeks. Then I quit having chills. It was a fine country, we made a fine crop. [?] No'm, I never been to a movie. I have heard the preacher tell about it [food]. He was telling about eating so many different things. [?] I don't have anything electric except like iron, radio. They gave demonstrations up here at the store last year. I just learned some of the things. We have a ice box. The ice man comes by here three times a week.

[?] I hear it from white folks and from the radio. I listen to the Farm and Home Hour. Freddie (my indi*vid*jal son) can just hear things on the radio and just understand it. At first my husband didn't want me to get the radio but my son Freddie wanted it so. He say he will pay the first $5 on it, so I said go on down to the store and get it. I paid the other $20, paid it up in three months. The storeman said we were the first to pay for our radio. Freddie was full of politics. [?] My daughter's boy is living with us, don't know any other home but this'n. He can pick 100 pounds of cotton most nearly any day. [?] Now I always give Helen and my daughter-in-law some kind of advice if they will take it. I have had a lot of expeerence of my own;

I'm always telling them things that is right. [?] At times, when I go over there (Glen School) to other things or meetings we talk about food. I don't see any reason why people don't learn more. Then I ustah go to P.T.A. every time it met. We have always had a car in the family almost, but before we had a wagon. I helped other people with what I know. I give some magazines that are given to me to the other people that want them. I don't know whether they can read or not. My children go to 'home eca' and bring their books home and I read their books sometime. I always tell people about sticking to just one kind of bread and lot of time I change and cook different kind of bread, they [my family] don't much like it but I just cook it anyway. You know they like fried foods. 'Brim bread' is ground with everything in it. 'Shorts' is real dark. It can be made at the mills because they just grind it all together. [?] No, I never would belong to P.T.A. I belong to BYPU at church. I have been in several different meetings held by white folks. I would have to go with them to the meeting and I pay attention to what is going on. My husband say he don't know what was said. I say to him, 'Don't you hear what he said?' He said, 'No, they wasn't talking to me.' I said, 'It was public.' Lots of people just let it pass them like that. I think there is lots of ways to learn these things. A good way to learn them is to read; a lot of them don't understand it. The Government had a lady going around here, teaching people how to read and she come here to get the names of people who can't read. She was from Thomswell, a WPA worker. The people that needed to learn would never come to the meetings. They would all meet here. We had a Christmas Saving Club. Some of 'em that never had any money had more than they ever had, but they could had more. I was the treasureman. When people got through work they would come every week and meet here. I was the one that started it. Anybody brought some, few didn't never put any in it. But the majority of us kep' it up. The one who brought money would catch it down in her book and the secretary would catch it down too. Lot was saved, some didn't save so much though. I didn't want to stay treasureman because it is a great responsibility for money, but to do this jest for accommodation and expeerence is all right. When we had it in Augusta they saved $5 or $10 every week. Didn't many that did read come to the meeting. [?] My daughter said when she finished Glen, she didn't want to go to school any more. But I say the more you learn the more you wanna learn. My first husband's father had never been to school a day in his life and he could read. He was the best in politics and he could jest beat me understanding it to death. I never did have a chance to go to school but I jest know now a lot more. Anybody around me I jest tell them that their children ought to go to school but there is jest so many people that don't send 'em. [?] Yes, all the children ought to go to school but some large boys don't. In the city they got so many other places to go and to hide out from school but here the parents won't send them. By making a habit of going, it gets exciting. I tell them lots of time there ought to be a law to force them to go. The vocational teacher, Robinson, tried to get these two boys to sign up to go at night. He's been here fo' five years. Some of the fellows never done anything but hole a plow and when night come they are running around somewhere where they ought not to be. One of my husband's sons is going with a girl who can't read and I think it is ter'ble. But to go get a girl that don't know as much as he knows! There is no excuse for anybody living right here. But I think she couldn't read practi'ly a bit. I have one boy who is fourteen years old, he went to school for a while then he felt like he had to work. But if anybody get near interested in anything they can do it. But when I come along, I were young and didn't have anybody to tell me then. My son grow up so fast and you know when a boy gets big he wants things, so he quit school. My other son went through the eighth grade. He works in a hospital in Augusta, and gets three good meals a day; he is jest getting too fat. He went from the vegetable-room to milk-checker. [?] Yes'm, I think the preacher helps to learn us about food we should eat. He said we should not eat so much fried food. But here we like everything fried; sometime

I tell them that the frying pans should ought to be throwed away. He go around every fourth Saturday and take dinner with 'em but not on Sunday 'cause he goes home. He been telling about how to grow some tomatoes; he tole me a new way to fix 'em and I been meaning to try that. [?] I have never seen a movie on nutrition. I been to see one at Glen but I could've gone in Augusta because we lived right there. But then I had my chil'un.

Susceptibility to Education, Advertising and Propaganda about Foods (IV)

[?] Yes'm, I have heard and tried to mix brown bread. I went to the store one day, and Mr. Harold asked do I get many eggs, and he say, 'We get 'em here not by the dozen but by the crates.' Lots of people don't use them, they sell 'em. My family could use 'em all, but sometime I do sell a few. At the school play it cost 25 cents for us all to go. They all want to go, but I say, 'Ah, you too little, you don't need to go so much.' One of my daughters said, 'Well, give me some eggs and I will sell 'em and get my nickel.' But I go find her a nickel so we can have the eggs for somp'in' else. So I guess that is a little sacrifice. I sell a pound of cream every Saturday; some time I swap a few things. [?] I change to this brown bread and I try to make them eat it and mo' eggs and milk. [?] We have plenty of sugar right now but we were out when they rationed it. I will have ripe peaches this month. [?] Yes'm, we have some cane growing, it's up now. And in the summertime they all like tea and drink it. I couldn't tell so much about the other folks' food habit. Miss Quillie tell me jest to tell them to save everything they can get their hands on, and she tell me to tell them 'cause she feel like I can get to 'em, and if I do this how much nicer it will be. Sometime it is hard to get 'em to get jest what you have, but sometime I tell 'em it is fo' their good and welfare. [?] The majority of the colored people think what the white people do is all right. My daughter say she know better than for me to ketch her with smoke in her mouth. They like to wear the colors like the white folks do. There is one thing I have learned—that right goes a long way and wrong don't go far. Where I ustah work, one night they had a big party and some got so drunk, and women too. They were well-to-do people there. The neighbor even called up about twelve and asked them to let the noise down. Such another drinking I never saw, they were drinking so hard they couldn't half eat their dinner and knocked ashes into full dishes of ice cream. The cook said she wasn't going to wash all those dishes, so she left. While she was gone a man come in the kitchen and gave me $2 so when she came back, now, I didn't have to give her one, you know, and I tole her, but I did give her one, and then helped her with the dishes. But you don't know what your children will do after they get away from home. But I say, the first thing put in them is the last thing to go out.

May 18, 1942

The Influence of the Social Structure upon Food Habits (VI)

[?] I has six girls and four boys. [?] At the table I don't want 'em to quarrel and I do think they ought not to reach all over the table and throw something across the table. My husband don't like for 'em to talk 'cause he hard of hearing. If they jest get mad, yes'm, I jest tell 'em to get up. [?] I don't think they ought to talk about bad things or dead things at the table. I don't like them to sing or whistle at the table. [?] Yes'm often I make 'em go wash their hands, then they say, 'I forget.' [?] Now this boy of mine, Freddie, he ustah be so timid about eating, he jest wouldn't eat noth'n at all and I tell him that he would have diebetes and now he will eat most anything. But he wouldn't eat noth'n but corn bread and syrup then. Now I had salad and spinach today, I mixed 'em. They don't like spinach and one of 'em say it is spinach. I say, 'I put some spinach in it but it ain't spinach.' [?] Everyone of us kinda have a special piece of chicken we eat, I like the back or neck myself. My husband get first choice when I tell 'im to, but most ever'body get what they want. I like to fix something when ever'body get his share. [?] Yes, I sortah try to fix more for the littlest one, but we always have plenty of milk, butter, and chicken and corn and most of 'um raised on foods we grow. [?] Yes'm, I'm really proud of my country hams; this year we sugar-cured four of 'em. [?] Jest covered 'um in sugar, pepper, and salt instead of all salt. [?] Yes'm, I like the wheat ones better than the white ones. But this year, we not going to have so much 'cause we jest got sixteen acres. [?] Most people in the country that go to the city do about the same and mostly eat the same. Of course, you can get the same things there. In a way they are green when they go to the city. One time this lady I wus working for, asked me to make some mayonise and I didn't no more know how. But she say we'll make it when she come back. So she say you mix this and beat it good while I pour this in. And you see she didn't know I didn't know how to do it. I didn't tell 'em I didn't know so when I learned they still didn't know the difference. [?] I don't think the people in the city eat so much fat meat, but when I go to the city mostly I jest make 'pop' calls 'cause I don't go much and I ain't there at mealtime so I don't know much about how they eat. I happened to kinda know how to eat myself, when I went to the city, but when I get home I can eat like I want to. And I tell you another thing, they is a whole lot of people in the country that do like the city folks 'cause the city people have brought it to the country. When we started to have lights, my husband say we ain't going to have lights; I say we is. He say they ain't no need to, we got along so far without it. I say no need to stay in the same rut all the time, so we get lights. [?] If some of us ain't ashamed of the way we eat, we ought to be. They always drink out of the same dipper 'cause they have done that all of their lives. But I expect my chil'un to do better than me but I teach them what I can. One time I wanted some cloth and I tole my two girls, if you can tell me how much will be left of this 50 cents you can have it. They figure and figure and then they commence guessing and I say, 'Ah, you don't know,' so we go on to the field and after while I say to Freddie, 'How much white cloth can you get for 50 cents at 6 cents a yard and how much be left?' He study a minute and then say, '2 cents.' I say 'Go get the 50 cents and get the cloth,' and it make the others kinda mad 'cause they didn't know. [?] The neighbors are right good about helping other folks. Now sometime I help lot of my neighbors and then they help me. But everybody begin to gather the corn and cotton about the same time. [?] Yes'm we borrow some things, but a big machine, we have to pay to use it. The neighbors sometime bring me things when they have too much of it. And when we kill a hog I always give my neighbors some. I make lye hominy and give all the neighbors some. When the ashes begin to get plum red, then the water begin to drip and the lye is mixed with the corn. Then the husk begin to come off the corn. I take it out and wash it, and wash it, and make a great big pot full. [?] Yes'm, I give things to white people and when I kill a hog I always give the Normans the brain and tenderloin. [?] I don't think any food is the white folks' food, 'cause it is anybody's that get it. When I was with the white folks in Augusta, I was little then. I slept in the same room with the other chil'un my size. Some time we would play 'blind man's bluff' and soon as they'd catch me they'd feel of my head and know who I is. I'd say, 'I ain't gonna play with you all no mo', it jest ain't fair, I'm going home.' But I never did. The next time they play I always play with 'um.

May 22, 1942

Attitudes toward Sources of Nutrition Information (V)

[?] Well, I don't hardly know; you don't know what they going to talk about, but I ain't a stranger to anybody myself. If anybody come and talk strange and funny, I feel like they up to something, you know. [?] Well, I like for any Government workers to come 'cause I feel that if anything is gonna benefit me, I feel like that time is valuable. [?] Well, all that I know, I do, when they get 'em, but anybody that are real good citizens feel like listening. [?] Well, my husband feel like they doing everything for the best. No'm, my husband don't have any education but he feel like the Government should help 'im some if they knowed his needs. I'm gonna do all I can while I can and when I can't then I expect somebody to help me. [?] Well, I were in town one day, and I heard some folks talking, and they wasn't colored either. They had been up to the Welfare Office, and they had some fruits and wus eating apples and talking and I said I'd heap ruther work for mine. [?] No'm, I don't think it is the majority of the people, 'cause I think the majority of people are good thinkers and know how to provide and there are a lot who jest don't know. I tell 'em in so many ways that Government have help 'um. Then I were up at the Welfare Office working one day and I don't know the people that come in and got clothes and everything. A man up there working said to me, 'You up here for something?' I said, 'No sir, I'm working for my living but anybody that help me help my children.' [?] Well, I could tell about myself but, well, I had think a older woman would know more about it 'cause she has mo' expeerence. [?] I don't know about the married woman, I don't think it matter about that though, but a older person have more better expeerence and mo' patience. [?] Some time it is people in a community, 'cause I figure if you know a person you know 'um, and that have a lot to do with it. [?] If a person give me a good talk, I don't know if he's wrong or not. I take what they say right, first. [?] I jest couldn't tell, with some it might be all right if they lived in the community, and then it would be all right for strangers, but with some it wouldn't be all right any way. [?] You take somebody that go off and learn and come back to teach, it don't have the same effect. [?] Well, they have a school supervisor sent by the Government and they keep her here, but the majority didn't like it. Mr. Robinson, I don't know how long he have been here but some are trying to get 'im out. They ought to do the right thing, and the thing that the Government ought to do is the right thing. [?] Well, I don't know; I have never heard any kick against anybody except this Supervisor, but the Occupational teacher, most everybody likes him. [?] Well, I think maybe they look to those who like to go to church and take care of their family and don't have any kinda doings in their home. [?] You take the Stranges and Hughes and the Heards, they are real smart now. [?] There is a family I would like for you to talk to. Her husband died and she is a widow; she have some boys and they are trying to help her to keep her place she is trying to buy. [?] Yes'm, they have to look up to the landlord, and you can be a leader if you are not a landowner. Freeman Jones is a fine family; one of their girls teach at the school. [?] Yes'm, I think they do, yes ma'am, but in some ways a lot of 'em kinda think sometime that a fellow who got a whole lot ought to help the other fellow. [?] Yes'm, they try to have something, but this family right over here, the flies are nearly taking them. You take a person with a large family and don't have any way to make anything. Maybe some make a $1 a day and maybe they don't. [?] No'm, some say you can put out disinfectant to keep the flies down, but I don't know. I have screens but the flies still come in, but I can't keep 'em all out because I don't have a good house. After mealtime I spray and shut the house all up and for the next day or two they ain't as many. [?] Yes'm, my daughter have screens 'cause I let her help me take in washin'. Now my husband's son don't have screens and the flies are sho takin' 'em. It cost about $5 to have all the house screened, I guess. [?] No ma'am, I think it would be a help to the lower class if you would go and see 'em; I think they would be ashamed for anybody to come and see 'em in this fix. [?] If you did go and they resent you, you could jest say, I was jest trying to help you. [?] I try to help 'em a lot and everybody talk about 'em so much. [?] But I feel like you are to help those who are down. Some are really pore, we pore too, I know that. [?] I don't think I would object to anything you would say. Yes'm, this way if I do anything wrong or if I make a error it is from the head and not from the heart. Yes'm, I'm always willing to be corrected. [?] No'm, not very much, not any kind. I don't pay much attention to 'em. I pay cash for what I get, I tell 'em. Then I can get it down at the store jest as cheap and sometimes cheaper. [?] Yes'm, when I have time, I listen to the Farm and Home Hour. [?] I save clippings of good recipes, when I see 'em.

June 4, 1942

Personal Experience and Food Habits (XI)

[?] Yes'm, I have had things to make me sick but I think it was my stomach already upset. I ate some white peas that made me sick, but I eat 'em now, but I don't love 'em like I ustah. I ate a great big bowl of 'em [?] I don't specially love peas but I can eat 'em [?] I don't know of anything else, yes'm, there is rabbits and 'possums that make me sick. [?] I like squirrel and bird. I jest clean the rabbits and 'possums so much. I think that is what made me sick. [?] I have heard such and such would kill you if you ate it but I don't think anybody ever did scare me about eating things. [?] Two of my boys didn't eat anything much, but I would tell 'em they would have diabetes and soon they got so they would eat. [?] When I was with the white folks, I jest eat after they get through but I eat with the chil'un and I ate what they ate and I think that is why I learn to eat most anything [?] I have always eaten fat meat 'cause all the country people usually eat it. [?] Most country houses are so ill-convenient and don't have a closet, and if you were in shape to buy a little fresh something, you don't have any place to keep it. If I go to Thomswell and get something, I have to come home and eat right away 'cause we don't have a place to keep food cold; it is ill-convenient. [?] A lady came here once that was working with PWA work and she said something about the flies and puttin' somethin' out fer 'em. [?] No'm, I don't remember when my chil'un won't eat fat meat. [?] Usually you start 'em to eat it, most of mine would like it. Just kinda' mash it up and in fact that is all they have in the way of meat. I never would feed 'em so much meat but I tole 'em it was good fer 'em. [?] Yes'm, I give 'em cow's milk after I weaned 'em. [?] I have weaned 'em about one year old. Now my last baby I didn't let him suck after he was about nine months old. [?] Yes'm, I have seen things that turn me against things. I have had people offer me things and I jest couldn't eat it, I can't stand anything that is the least bit sour 'cause we have hogs that can always eat it. [?] Some people try to keep milk from one meal to another, now like they had milk that morning and by supper it is soured. Last August we had a spring to set the milk in and it would keep good and cool. [?] But if you haven't got any to keep milk cool, it sho' ain't good. You can skim the cream at night and by in the morning the night's milk is ready to churn; I churn every other day. [?] I have had a receipt for cottage cheese. I jest never have made any. [?] It is hard for me to get the first down payment on a refrigerator. [?] You can get 'em from $100 on up. [?] You see, if you cook anything, now like Sunday we cooked beans and went to church and we had some left over from dinner for supper but they were soured. [?] A refrigerator would mean all to the milk and butter. It is a whole lot disconvenient not to have ice. But we jest have to cook in the kitchen and eat there when it is so hot right after I finish cooking dinner, it is so uncomfortable. But with the flies and the milk hot, you can't rest while you are trying to rest to go back to the field. [?] I believe celery and olives are the nastiest thing I have ever ate. One time this man went to a place to eat and they passes him the olives, and he said, 'Pass me another one, this one is rotten,' and they passed him another one and it taste just like the first and he said, 'Well, maybe it's me.' [?] I learn to like carrots, I know my folks like 'em. [?] Here for the last year or two they have raised carrots and I learn to love 'em and asparagus. I like the canned asparagus better. [?] I think maybe they like squash. [?] No'm, nothing that I have changed to now; three or four years ago I have heard I couldn't eat things 'cause they'd give me indigestion but I have not been bothered with it for the last eight or ten months. After I got my yeast tablets, and I take 'em till I get well, then I stop. [?] Yes'm, I have had bad luck with raising things but not enough to dis-encourage me. Now last year we didn't have a good garden 'cause it was dry. Now I had this fall garden last year and I had lots of things and give some to Miss Quillie and my neighbors. It come up in September and then the frost kill 'em. [?] I don't know, I have been trying to raise some celery but I can't get it to do much. [?] No'm, I don't think anything too much trouble to raise. [?] Potatoes and sweet potatoes is a lot of trouble sometimes, beans is a lot of trouble and you can't get a good stand; right now my beans are drying up at the bottom, and then the leaves begin to turn brown at the bottom and dry out but I have never get disencouraged. [?] Now last year I tried drying some okra and it was real nice so this year I'm going to try some more. [?] I dry apples and peaches and okra. [?] Well, more of the others—I already know about them. Cauliflower, I never did learn to like that. [?] I was born, reared, and raised in Lincoln County, then I went to Waynesboro for eleven months. But I guess they ate like we do, they ate kinda scanty and talk more like country down there. [?] We made the best crop we ever made down there. It was near a long bridge not any wider than the road and the river was full of logs down there, you could walk across it just from one log to another. But we gather our crop and everybody catch malaria and so we had to move. I see 'em have that fever so bad they jest have hemorrhages. The doctor told my husband he couldn't live there 'cause of his health. My husband was from up north and he couldn't stand that weather. The doctor seem to think a lot of my husband. He was a great worker. [?] We just have great corn way up, but the boll weevil got bad and most everybody had to leave. [?] Yes'm, it really is good land, my husband ustah make fifteen or sixteen bales of cotton easy. [?] It is way back down and a little old school in the woods. We had a pasture and the place fixed up real good and we had the great spring on the place and it runs through the pasture. The creek runs into Little River and that runs into Savannah. It had fine timber and plenty of wood. [?] Yes'm, some of my chil'un put on long pants to work in the field and sometimes when they are around here they put on their basketball suits and play around here and my husband see 'em and say you might as well be going around here naked as to have that on, but they wear 'em anyway some.

June 3, 1942

Food Habits and Economic Conditions (VIII)

[?] Well, yes ma'am, now a lot of people could. Well, this family over here, now, have plenty of vegetables and her husband is smart and industrious as he can be, but they don't have enough. He get paid for extra work. He feel like when the man ask him to work, he hafta. [?] It takes somebody that know how to work in the garden, it's tedjius you know. [?] Well, I work about once a week in my garden, I guess that's pretty often. [?] No'm, I never have esjemate the time it takes me to work in my garden; you have at least one day a week to work it. It just take the full day. [?] You feed your pig in the morning when you go to the field and at dinner when you go to the field; they should be feed about three times a day. And a cow should be feed about two times a day. [?] You take a young woman with a young baby like Helen, my daughter, they can't work in the field with the baby, or if they do they have to leave the baby in the house with the chil'un and the flies is awful. [?] I have four grown cows and I sell cream every Saturday at Thomswell. [?] Well, I guess Mr. Vaughn just gave the money to the ones who had put in for it. [?] It is not much trouble to have a orchard. I canned some peaches yesterday. [?] If everybody set out a orchard everybody would have one, but some are just afraid they are going to do somethin' for somebody else. [?] Now John don't have a cow, but he could get one, but they charge him 10 cents on a dollar. He said he is jest gonna git it from the Government. [?] I'm kinda stingy anyway myself, but you hafta be if you have anything, but we still don't have much. When I git a little heifer I make her pay for herself by selling milk and butter, like that, you know. [?] Some colored people that live on Mr. Warren's place look like they are grown boys and don't never go to school, but they are good workers. I don't know why his chil'un don't go to school. They don't have any edjucashun but still they ain't ignorant. [?] Mr. Norman tell his hands to have a orchard. But lot of time people don't do it because they say they don't have the time. [?] That's true, yes ma'am, so don't know who to blame, the Warrens or the colored family. [?] Lot of 'em don't take any interest in the people that live on their place and then the people don't take any interest in their landlord. [?] Some of 'em put it off on the circumstances. [?] Now you take Jo, Helen's husband, he get $7 a month to run on. He have four chil'un and a wife. Now he try to raise a garden and he have a cow. Last year he made one bale of cotton. [?] No'm, I'm not able to help 'em finanshuly but I help them all I can. He borrow that $7 a month. He ask Mr. Mason could he get him a little more money and he couldn't. [?] No'm, I don't know what the others git. If you get a crop you 'bliged to work it and can't work for nobody else. [?] No'm, we don't borrow so much, and I knock about and have a little. [?] Let me tell you how we ustah borrow. When we first came here, there was fifteen in the family and we borrowed $15 a month; cos it seem like a lot but it was very por' living. That was eight years ago. We have built on to the house, it was jest a little shed then. John lived here then. I left my cow with Jo and Helen but she was a old cow so we sold her. [?] If it wasn't fer my management, my husband don't know much about it; if it wasn't for me, I don't know, we wouldn't have as much. When Winnebelle gradchated, I spent $5 on her, and that come out of my own money, not the farm money. When the rental check come it was jest for $1.50 and that won't buy a print dress. [?] It is good that we make everything we eat. My husband is a por' management. I buy all the chil'un clothes but he gets the credit. He say, well, he does the best he cans and I say, 'Maybe you does.' But you know, the boys won't stay at home when it is por' management, por' management makes 'em want to leave home. When they work all summer and make right good and they want to buy a car and he don't want 'em to, of cos they don't like it. After they work all summer they git about $10 and that won't do 'cause they are grown boys. [?] My chil'un earn their food in the field and chil'un that are off working in town, what they send me I take it and git the chil'un clothes. [?] Didn't any of 'em want to leave the farm but they ain't gonna stay on when they don't have any money. He had one son of his own and two of mine. His own son wouldn't ask for money. I ain't saying he took the money but the farm was in his name and the boys didn't get any money. But his own indi*vid*jal son ask me to ask him for money. [?] All of the boys subject to the army and they didn't know whether to get a farm or not. [?] A lot of people go and buy meat and bread and a big long piece of fat-back when I could take the money and git better things. My husband jest buy some lard and flour and black molasses and a great long piece of fat-back, which is old timey. [?] Yes'm, a lot of people think the same way. [?] Yes'm, I help my husband git in such good shape but I don't tell nobody that. He lives a lot better than ustah. His house is kept better and the food fixed better. When I come here, the chil'un jest wasn't ustah my way of fixing so it wus hard fer me to get 'em ustah it. [?] Mrs. Bessie and John don't get much, but they have seven or eight in family. But he borrow some before his check come—you know, this Government money–and the man he borrowed the money from take the check and bought flour. [?] I reckon the flour wus for the family, anyway the chil'un needed some clothes and they didn't git any. [?] They's a lot that don't feel satisfied but everybody has got somebody on his place. And a lot of 'em would do better if they could. They say, 'I don't know that man over there, and I do know the one I'm with now, and this land is good.' [?] They git a colored person who hasn't got much edjucation and they get him just dipple-dapple along and he don't understand it. They take his money and tell him to trade it out at the store and then they don't put it down right. But I don't dapple much in that. But he couldn't read, so he don't know what he got and what he didn't. [?] Now, they have a book and you get a book, so each can keep up with what they buy and borrow. [?] Mr. Mason is jest as honest as he can be, but he don't let Jo have much. [?] It wus jest after I come up here that they didn't give 'em the rental check at all. [?] No'm, a lot of 'em don't know about credit, I tell you the truth. [?] Yes'm, I think some of 'um are gonna try the Government plan, and somebody say it ain't no good, the Government won't let you do nuthin'. [?] Well, I don't know, 'cause I don't know so much about the people right in here. [?] Yes'm there is a lot of people right here, if they jest had a ice box they would try to scuffle to buy ice, they would sell eggs or somethin.' [?] Well, I talk with John down here 'cause he is good and in right good condition. Well, he don't have much to buy clothes with, and what he do git, they still 'bliged to have to buy somethin' they eat. [?] But he is gonna try the Government plan straight out next year, I have heard him say that. [?] Well, I think most of 'em have tol'able fair cooking utensils. [?] No ma'am, I don't have a pressure cooker but they are specially good to can with. [?] Yes'm, I have a big wood stove. [?] I can beans in a lard can, I would use the pressure cooker for that. [?] I can peaches the old-timey way. [?] No'm, I had to buy a lot of cans last year and I'm gonna have to buy this year. I didn't can any tomatoes last year but I am this year.

June 4, 1942

Attitudes toward Live-at-home Practices (IX)

[?] I believe in the live-at-home. [?] Well, a lot of people do this, when he is a renter, that a man want so much cotton and want him to plant so much cotton and he will go plant a whole lot of cotton and he can't get anything much out of it, then the white man will have to loan 'em some money. [?] Yes'm, he always live a year behind. [?] You can't half work without any food much. Plenty of 'em come to the house and eat a little fried meat and bread, you can't work like that. [?] We don't have any corn, on account of the drought, but if we had planted it early enough we would had some. [?] If the corn hada been planted when the rain came, we woulda had plenty. Lot of time you are your own depriver, but it is the way you do things. You can't go on jest nuthin'. I hate to prepare a meal when we don't have much to eat. [?] Mr. Norman don't plant corn but ever' other year, 'cause he get half of all his renters'. [?] But if we don't make any corn the landlord has to feed the horses and cows. [?] That's why a lot of people would do better if they had things of their own, 'cause they think they are doing it for somebody else. [?] That's why I say some people ain't gonna have nuthin' no matter what. I tell my chil'un that a person that will be faithful over a little will be faithful over a heap. [?] I believe that somebody will help you if you try to help yourself. [?] Well, the gen'al practice that lot will try to have something at home, some claim they ain't got the stuff they need; I couldn't tell, some maybe ain't, I don't know. [?] When my first husband and me marry, we don't raise anything but cotton and I get 'im to raise some corn when we have one baby, and then we have two chil'un and I get 'im to raise some cane, but I don't get 'im off of that cotton. [?] We don't live but with two white families and we were married twenty-one years. [?] We live in Lincoln County, then one year in Burt County. [?] Yes'm, I make brooms, bed spreads, and soap, and all my patchwork and I make my quilts. I made one quilt and a lot of people come here to look at it. [?] Yes'm, I started a shuck rug in the summer time. Yes'm, I have made a shuck hat; they were stylish and I jest think maybe I'll make another one. [?] You sew the shucks together and then come back and make a layer, then another, then you make the crown, but I forgot how to do that. [?] No'm, shucks don't break. [?] Yes'm, I knit a little and crochet a little. Winnebelle ask me one day to show her to crochet and I said I can't learn you when I forget myself. [?] I make all my sheets and pillow slips and curtains and all my everyday towels, I make my towels out of guano sacks. I made a dress once. It was a swagger, it was real white and with buttons, down the front. [?] I did make all my boys' white pants and I kinda' got tired of 'em befo' they wore out. [?] Yes'm all my boys have guano sack pants. [?] Sometime when I would be real busy in the field I would get somebody to do some sewing for me. [?] No'm, I don't know how to bottom chairs but I believe I could. [?] I have made these little pot holders and little aprons. [?] Winnebelle saw some shoes in a book and she set down one Saturday and made some jest like 'em as good. [?] I have made some furniture but I'm no carpenter. Maybe if I had something to make things out of—now those porch chairs over at Miss Annie's and Miss Quillie's, I believe I could make 'em. [?] No'm, my chil'un like to do things like that. But they are like me, they can't make 'em very good 'cause they haven't got anything to make 'em out of. [?] Well, I feel if you have things to make 'em out of, you don't need to buy 'em, if you make things that will do well and look well; but maybe they would buy 'em if they were in shape to buy 'em. [?] I believe this now, there are some things that they had ruther make themselves and some they had ruther buy if they had the money. [?] I like to make 'em 'cause I think that's industrious. Some of 'em don't have the things to put 'em together with. [?] I went up to the store and bought the cloth to make a quilt. I wanted to have all the cloth jest alike, so I go on and make a sacrifice to get it all alike. [?] I know how to make the lye hominy. [?] You put up some sacks and lay the ashes there, and set something up to drip in, and then it will begin to drip and it will get just as red. [?] You have the corn already in the pot and pour the lye in there and get it so the husk will come off. Then you have to wash and wash it till the water is clear. [?] You could put so much in there that it would bring the husk right off.

June 3-4, 1942

Rationalization of Dietary Deficiencies (X)

[?] I don't know, some landlords might not let 'em have all the garden they want. [?] Lot of 'em don't get any seeds. [?] Lot of people don't want the colored chil'un to go to school. But lot of 'em make the chil'un stop school to gather crop. [?] Yes ma'am, they do do it, they jest pick up and leave in the middle of a year. [?] Mr. Norman is kinda' high strung. But him and this colored man jest had a few words about the mule. Mr. Norman said he hit the mule and he said the mule needed hittin' and they had words, so he jest up and left. [?] No'm, he didn't have any chil'un—jest his wife. [?] I don't know, the landlord furnish half the fertilizer and the plow. [?] I don't know why they don't drink milk, unless they don't have a cow. [?] Oh, that's jest silly; who ever heard of anybody not liking milk or it not sitting right on their stomach? [?] Well, you have to do somethin' about the bugs. [?] I think most everybody cans. I like blackberries canned.

Food Practices and the War (XIII)

[?] Yes'm, always I bought sugar about one hundred pound, and flour by the barrel, sometime two barrel. We buy lard about fifty pound. [?] We will raise as much lard as we can. We have three hogs and we can make about enough lard out of them. We will have enough meat to last. [?] I like the black molasses better than the cane syrup. We have to buy the black molasses, and we never did buy any dried beans or peas cause we usually raise 'em. [?] We usually buy what we need at the store, but don't buy much at the store except soap and salmon. [?] My husband usually buy what we need at Westmore store. [?] Yes'm, I usually tell 'im what to buy. [?] Maybe we buy mackerel once a week in a can and two or three cans at a time. [?] If I had to buy all these things, if I wus going to run the farm and I was going to get $50 for a year, I would get $25 to begin with and I'd buy one carton of salmon and some tomatoes. [?] Well, the man think you want to put on the britches if I wanted to buy all the things. [?] I would buy a whole lot better with the same money. [?] I tole my husband I could beat him to death buying, but I didn't want to. [?] He didn't like much for me to tell him that. The last husband and me made eighteen bales of cotton the the first year we married, then nineteen, twenty, twenty-four, twenty-six, and last year ten bales of cotton. Lot of times I have had to make my husband real mad 'cause he would go to the store and get one package of soda or somethin' and I would say, 'Get a quarter's worth,' but he jest get one little package. [?] We buy about one hundred pound of salt in the winter, but if we give out in the summer we jest buy about ten pound. In the winter we salt down our hog meat and salt our cows some. [?] Yes'm, I send a bill when I send my chil'un to the store. [?] I won't send my chil'un unless I know what the price is. [?] Yes'm, we have to cut out some, 'cause they gone so high. [?] Mackerel first ustah be 10 cents and now they are 15 cents straight. [?] Yes'm, the last lard we bought was real high, we bought twenty-four pound for $4.50, I think. At that rate I would say $9 for 50 pounds, and that would last us the balance of the summer. [?] Yes'm, I have thought about using hard syrup for substitute. [?] I took a whole lot of the peaches and mashed 'em up and canned a half-gallon. [?] Yes'm, if the lard gets higher, I will have to keep my butter. [?] I'm not 'bliged to sell the cream. [?] I sold $1.02 worth last Saturday but I been gettin' about 80 cents to 90 cents for my butter. [?] No'm, the traveling grocery truck don't bother me, I don't look at 'em much. [?] Last fall I sold butter in Atlanta to some relatives. It helps me out with the chil'un going to school, but if I couldn't sell it, I could use it. [?] I get three pound of butter already this week, and I got churning I got to do now. [?] I could use all my eggs, my crowd really loves eggs, but I sell some—they don't eat as many as they could 'cause I sell 'em. [?] I could not keep the ice so I couldn't keep the butter. [?] Yes'm, I would be glad to have a kerosene stove but people here can't have one. [?] They don't keep 'em warm in the winter. [?] It would be so much better if I could have a refrigerator. I one hundred times ruther have the refrigerator instead of the stove, 'cause the refrigerator would be better in the summer. [?] I takes 25 cents worth of ice every two days. [?] Just like it was for the car, my husband thought the boys ought not to have it. The boys did all the work, and they wanted a car, and it only cost $140, and they were so dis-encouraged. But then they bought it. [?] I have not been a beggar but for work. You are rich when you have your health and strength. [?] I pay 75 cents a week for ice. [?] In the spring of the year I think I will save up and make the down payment on the refrigerator, but all my chil'un are in school then and I have to look after them. [?] Miss Quillie is real anxious for me to get a refrigerator. Last year I raised a lot of chickens but this year I don't have but fifteen. I haven't had a brooder to put the chickens in. [?] Now Vajinjer [Virginia] was in school and she couldn't get any fresh vegetables and milk but about once a week when she come home. Now if she could go back and forth to school from home and get the food and milk she needs. [?] Last year they were jest shore they'd get a bus, but they hadn't got one. [?] Vajinjer is about sick now, and I feel like if she had good food she wouldn't have been so sick. [?] She didn't eat enough food to keep her body strong.

June 4, 1942

Chief Lines of Communication for Nutrition Information (VII)

[?] Well Lawd, it don't need any newspaper; I don't hardly know though. [?] Well, if you get the right kind of news, but I tell you for myself, I would try to take it to somebody like John and Bessie, and then I talk with Jack and his people, and Helen 'cause she natchuly is my child, and then Turner's 'cause I'm interested in them and they are kinda backwards, and I know I seem a little better than them and they seem to want to know, and they don't get offended at what I say. And Ella Teasley and Ola Jones, and she is always talking about things. [?] Well, Miss Ola Jones and Ella Teasley. [?] I'm a Baptist, always have been. [?] And Mr. Ly Sharon, and the Barnes, and Mr. Robinson, and the Heard's, and Ida Hunt. [?] I have never been to see Bertha Norris but she been here. [?] Now I ustah visit Ben Gaines, they are good friends of mine. [?] Kattie Bell Curry, I know them well.

[?] Well, first I would go to John and Bessie's or Jack and Helen's, I see them at dinner time. [?] No'm, not much visiting on Sunday, 'cause I can't walk so far. [?] Then I go to see the Ben Hughes, and they are the nicest people. They had one daughter to finish school here and went to Albany and finished; now she is a schoolteacher. [?] Maybe some don't care so much for anybody but themselves. [?] I have lived around people that were disagreeable, but I remember having a white woman get mad at me. They came here from Tennessee, and seem to have a lot at first. She come here one day and want me to wash some for her, so I already washing, so I say for her to bring 'em on over. She does, and I put a few pieces of hers in the pot with two pieces of mine. And she come in and see 'em and she say she didn't want any nigger's clothes in the company with hers. So I jest take hers out and finish mine 'cause I was washing mine first. And then this white man come and jest cuss me out. But I have learned to shun things like that. [?] Well, the news ought to go a long ways. I guess about Mr. Lance Turner's, and then Easton Ruckley, I see them a lot. It would go to Vincent Brown and to Ben Hughes, that far that way. Then say the creek in the Glen community would be as far that way, then towards Elberton below the Warren's down to the creek. [?] Not many of 'em take the paper. [?] No'm, lot of 'em don't have a radio 'cause they don't have electric lights. [?] Mr. Norman say he pay for all the material for the lights and half the work and he don't care how long you stay there. [?] We have had lights five years, it cost about $1.50 a month. [?] Yes'm, my husband pay the bill. [?] The colored go to Shiloh Methodist, Maple Spring, and Glen. [?] Yes'm, the biggest majority are churchgoers. [?] I don't feel like we lose anything by getting lights. [?] It look real funny when I go somewhere when they don't have lights. You have to hole the lamp around for everything. [?] Vocational teacher and at church and at school is important places. One man in Elberton said Mr. Robinson was doing better than any body that has come here.

Changes in Food Habits—Old Ideas and Habits (XII)

[?] Well, a lot of old people, like Mrs. Bessie Blackwell. When they have this baby, they will eat bread and butter a whole month 'fraid they will die. And won't take the ashes up out the fireplace and won't comb her hair and jest perish 'em to death almost. [?] I was down to Miss Quillie's and she was out in the garden, so I jest go in the garden and Miss Quillie say she don't have any Irish potatoes, and somebody say they planted 'em on the wrong moon. Her's was blooming and when they blooming they is supposed to be some. But she looked and couldn't find any, so I jest reach down and get two big ones, and she said, 'Get me two mo',' and I jest do it. But she jest look under the wrong plants maybe. [?] I know this girl to finish school at Thomswell and she was having these very bad spells and we went to see her, found out that she was very superstitious and her sister prayed about somebody poisoning her sister. The doctor went to see her and didn't go back 'cause they wasn't anything wrong with her. We didn't go back either. [?] From what I could see it was her nerves and they talked about she was poisoned somehow. [?] I jest about soon pick blackberries off the graveyard. Why no, nobody here would pick 'em off the graveyard. [?] No'm, I don't know of anybody that makes ash cakes. [?] There was a old woman about one hundred years old, she was blind and I lived right by her, then I went away and married. Then a long time after I went back and she knew me. She has the best recollection and couldn't even see you to know who you wus. [?] No'm, I don't know of anybody that still grinds his own coffee, but my grandmother ground her own."

Appendix D

SUMMARY OF 1940 CENSUS DATA AVAILABLE FOR THOMS COUNTY, GEORGIA

Population

For the county as a whole there has been a slight growth from the 1930 population (15,174) to the 1940 population (15,512). Slight changes have occurred in the two districts studied comprising Westmore and Glen: Macon (Westmore) decreased from 2021 in 1930 to 1976 in 1940; Smith (Glen) increased from 1176 in 1930 to 1371 in 1940. Thomswell, the county seat, increased from 2048 (1930) to 2372 (1940). This section does, therefore, not share the considerable population losses of many rural sections to the towns and cities.

General social and economic data

There are 2308 farms in Thoms County; about one in every four is operated by a Negro (1827 White operators, 481 non-White operators), while for the state as a whole, one farm in every three is operated by a Negro. In Westmore, however, there are 10 White landowners, while in Glen there are just as many Negro landowners. The average acreage of the farms in the county is small (64.7), which is to be contrasted with the average acreage for the state (109.6) and the acreage tested in the Greene County plan (over 100) as being the minimum necessary to farm successfully. The average farm value ($1765) is also smaller than the state value ($2223).

The rate of tenancy in the county is large (71.3), even for Georgia, where the average state rate is 60.1. This high rate is less significant, however, when one takes into account the fact that this tenancy is almost invariably *long-term* tenancy, particularly in the communities studied, where tenants stay on a place sometimes for a lifetime.

The enumeration of the farmers in the various tenure classes of Thoms County is as follows:

All White operators	1827
Full owners	556

Part owners	56
All tenants	1214
Croppers	502
Non-White operators	481
Full owners	46
Part owners	4
All tenants	431
Croppers	305

It is noteworthy that the average total value of farm products sold, traded, or used by farm households in 1939 was only around $300 per farm.

Cash-crop farming, therefore, does not necessarily bring in sufficient cash to maintain that standard of living designated by nutritionists as minimum.

Cotton is a million-dollar crop in Thoms County ($1,121,-693), while the value of vegetables grown for sale and use ($69,959) nowhere approaches this amount. The universality of cotton as a source of income is further indicated by the fact that 99 percent of farms reported it, while 1.6 percent of farms reported vegetables, 6.3 percent reported fruits and nuts, and 1.9 percent reported horticultural specialties. Livestock, however, ranks high (64 percent) and dairy products were reported as a source of income by 20.8 percent of the farms. Cotton is regarded as a major source of income by 2185 farms of Thoms' 2308 farms, and these cotton farmers get 73.7 percent of their income from the cotton and 21.1 percent of it from farm products used by the household. In other words, cotton tends to displace home-grown products from family income.

Further, it is important to note that as the income rises, the number who *use* farm products increases; quite frequently the lowest income farms do not use farm products, while the farms with incomes of $1000 to $1499 all use farm products.

Food production

We are chiefly interested here, of course, in the data for food production. To summarize, we may say that most farms of Thoms County's 2308 farms keep hogs (1849), most have calves (1924) and cows (1819) for milk (1805), most churn butter, most keep poultry (2165) and eggs (2017), most grow corn (2226) which is harvested for grain (on 2214 farms), most butcher animals (2050). A large number grow winter wheat (1434) and sweet potatoes (1386), though fewer grow Irish potatoes (968).

Deficiencies are evident in the number of the total farms (2308) which report beef cattle (98). Very few sell whole milk (33), cream (46) and butter (425), though this situation may be nutritionally advantageous. Very few keep sheep (6), turkeys (91), ducks (428), geese (13), guineas (66), and bees (189). Few farms harvested sorghum for syrup (517). Only 23 farms reported any small fruit harvested for sale, and these were mostly strawberries (1689 quarts).

About a fourth of the farms (697) reported any orchards, nut trees, or vineyards at all, and about a fourth reported pear trees (503). Half reported apple trees (1206 farms), about a fifth had cherries (428 farms), and there were a few farms having plum trees (331), grapes (384), and figs (390). There are many farms with peaches available (1332).

About half of the farms reported automobiles (1004), and these were mostly 1931 model. The 59 tractors in the county give no competition to the mules. About half of the farms (1190) are within a quarter-mile of an electric distribution line; even so, electricity is more accessible than in the other communities studied.

Appendix E

DESCRIPTIVE DETAILS OF THE FOOD HABITS OF THE NEIGHBORHOOD OF WESTMORE, THOMS COUNTY, GEORGIA, PRESENTED IN TABULAR FORM

NOTE: *In the interest of succinctness, the data on the diet of Westmore and Glen, showing the correlations with various factors such as agricultural class, race, season, individual differences, are arranged in tables. Discussion and interpretation of the tables will be found under the appropriate topics in preceding chapters.*

Table I—THE FOOD SUPPLY—Gardens and Home-raised Food Crops

LANDOWNER		TENANT AND SHARECROPPER		WAGE LABORER	
White	*Negro*	*White*	*Negro*	*White*	*Negro*
Early summer and fall gardens. Early (May) garden: Asparagus, Lettuce, Radishes, Squash, Onions, Cabbage, Green beans, Peaches Summer (June-Sept.) garden: English peas, Field peas, Corn, Tomatoes, Okra, Butterbeans, Squash, Asparagus, Onions, Lettuce, Carrots, Spinach, Turnips, Turnip greens, Beets, Irish potatoes, Cabbage, Green beans, Cantaloupe, Grapes, Melons, Apples, Peaches, Plums, Strawberries, Pears, Cucumbers Fall (Sept.-Dec.): Collards, Turnip greens, Cabbage, Kale, Rape,	About the same as the White landowner.	The long-term tenant and sharecropper, and the farmer under close supervision (such as a Farm Security client or the tenant of an enterprising and conscientious landlord) usually has a good garden and raises most of his food supply. His garden and food crops have the variety and abundance of the typical landowner's. The short-term tenant and sharecropper, and the tenant of an indifferent or	The Negro tenant and share-cropper's garden and food crops depend in the same way upon the length of his tenure and the willingness and interest of his landlord. On the whole, however, he tends to have less of a garden, both in number of months and plantings and variety of vegetables, and much less of a fruit supply. He tends not to grow his wheat.	May manage to have a garden. Feels more dependent upon his own food supply than does the sharecropper who is sometimes "furnished" by the landlord until the crop is sold. Cannot raise his own wheat, or much corn. Rarely plants a fall garden, because he expects to move when crop is done.	Same

Table I—THE FOOD SUPPLY—Gardens and Home-raised Food Crops (Continued)

LANDOWNER		TENANT AND SHARECROPPER		WAGE LABORER	
White	*Negro*	*White*	*Negro*	*White*	*Negro*
Mustard, Sweet potatoes, Corn meal, Wheat, Grits, Peanuts, Honey, Sorghum		extremely exploitative landlord, tends to have no garden, or at least a poor one.			

Table I—THE FOOD SUPPLY—Meat

LANDOWNER		TENANT AND SHARECROPPER		WAGE LABORER	
White	*Negro*	*White*	*Negro*	*White*	*Negro*
Hogs killed as needed, usually in the fall. Hams cured and smoked. Side-meat and fatback, neck bones, feet, and jowls salted. Chitterlings eaten. Fat cut off and made into sausage and lard. Head sometimes made into souse. A calf sometimes killed and canned for home use. Some of it may be	Uses hog-meat and beef about as much as the White landowner. Is apt to use more of the parts of the hog and waste less.	The White tenant and sharecropper usually supplies his own hog meat. Sometimes he raises the landlord's hogs and then gets his share at the killing. White tenants and sharecroppers	The Negro tenant and sharecropper may raise his own hogs, and occasionally a calf, but sometimes raises hogs on shares with the landlord and has to give him half. Usually he	Usually raises and kills his own hog, or gets some of the landlord's for helping him butcher.	Same

Table I—THE FOOD SUPPLY—Foods Sold

LANDOWNER		TENANT AND SHARECROPPER		WAGE LABORER	
White	*Negro*	*White*	*Negro*	*White*	*Negro*
Eggs, butter, milk, cream (sweet and sour), vegetables and fruits (if convenient, but most landowners do not have to stoop to this, they feel). Some raise chickens for the market, some raise beef cattle and hogs, corn, soybeans.	Eggs, butter, milk and cream. May have a few pigs to sell, or a calf.	Tenants also tend to sell their eggs and butter (if they have a cow) for cash to buy the things they think they need more, such as matches, soap, kerosene, or to provide a little more variety in their diet. The sale of food is the only source of cash income for most of the year.	Because the Negro tenant or sharecropper's food supply is probably lower than the White's you would expect that he would have to eat his eggs or butter or vegetables rather than sell them. Actually, the strong psychological need he feels for a little "cash" with which to buy a few "luxuries" or variety in his diet makes him sell his eggs and butter and cream rather than eat them.	Rarely has anything to sell. The wage laborer isn't under the same terrific psychological need for "cash" as a symbol of freedom, as the sharecropper or tenant, because he is paid in cash every week, except when he is laid off.	Same

Table I—THE FOOD SUPPLY—Purchased Foods—Foods which could be produced at home

LANDOWNER		TENANT AND SHARECROPPER		WAGE LABORER	
White	*Negro*	*White*	*Negro*	*White*	*Negro*
Canned pears, Celery, Cauliflower, Cheese, Molasses, Sorghum, Honey (sometimes), Flour (sometimes), Loaf-bread, Cereals (usually cornflakes).	Flour, Molasses, Honey, Cheese, Some Canned Fruits, Vegetables, Loaf-bread, Cereals (usually cornflakes)	The White tenant and sharecropper buys all that the landowner buys, when he can afford it, and often has to buy more canned goods, because his wife does not can enough to last the winter through for the family. He usually has to buy his flour.	The Negro tenant and sharecropper also has to buy a good portion of his food supply which he could have raised at home, if all circumstances permitted. His range of choice is more limited. Sometimes he can afford only the barest necessities: flour, corn meal, fat back, lard.	Buys most of his food from current wages. Has to go without necessities when it's the off season.	Same. Is probably worse off than the White wage laborer, because his wages are apt to be lower.

Table I—THE FOOD SUPPLY—Purchased Foods—Foods which could not be produced at home

LANDOWNER		TENANT AND SHARECROPPER		WAGE LABORER	
White	*Negro*	*White*	*Negro*	*White*	*Negro*
Canned pineapple, Dates, Bananas, Oranges, Grapefruit, Fish (fresh and canned), Coffee, Tea, Chocolate, Corn syrup, Nucoa, Rice, Soft drinks (Coca-Cola, Pepsicola), Sugar, Canned milk.	Some canned fruits and vegetables but not as much of a variety as the White landowner might buy. Coffee, Canned fish (salmon, mackerel), Corn syrup, Rice, Soft drinks, Sugar, Canned milk	The highest type of White tenant and sharecropper allows himself the same purchases as the landowner. The poorer-off tenant or sharecropper most often has to do without.	Same as for the White tenant or sharecropper.	Buys what luxuries he can, but is usually limited to Sugar, Corn syrup, Flour, Cornmeal, Coffee, Fatback, and Lard.	Same as for White wage laborer.

Table I—THE FOOD SUPPLY—Preservation of Food: Canning

LANDOWNER		TENANT AND SHARECROPPER		WAGE LABORER	
White	*Negro*	*White*	*Negro*	*White*	*Negro*
Usually cans an ample yearly supply of vegetables and fruits for the family, maybe 200-400 quarts. Cans	Is apt to can less in quantity and variety than the White land-	The White tenant and sharecropper may can as much as the landowner	The Negro tenant family does even less canning, as a rule, than the	Does very little canning. Too mobile. Hasn't the equipment.	Same

Table I—THE FOOD SUPPLY—Preservation of Food: Canning (Continued)

LANDOWNER		TENANT AND SHARECROPPER		WAGE LABORER	
White	*Negro*	*White*	*Negro*	*White*	*Negro*
mainly: Tomatoes, Corn, Lima beans, Green beans, Peaches, Pears. Makes preserves of peaches and pears. Makes pickles and relish. Very few have pressure cookers. Most use cold-pack or open top method.	owners. Depends upon individual initiative and experience.	if the tenure is well-established and the family is not moving from farm to farm every year or two. Canning, however, is always secondary to the cash-crop in the life of the tenant family. When it requires attention, the canning has to wait, even though the season is just right. Farm Security clients usually are given a pressure cooker for canning. Others use older methods.	White. Many know how to can only tomatoes. Lack of jars is a problem with some. Few pressure cookers. Many use the washpot method.	Has no fruit trees, as a rule.	

Table I—THE FOOD SUPPLY—Meat (Continued)

LANDOWNER		TENANT AND SHARECROPPER		WAGE LABORER	
White	*Negro*	*White*	*Negro*	*White*	*Negro*
dried. Depends upon number in family and liking for beef.		sometimes raise and can their own beef.	butchers for the landlord, or maybe helps several others in the neighborhood, and is given certain cuts for his services, such as the head, or neckbones, chitterlings, pig's feet.		

Table I—THE FOOD SUPPLY—Poultry and Eggs

LANDOWNER		TENANT AND SHARECROPPER		WAGE LABORER	
White	*Negro*	*White*	*Negro*	*White*	*Negro*
Chickens—a flock anywhere from a few to 50 or 200. Eggs available for home use, but often sold instead of eaten.	An ample supply of chickens and eggs—eggs more often sold than eaten, as with	The number of chickens kept by the tenant or sharecropper also depends upon the length of	Negro tenants and sharecroppers also keep chickens and use or sell the eggs.	Usually has a few chickens. Has to eat his eggs more often than sell them.	Same

Table I—THE FOOD SUPPLY—Poultry and Eggs (Continued)

LANDOWNER		TENANT AND SHARECROPPER		WAGE LABORER	
White	*Negro*	*White*	*Negro*	*White*	*Negro*
	the White landowner.	tenure and attitude of landlord. Most tenants and sharecroppers do keep chickens and eat or trade the eggs.			

Table I—THE FOOD SUPPLY—Dairy Products

LANDOWNER		TENANT AND SHARECROPPER		WAGE LABORER	
White	*Negro*	*White*	*Negro*	*White*	*Negro*
Usually has one or several cows, so that one is always fresh when others are dry. Those who like milk usually have enough. Uses more buttermilk than fresh milk. Has plenty of butter, but sells a lot. Rarely makes cottage cheese.	Is apt to have less cows than the White landowner.	The tenant and sharecropper is less apt to have a cow than the landowner. It also is a function of his mobility and the attitude of the landlord. Many enlightened	The Negro tenant and sharecropper is far less apt to have a cow. Many Negro families have never known how to take care of a cow and tend to neglect it if they	Rarely is encouraged to keep a cow; usually is too mobile.	Same

Table I—THE FOOD SUPPLY—Dairy Products (Continued)

LANDOWNER		TENANT AND SHARECROPPER		WAGE LABORER	
White	*Negro*	*White*	*Negro*	*White*	*Negro*
		landlords are requiring their tenants to keep a cow. Some landlords provide their tenants with milk in exchange for services such as milking or churning. Most tenants have no place to pasture a cow.	manage to get one. On the other hand many Negro tenant families have charge of the cows and milk for the landlord, and receive some milk in payment.		

Table I—THE FOOD SUPPLY—Wild Foods

LANDOWNER		TENANT AND SHARECROPPER		WAGE LABORER	
White	*Negro*	*White*	*Negro*	*White*	*Negro*
In the fall hunts for squirrel, turkey, quail, rabbit. Very little fishing available. Blackberries and huckleberries gathered in summer. Poke greens in early summer.	Shoots wild game as does the White, and also eats 'possum more often than Whites. Fishes in the small streams and rivers and eats the catfish and other small fish caught there. Blackberries and huckleberries gathered in summer, scuppernongs and persimmons in fall. Poke greens in early summer.	The White tenant and sharecropper also gets his share of wild foods. He probably depends upon it for variety in his diet more than the landowner.	The Negro tenant or sharecropper and his family are the exploiters, par excellence, of the wild food supply. In the fall after the cotton is picked and sold, and farm chores are lowest, he hunts in the woods with his hounds. His wife and children gather berries and nuts and fruits in season, and fish whenever there's a puddle to drop a line in.	Depends upon the wild food supply in same way.	Same

Table I—THE FOOD SUPPLY—Foods Sold

LANDOWNER		TENANT AND SHARECROPPER		WAGE LABORER	
White	*Negro*	*White*	*Negro*	*White*	*Negro*
Eggs, butter, milk, cream (sweet and sour), vegetables and fruits (if convenient, but most landowners do not have to stoop to this, they feel). Some raise chickens for the market, some raise beef cattle and hogs, corn, soybeans.	Eggs, butter, milk and cream. May have a few pigs to sell, or a calf.	Tenants also tend to sell their eggs and butter (if they have a cow) for cash to buy the things they think they need more, such as matches, soap, kerosene, or to provide a little more variety in their diet. The sale of food is the only source of cash income for most of the year.	Because the Negro tenant or sharecropper's food supply is probably lower than the White's you would expect that he would have to eat his eggs or butter or vegetables rather than sell them. Actually, the strong psychological need he feels for a little "cash" with which to buy a few "luxuries" or variety in his diet makes him sell his eggs and butter and cream rather than eat them.	Rarely has anything to sell. The wage laborer isn't under the same terrific psychological need for "cash" as a symbol of freedom, as the sharecropper or tenant, because he is paid in cash every week, except when he is laid off.	Same

Table I—THE FOOD SUPPLY—Purchased Foods—Foods which could be produced at home

LANDOWNER		TENANT AND SHARECROPPER		WAGE LABORER	
White	*Negro*	*White*	*Negro*	*White*	*Negro*
Canned pears, Celery, Cauliflower, Cheese, Molasses, Sorghum, Honey (sometimes), Flour (sometimes), Loaf-bread, Cereals (usually cornflakes).	Flour, Molasses, Honey, Cheese, Some Canned Fruits, Vegetables, Loaf-bread, Cereals (usually cornflakes)	The White tenant and sharecropper buys all that the landowner buys, when he can afford it, and often has to buy more canned goods, because his wife does not can enough to last the winter through for the family. He usually has to buy his flour.	The Negro tenant and sharecropper also has to buy a good portion of his food supply which he could have raised at home, if all circumstances permitted. His range of choice is more limited. Sometimes he can afford only the barest necessities: flour, corn meal, fat back, lard.	Buys most of his food from current wages. Has to go without necessities when it's the off season.	Same. Is probably worse off than the White wage laborer, because his wages are apt to be lower.

Table I—THE FOOD SUPPLY—Purchased Foods—Foods which could not be produced at home

LANDOWNER		TENANT AND SHARECROPPER		WAGE LABORER	
White	*Negro*	*White*	*Negro*	*White*	*Negro*
Canned pineapple, Dates, Bananas, Oranges, Grapefruit, Fish (fresh and canned), Coffee, Tea, Chocolate, Corn syrup, Nucoa, Rice, Soft drinks (Coca-Cola, Pepsicola), Sugar, Canned milk.	Some canned fruits and vegetables but not as much of a variety as the White landowner might buy. Coffee, Canned fish (salmon, mackerel), Corn syrup, Rice, Soft drinks, Sugar, Canned milk	The highest type of White tenant and sharecropper allows himself the same purchases as the landowner. The poorer-off tenant or sharecropper most often has to do without.	Same as for the White tenant or sharecropper.	Buys what luxuries he can, but is usually limited to Sugar, Corn syrup, Flour, Cornmeal, Coffee, Fatback, and Lard.	Same as for White wage laborer.

Table I—THE FOOD SUPPLY—Preservation of Food: Canning

LANDOWNER		TENANT AND SHARECROPPER		WAGE LABORER	
White	*Negro*	*White*	*Negro*	*White*	*Negro*
Usually cans an ample yearly supply of vegetables and fruits for the family, maybe 200-400 quarts. Cans	Is apt to can less in quantity and variety than the White land-	The White tenant and sharecropper may can as much as the landowner	The Negro tenant family does even less canning, as a rule, than the	Does very little canning. Too mobile. Hasn't the equipment.	Same

Table I—THE FOOD SUPPLY—Preservation of Food: Canning (Continued)

LANDOWNER		TENANT AND SHARECROPPER		WAGE LABORER	
White	*Negro*	*White*	*Negro*	*White*	*Negro*
mainly: Tomatoes, Corn, Lima beans, Green beans, Peaches, Pears. Makes preserves of peaches and pears. Makes pickles and relish. Very few have pressure cookers. Most use cold-pack or open top method.	owners. Depends upon individual initiative and experience.	if the tenure is well-established and the family is not moving from farm to farm every year or two. Canning, however, is always secondary to the cash-crop in the life of the tenant family. When it requires attention, the canning has to wait, even though the season is just right. Farm Security clients usually are given a pressure cooker for canning. Others use older methods.	White. Many know how to can only tomatoes. Lack of jars is a problem with some. Few pressure cookers. Many use the washpot method.	Has no fruit trees, as a rule.	

Table I—THE FOOD SUPPLY—Preservation of Food: Storing

LANDOWNER		TENANT AND SHARECROPPER		WAGE LABORER	
White	*Negro*	*White*	*Negro*	*White*	*Negro*
Sweet and Irish potatoes, Apples, Corn (to be ground later into meal or grits).	Same	Same as the landowner.	Same	May store some potatoes and corn.	Same

Table I—THE FOOD SUPPLY—Preservation of Food: Drying

LANDOWNER		TENANT AND SHARECROPPER		WAGE LABORER	
White	*Negro*	*White*	*Negro*	*White*	*Negro*
Very little drying of fruits and vegetables practiced, but sometimes dries apples, peaches, okra.	Same	Same as the landowner. Sometimes dries fruit for the landlord, and is paid in kind.	Same	Doesn't have fruit trees—can't do much drying.	Same

Table I—THE FOOD SUPPLY—Preservation of Food: Refrigerating

LANDOWNER		TENANT AND SHARECROPPER		WAGE LABORER	
White	*Negro*	*White*	*Negro*	*White*	*Negro*
Apt to have some method of refrigeration, either electric, kerosene, or bought ice. Can preserve many foods otherwise spoiled. Makes milk more palatable and therefore more desirable.	Apt also to have some method of refrigeration.	The tenants and sharecroppers, except the most fortunate ones, have no refrigeration. A few manage to buy ice during the hottest months. Others have to keep butter and milk in the well, or a cool pit.	Apt to have less facilities than the White tenant.	No refrigeration, as a rule.	Same

Table I—THE FOOD SUPPLY—Preservation of Food: Saving Left-overs

LANDOWNER		TENANT AND SHARECROPPER		WAGE LABORER	
White	*Negro*	*White*	*Negro*	*White*	*Negro*
Left-overs usually saved and used again. Left-overs from mid-day meal often eaten unheated for supper, as among other classes.	Same	Meals usually cooked two or three at a time, especially in hot weather when the cooking is done in the early morning and the kitchen not heated up again during the day, or in the busy season when the women are working in the fields all day. What is left from one meal is consumed at the next—very little waste, never enough to fatten the hounds.	Same	The wife of the wage laborer, unless she is hired too, is not under the same obligations to work in the fields from sun-up to sun-down during the busy seasons, as is her husband. She can cook meals more regularly, but then he is not there to eat them regularly. She also tries to cook as little as possible when it's hot.	Same

Table II—Basic Summer Diet in Westmore and Glen Communities, Thoms County, Georgia

Hot breads at least once a day	Sweet milk—if it can be drunk before it sours
Corn bread	Butter
White biscuits	Rice or grits
Fat meat—cooked with vegetables to season them, then eaten	Cabbage
Ham—if any is left from the fall and winter hog-killing—several times a week	English peas
Chicken—fried chicken nearly always on Sunday—sometimes 2 or 3 times a week	Beans
Eggs	Squash
Canned fish—salmon or mackerel—several times a week	Corn
Buttermilk	Salad greens (turnip or wild poke)
	Irish potatoes
	Peaches
	Apples
	Iced tea
	Coffee

By "basic" we mean those foods and practices which were found in every class and caste group, though not necessarily in every family.

Table III—Seasonal Deviations from Basic Diet

FALL	WINTER	SPRING
Sweet potatoes. By late fall, no vegetables left in garden except collards, turnips, cabbage, mustard, rape, kale, carrots, onions, beets. The last six are uncommon. After first very cold weather, in November usually, hogs are butchered, and there is more and fresher supply of hog-meat. The brains, tenderloins, liver and "chit'lin's" are eaten fresh right away. Other parts are salted away. Sausage is made. If a calf is killed, some of it is eaten fresh, and the rest dried or canned. Beef is more frequent in the diet for a while. The hens don't lay	Sweet potatoes. Winter garden of collards and turnips generally. The more enterprising have mustard, rape, kale, carrots, onions, and beets all winter. Very few grow all the kinds of vegetables it is possible to grow. Ham, sausage, fat-meat, souse. Beef more frequently, if a calf has been canned. Less eggs and chicken. Sweet milk. Rest of the diet same as in fall.	Sweet potatoes—supply may have given out by spring. Winter garden of collards and turnip greens has probably given out. No fresh fruits or vegetables except wild poke greens in late spring. The supply of canned fruits and vegetables has probably given out, and they must buy canned tomatoes, peaches, pears, pineapple, etc. Hens have probably not started to lay yet. No fryers yet. Hog-meat and beef supply probably gone. Hunting season over—no wild game. Late spring (March

Table III—Seasonal Deviations from Basic Diet (Continued)

FALL		SPRING
as much, so eggs are less plentiful. The milk doesn't sour as quickly, so more of it is drunk fresh. More canned fruits and vegetables are eaten, chiefly peaches, beans, corn and tomatoes. Dried field peas. Rice, corn bread, grits, white biscuits and sweet potatoes form the bulk of the diet. Hot breads cooked 3 times a day usually. Wild game and fruits as procured: turkey, quail, squirrel, rabbit, 'possum (chiefly among Negroes), scuppernongs, persimmons, black walnuts, hickory nuts, chinquapins.		15-May 15) is the lean season. Many of the poorer families say they have only bread and milk to eat until the garden comes in. Cash is scarce then, too, so they cannot buy much.

Table IV—Class Deviations from Basic Diet

LANDOWNER	TENANT AND SHARECROPPER	WAGE LABORER
Wider variety of vegetables in gardens: asparagus, lettuce, radishes, butter-beans, spinach, kale, rape, cucumbers, carrots, cantaloupes, strawberries are the rarer items apt to be found. They also buy occasionally cauliflower and celery, and the fancier canned fruits such as pineapple, and fresh fruits such as dates, oranges, grapefruit, and bananas. They buy loaf bread. They have meat and	Apt to have less of a variety of vegetables and fruits, both in their gardens and in what they are able to buy. They probably do not have much of an early or fall or winter garden. Probably have no fence for winter garden, which the stock destroys. They have less time to can, and therefore the quantity may not be sufficient to tide the family over the winter and spring. Fewer buy canned fruit.	Diet more restricted in variety and amounts of most foods, depending upon the presence or absence of a garden, hog, and cow, which depends upon length of employment and attitude of employer. Cash available for small purchases when there's work (a week of rain, or off-season cuts off the cash) but bulk of diet consists of corn meal, white flour, fatback, lard, collards, potatoes, cane syrup, or black molasses. Diet

Table IV—Class Deviations from Basic Diet (Continued)

LANDOWNER	TENANT AND SHARECROPPER	WAGE LABORER
eggs more frequently; ham, sausage, bacon, beef, fish, chicken. They usually have more milk and butter. They probably have more different kinds of fruit and nuts; plums, pears, cherries, melons, pecans. They also probably eat more white flour, corn bread and grits, potatoes and rice—but this does not result in a greater proportion of carbohydrates to the other kinds of foodstuffs in their diet because amounts of the others are increased too.	Thrifty families tend to sell their eggs and cream and butter, so their diet is often deficient in those things. They rely more upon wild game in fall, especially the Negroes. They are apt to have less milk and butter. Some of them have their own wheat ground at the mill, part of it as whole wheat which they then make up into biscuits called "brim bread," and eat occasionally. Cream gravy, made from fried fat-meat, eaten for breakfast by some families. The proportion of carbohydrates to other classes of food is probably higher among this group than among landowners.	apt to lack milk and citrus fruits. Wage laborer's diet probably better in eggs and butter (if he has chickens and a cow) than the sharecropper's because he isn't tempted so much to sell for cash.

Table V—Racial Deviations from Basic Diet

WHITE	NEGRO
White families—landowner, sharecropper or wage laborer—apt to have more purchasing power, and therefore slightly more variety in their diet. Tend to buy more packaged and ready-prepared foods, such as cereals, loaf bread; more luxuries, such as canned pineapple, oranges. Can buy more meat and eggs and milk when their own supply is exhausted; green vegetables out of season. Probably use a little less fat-meat in their cooking and prefer their foods less greasy (but this is more a matter of individual preference—	Negro tenant, sharecropper and wage-laborer families, having poorer gardens, both in variety, number of plantings and number of months of year, and poorer orchards (if any), and probably no cow, have a more restricted diet than do whites of same economic class. There are some notable exceptions, depending upon individual initiative and attitude of landlord. What differences there are in diet are economically conditioned rather than racially conditioned. Cultural differences in diet which have come to be associated with the Negro (such as eating the more humble

Table V—Racial Deviations from Basic Diet (Continued)

WHITE	NEGRO
many who can afford better and leaner cuts of meat still prefer the taste of fat-meat).	parts of the hog, or eating more greasy foods) are results of economic circumstances of long standing. The Negro's whole attitude of indifference, laziness, thriftlessness, when it is found, is largely a reflection of the hopelessness of his economic position. A whole habit of mind and personality is thus engendered which lasts over for several generations, perhaps, as a cultural inheritance. Swift change in economic circumstances cannot sweep away this cultural heritage all at once. The older Negro diet consisted of the coarser foods such as dark flour, yellow corn meal, black molasses. But as the Negro tends to improve his economic position, he also tends to take on the White man's food habits, and to replace the traditional foods with white, self-rising flour, white cornmeal and corn syrup—none of which is as good nutritionally. The Negro exploits the wild food supply—game, fish, berries, nuts—more than the Whites. The Negro baby is often given a pacifier of fat-meat when he cries. This may entrench in him early the taste for fat-meat. Negro babies are also early fed "a streak of fat and a streak of lean" (hog-meat, a kind of bacon, but not crisped).

Table VI—Individual Deviations from Basic Diet

FOODS MOST OFTEN CLAIMED TO DISAGREE WITH SOME INFORMANTS	FOODS ESPECIALLY DISLIKED BY SOME INFORMANTS
English peas	Carrots
Cabbage in summer	Yellow corn meal
Cucumbers	Whole wheat flour and graham biscuits
Beef—lean meat	Sweet milk
Fat-meat	Squash
Strawberries	Celery
Raw vegetables	Turnip-greens
Bananas	Wild game
Sweet milk	Rare meat
	Chicken
	Fat meat
	Beef
	Oatmeal
	Dried fruits
	Under-cooked turnip-greens or cabbage (less than two hours)
	Under-cooked peas or beans (must cook all morning on back of stove till dried out)
	Vegetables without catsup

Table VII—Circumstantial Deviations from Basic Diet (ideas of what the diets of persons in certain circumstances should be)

MENSTRUATION	PREGNANCY	POST PARTUM
"A menstruating woman should not drink buttermilk because of the odor it gives."	"Plenty of milk and eggs, and bread and butter." "Plenty of milk, vegetables, fruits and meat." "Best for a pregnant mother to eat several times a day, but no fattening foods." "Don't know exactly what they eat, but I know a pregnant mother has got to be keerful what she eats." (This woman had had one child.) "I ate anything I wanted when I was having my 14 children."	"Bread and butter." Coffee "Something light like rice and grits." Soup and toast Eggs No cabbage No meat or canned meat No fish No potatoes ("they're heavy") (All such foods are supposed to "make the milk come too fast," or else may hurt the baby—such as potatoes which when eaten by the mother give the baby colic). "The mother should eat what she wants, and mostly what she craves." "Eggs, milk, and oatmeal." "More milk than usual." "The doctor says a woman after childbirth should eat only bread and butter—no buttermilk." "Meat isn't good for a woman right after childbirth."

Table VII—Circumstantial Deviations from Basic Diet (ideas of what the diets of persons in certain circumstances should be) (Continued)

SICKNESS AND CONVALESCENCE	INFANCY	CHILDHOOD
"If he has a fever, he should have liquids." "If sick from the waist up, can eat most anything, but if sick from waist down, you have to be more careful." "If not much temperature, give 'em some meat and a lot of milk—just pour milk down 'em." "Coffee makes 'em restless." "Soup and crackers and milk." "A sick person shouldn't eat the same things they do when up and going." "Should try a liquid diet for getting well."	"Babies should be fed something like grits and oatmeal—no solid food." "My baby (2 years old) likes coconut puddin', oatmeal and candy—he gets 5 cents' worth ev'y day. He likes meats of all kinds—don't like bacon much, prefers beef. He gets castor oil about once a week. He wuz weaned just recently—ain't completely weaned yet—he still thinks he ought to have it. He liked lean meat before he wuz weaned. Lots of things the baby can't eat: English peas make him sick—dried beans too. Blackberry wine is good for dysentery when he's got it. The doctor said to feed the baby prune juice, eggs, orange juice, and some cod liver oil." "The doctor told me never to give my babies anything to eat till they were a year old and had started to walk. I tried to feed my twins on bottle milk, but it made one of them sick, so I went back to breast-feeding. After a year, I started 'em out on what I was eating. I never tried to make 'em eat fat meat." "Oatmeal and soup."	"Pot likker good for them, fruit juice too." "Shouldn't have meats, 'cause it ain't good for 'em comin' up." "Young children can eat whatever their elders eat." "My daughter never stopped till she had drunk 3 glasses of milk at table. She liked turnip greens pretty well. She wanted too many sweets, but I didn't give her much." "Young children shouldn't have much meat and cabbage—no English peas, not much candy." "Young people shouldn't eat hard fried ham." "Maybe children and babies shouldn't eat what their parents eat, but sharecroppers can't always choose what they'd like to eat. At this time of year (spring) they have to take what they can get. The babies usually have to start eating just what the older people eat."

Table VII—Circumstantial Deviations from Basic Diet (ideas of what the diets of persons in certain circumstances should be) (Continued)

SICKNESS AND CONVALESCENCE	INFANCY	CHILDHOOD
	"All my children are breast fed—breast fed till they had all their teeth and could eat anything I could." "I gave my babies 'pot likker,' specially when they were sick." "Babies should be started on a little bacon (fat meat with a streak of lean) when they are weaned. I raised 10 children that way." "I fed my baby on cow milk, karo syrup, puff wheat, and oatmeal—started him eating before he was weaned."	
ADOLESCENCE	**HARD WORK**	**OLD AGE**
"High school children eat too many sweets and Coca-Colas." "My boy would always eat a big iced-tea glass full of milk and bread and fill his plate full of vegetables. He usually had two glasses of milk and two platefuls." "I always have tea for supper, and I know it's not good for the children." "Chil'un don't like much breakfast, but eat a big supper."	"My husband thinks vegetables and corn bread and milk would keep up his strength." "My husband has to have a good substantial breakfast—he is a great lover of meat."	"Should eat like a baby. They have to be keerful and eat light foods, like bread and corn bread, oatmeal and cereals. Beans is heavy. Aunt Cilla (over 80) can eat her cabbage only when it's cooked in water and the water drained off and butter on 'em." "Old people is just like babies—can't eat dried peas and beans." "Old people ought to have a diet that would give them their vitamins." "Old people should eat very restricted diet and cut down on the amount of different things."

Table VIII—Foods and Remedies for Diseases, and Diseases Caused by Foods

For Colds: "When I take a cold, I go to the water-bucket and drink and drink all I can hold." "When I have been eating too much it will give me a bad cold." "Cod liver oil and citrus fruits, also castor oil." Sage tea. Onions.

For Anaemia: "Eat liver and rest about two hours after eating." "Green vegetables are good for the red part of the blood."

To purify the blood: Sulphur and molasses. Sassafras tea. ("The red roots are the good ones, but the white roots will make you blind, the old people say.") Roesmary tea.

For the digestion: "Turnip greens and tomatoes are good." Black Draught.

For constipation: Senna leaves, fruit laxative, calomel, milk of magnesia, salts.

As a tonic to build up the strength: Vim Herb.

In the spring: Poke salad, Sassafras tea, Rosemary tea, Sulphur and molasses.

To relieve fatigue: Milk.

To soothe the nerves: "Onions, lettuce and poppies." Cardui's ($1.50 a bottle).

To draw soreness after childbirth: Castor oil with a drop of turpentine.

For rheumatism: Lorde's Bitter Tonic.

Foods which make high blood pressure: Pork and fat-meat. Lean beef, sweet milk.

Old Remedies, now mostly out of use.

"Spring tonic" to purify the blood:	Wild cherry bark, Rusty nails, Wild arsenic root } in whiskey
	Sulphur and molasses or sugar
After exposure to the measles or *"Getting ready for the measles":*	Sassafras tea
	Alder-tag tea
For worms	Jerusalem oak seed in syrup candy
For colds:	Sage tea
	Heart-leaf in syrup candy
	Hore-hound candy (hore-hound in molasses)
	Pine-top tea
	Pine-rosin pills (after a wagon has run over the pine-root)
	Whiskey and rock candy
For babies with hives:	Catnip tea
For sore mouth:	Chew yellow-root
For malaria:	Bone-set tea
For young girls:	Tansy tea (some old women used to wear it in shoes)
For dysentery:	Blackberry wine
For kidneys:	Pine-rosin pills
For abortions:	Pennyroyal (herb)

Table IX—Trends in Food

NEW FOODS	PURCHASED FOODS		FOODS DROPPING OUT OF USE
	Foods which could be produced at home	*Foods which could not be produced at home*	
Celery Carrots Cauliflower Cottage cheese Loaf bread Packaged cereals Packaged beverages (postum, cocoa, coffee, etc.) Soft drinks Aspic salads Canned food: soups, macaroni, salmon, fruits—pineapple, citrus juices Oranges Grapefruit Corn syrup Nucoa and other oleomargarines	Butter Beef Dried beef Loaf bread Canned soups	Packaged cereals, usually cornflakes Packaged beverages (cocoa, coffee, malted milk, etc.) Macaroni and spaghetti Canned pineapple Fish	Lye hominy Wild foods (except fish among Negroes) game, fish, berries, poke Souse Herb teas and remedies Molasses, sorghum Home-ground flour and meal Dried fruits Home-churned butter

Table X—Typical Menus in Westmore

WAGE LABORER	TENANT AND SHARECROPPER	LANDOWNER
Breakfast	*Breakfast*	*Breakfast*
Eggs or oatmeal or grits Hot biscuits Coffee or cocoa (Peaches in season)	Cornflakes and cream-gravy, or eggs and bacon (or ham in winter), or fat meat, ham, or sausage Hot biscuits and butter Coffee or cocoa	Fruit or fruit juice or tomato juice Cereal and milk or grits Eggs and bacon or ham Toast or hot biscuits and butter Coffee or cocoa
Dinner	*Dinner*	*Dinner*
Eggs or meat (fat meat usually, sometimes sausage, ham, beef, fish, or chicken) Sweet or Irish potatoes or rice Cabbage or "greens," cooked with fat meat Corn bread Milk or buttermilk	String beans Lettuce and onions Shoulder-bone Corn bread Biscuit Butter Milk or buttermilk or iced tea Canned peaches or cane syrup or black molasses	Chicken or ham or beef or canned fish Turnip greens or spinach Potatoes or rice Hot biscuits — whole wheat one day, white the next Butter Canned peaches Buttermilk or milk or iced tea
Supper	*Supper*	*Supper*
Vegetables left over from dinner Bread (hot biscuits or corn bread or biscuits left over from breakfast and dinner) Honey or syrup	Winter: Corn bread or biscuits Milk or cocoa Sometimes meat or hot soup Summer: Left-overs from dinner Iced tea or milk	Vegetables, usually warmed over from dinner Milk or buttermilk or hot cocoa Biscuits and butter Canned pineapple or pears or peaches Honey

Index

A

Abstemiousness, attitudes toward, 29
"Acid" foods, 74
Adequacy of diet, 56
Adolescence, and diet, 253
Adults, and children's food, 36; and food habits, 85
Aged people, foods required, 168
Agencies, transmitting foodways, 68
Agricultural classification, 25
American Medical Association, nutrition policy, 21
Anglo-Saxon heritage, and food habits, 95
Animals, as sources of food, 33
Anxiety, and digestion, 148
Appearance, of food, 48

B

Basic diet, deviations from: circumstantial, 251; class, 247; individual, 250; racial, 248; seasonal, 247; summer, 246
Behavior, eating, 66; foodways based on, 136
Balanced diet, ideas of, 60
Bennett, John W., cited, 135
Biological need, and food, 42
Black, John D., cited, 165, 173
Blood tests, ordinance for, 144
Blood tonic, medicines, 144
Borgeson, Gertrude M., cited, 85, 93
Bossard, James H. S., cited, 65, 77
Bread, remarks about, 58
Breakfast, typical, in area, 256
British, food complaints, 17
Bruch, Hilde, cited, 147, 161
Bureau of Agricultural Economics, cited, 48, 55
Burton, Robert, cited, 34, 35, 40

C

Candy, cravings for, 156
Canning, and food supply, 241; attitudes toward, 143
Catering pattern, 116
Cavaliers, and food habits, 95
Chicken, preference for, 156; serving of, 124; supply and use, 235
Children, and diet, 252; and food habits, 85; attitudes of parents, 122; craving for sweets, 156; food for, and for adults, 36; parental control of food, 66
Chiropractor, and food habits, 74
Citrus foods, sentiment toward, 151; use of, 74
Class, as arbiter of friendly relations, 71; differences, and food pattern, 63; distinctions, 129; social forms, 121; structure, and diet, 64
Classifications, race and agricultural, 25
Climate, effect on diet, 60
Colds, medicines for, 144
Color, of foods, 48
Community, attitude toward food crops, 68; research in, 24
Conflicts, food, individual and majority, 50; nation and region, 50; rural vs. urban, 106; within the region, 51
Conformity, regional, 136
Constipation, anxiety over, 148
Consumer, food choices, 17
Consumption, shifts in, 166
Cotton, and food, 63
Crops, cash, 63; home-raised, 233
Culture, influence on food habits, 20, 95, 98, 197; Southern, 95

D

Dairy products, supply and use, 236
Data, source of, 22
Deficiencies, dietary, 141, 196, 223
Demonstrations, effectiveness, 88
Dickins, Dorothy, cited, 69, 77, 87
Diet, adequacy, 56; balanced, 60; basic, 76 (*see also* Basic diet); and class structure, 64; climate and, 60; colonial times, 101; deficiencies, 141, 196, 223; in South, 19; innovations, 90; levels of, 63; meat, 34; race relations and, 71; restricted, 166; Stigler diet, 168; (*see also* Food)
Differentiation, in foodways, 129
Digestion, and anxiety, 148
Dinner, typical, in Westmore, 256; Sunday, 125
Diseases, foods and remedies for, 254
Doctor, effect on food habits, 72, 73
Documentary photography, 25, 27, 177
Druggist, effect on food habits, 75
Drunkenness, attitudes toward, 137
Duncker, cited, 70, 86
Dynamics, food habits, 89; individual preferences, 91; local contacts, 91; outside contacts, 90

E

"Eating to excess," 30
Education, accent on, 108; change of food habits, 88; for nutritional light, 172
Eggs, source of income, 111; supply and use, 235
Emotion, and food consumption, 147

F

Family, effect on food pattern, 65; food preferences, 122; new foods for, 167
Farmer, frontier, 99; Master, in Georgia, 104
Father, food decisions of, 64
Field data, source of, 22
Fish, remarks about, 58
Flour, enriched, 77
Food, and daily routine, 61; and family relations, 65; and social interaction, 31; appearance, 48; as source of danger, 30; attitudes toward, 38; aversions, 47; basis of selections, 42; British, 17; children's and adults', 36; choices, factors in, 41; citrus, 151; conflicts, 50; diseases caused by, 254; emotion-centered, 147; folk beliefs, superstitions, prejudices, fads, 193, 228; for aging population, 168; for new types of families, 167; habits, *see* Food habits; home-grown, 110, 112; innovations, 90; "light" and "heavy," 158; liked or disliked, 250; natural, 159; pattern, 18, 63; practices, 193; pricing of, 169; processed, 35; production in Thoms County, Ga., 230; psychological and physical reactions, 92; public use of, 144, 166; purchased, qualities of, 111; purity and light color, 36; ranking of, 152; rarity, cost, and effort, 36; refined, 159; relation with friendship, 68; religious restrictions, 29; rural (and urban), 37, 159; sanctions, 52; saving left-overs, 245; social approval or disapproval, 29; sold, 239; sources of knowledge and superstitions, 194, 204; Southern, 63; standards for, 138; store-bought, 63, 110, 111; storing, 243; supply, Table I, 233-245; surplus sales, 110; susceptibility to education, advertising and propaganda, 194, 209; taboos, 30; taste and flavor, 46; temperature, 46; texture, 46; trends in, 255; war practices, 197, 224; women's and men's, 37; world planning programs, 164; (*see also* Diet)
Food habits, 56; and pellagra, 140; and Southern culture, 95; children, 85; conditioned by personal experience, 197, 215; culture and, 197; dynamics of, 89; economic influences, 196, 218; education and, 88; influences of social struc-

Index

ture on, 195, 210; interviews on, 193; wage-laborers, 102
Foodways, and food habits, 49; different areas, 20
Frazer, James G., cited, 31, 39
Friendship, relation with food, 68
Frontier farmer, 99
Fruits, citrus, 74

G

Gardens, kinds of, 233; lack of, 142
German Flats, South Carolina, 7, 22, 27, 83, 84, 88, 138, 141
Gesell, Arnold, cited, 41, 54
Gillett and Rice, cited, 87
Glen, *see* Thoms County, Ga.
Gluttony, attitudes toward, 29
Government, effect on food habits, 72
Grapefruit, pink, 48; use of, 18

H

Habits, food, *see* Food habits
Health, ordinances, 144
"Heavy" foods, 158
Home economics, value of, 107
Home-grown foods, sale of, 110, 112
Hospitality, and visiting, 118
Household arts, 100

I

Income, and nutrition, 171; from eggs, 111
Indigestion, medicines for, 144
Infancy, and diet, 252
Informal contacts, and food attitudes, 70
Interviews, case material, 198; conduct of, 24; on food habits, 193

K

Kluckhohn, Clyde, cited, 146
Koos, Earl, cited, 69

L

Landlord, delicacies given to, 134
Landowners, canning by, 241; dairy products, 236; defined, 27; deviations from basic diet, 247; food drying, 243; food storing, 243; foods not produced at home, 241; foods produced at home, 240; foods sold, 239; gardens, 233; meat, 234; poultry and eggs, 235; saving left-overs, 245; typical Westmore menus, 256; White, classification of, 25; wild foods, 238
Laxatives, use of, 148
Lewin, Kurt, cited, 86, 87, 94
"Light" foods, 158
Linton, Ralph, cited, 108, 115
Living-at-home practices, 99, 196, 221
Lowenberg, Miriam E., cited, 46, 55

M

Macaulay, on Samuel Johnson, 65
Magazine subscribers, 93
Malaria, medicines for, 144
Mandeville, John, cited, 40
McCay, Jeanette B., cited, 88, 94
Meals, for smaller families, 167; regularity, 126
Meat, as emotional disturbance, 32; as preferred food, 35; diet of, 34; kinds used, 234; reaction to, 154; remarks about, 58
Medicines, patent, 144, 149
Men, rural, food preferences, 102
Men's food, and women's, 37
Menstruation, and diet, 251
Menus, typical, 256
Middlemen, intervention of, 19
Milk, attitudes toward, 142; reaction to, 153; refrigeration and, 153; remarks about, 58
Money, factor in diet, 65
Mother, food functions of, 66
Motion pictures, and nutrition, 25, 28, 84
Mouth, basic tastes, 46

N

National Nutrition Conference, cited, 8
National Research Council, cited, 8, 27, 77, 93, 162
Negroes, and food distinction, 132; attitudes of Whites toward, 71; canning, 241; cravings for sweets, 156; dairy products, 236; devia-

tions from basic diet, 247; food drying, 243; food storing, 243; foods not produced at home, 241; foods produced at home 240; foods sold, 239; gardens, 233; meat, 234; owners, and diet, 64; poultry and eggs, 235; saving left-overs, 245; typical Westmore menus, 256; wild foods, 238
Nutrition, adequate, 23, 65, 110; information on, *see* Nutritional information; knowledge of, 139, 193; method of study, 23; policy of A.M.A., 21; standards, 138; through education, 172
Nutritional information, adequacy of, 57, 60; attitudes toward sources, 194, 212; lines of communication, 196, 226; spread through friendship, 68

O

Old age, and diet, 253
Olmsted, Frederick Law, cited, 101, 104, 111, 115
Owners, and diet, 64; and telephone communication, 79; child feeding, 123; food needs, 110; relations between, 71; work attitudes, 119

P

Patent medicines, 144, 149
Pattern, food, 18
Peas, attitude toward, 157
Pellagra, and food habits, 140; cases, 57; medicines for, 144; prescription for, 73
Periodicals, and food policies, 81
Philippine Committee, report on rice, 165, 173
Philosophy, Southern, 117
Photography, documentary, 25, 27, 177
Plantation unit, 81, 93
Pork, eating of, 33
Post partum, and diet, 251
Poultry and eggs, supply and use, 235
Pregnancy, foods during, 73, 158, 251
Pricing, of foods, 169
Primitive societies, food ideas, 30
Processed foods, prestige of, 35
Protestantism, and food pattern, 97
Purchased foods, 36, 111, 240
Purity and light color, foods, 36

R

Race, classification, 25; distinctions, 132; relations, and diet, 71
Radcliffe-Brown, A. R., cited, 19, 26, 52, 55
Radio, influence on food habits, 84
Rats, food experiments with, 42
Refrigeration, and use of milk, 153; problem, 61
Region, conflicts within, 51
Regularity, anxiety over, 148
Religion, and food pattern, 97; restrictions on food, 29
Remedies, for food diseases, 254
Renner, H. D., cited, 43, 46, 55, 65
Research, in communities, 24
Rice, and Gillett, cited, 87
Rice, Philippine Committee report, 165; preferences, 48
Richards, Audrey I., cited, 128, 162
Rural community, and food attitudes, 68
Rural foodways, negative attitudes toward, 112
Rural society, conflicts of value, 50
Rural South, study of, 22

S

Sanctions, food, 52, 86
School, and food habits, 72; center of activities, 108
Science, and food values, 51; food discoveries in, 89; nutritional, 21; *vs.* tradition, 105
Seaford, North Carolina, 7, 22, 24, 26, 73, 75, 82, 88, 93, 113, 117, 138, 140, 153, 156
Shakespeare, witches' brew, 32
Sharecroppers, and communication, 81; and cotton crop, 63; and diet, 64; and food distinctions, 133; canning, 143, 241; catering to husband, 124; child feeding, 122; class relations of, 71; dairy products, 236; defined, 27; devia-

Index

tion from basic diet, 247; food drying, 243; food needs, 110; food storing, 243; foods not produced at home, 241; foods produced at home, 240; foods sold, 239; foodways traditionalism, 102; gardens, 233; impact of urban innovation, 106; land rental, 130; meat, 234; nutritional knowledge, 139; poultry and eggs, 235; saving leftovers, 245; typical Westmore menus, 256; wild foods, 238; work attitudes, 119
Shock treatment, and eating, 44
Sickness, and diet, 252
Smell, and eating, 42
Sobriety, value of, 137
Social distinctions, in foodways, 129
Social forms, 121
Social interaction, and food, 31
Social relations, affability of, 116; and foodways, 62
Social structure, and food habits, 195, 210
Socialization, and eating behavior, 66
Societies, primitive, 30; rural *vs.* urban, 50; values in food patterns, 95
Soldiers, food preferences, 35
Sorokin, Pitirim A., cited, 30, 39, 55, 162
South, diet in, 19
Southern culture, and food habits, 95
Southern hospitality, 68, 116
Soybeans, consumption, 87
Spencer, Herbert, cited, 39
Standards, for food, 138
Staples, cost of, 169
Stefansson, V., cited, 34, 40
Stigler diet, 168
Store-bought food, 63, 110, 111
Storekeeper, effect on food habits, 75
Stratification, social, 129
Sunday dinner, 125
Supper, typical, in Westmore, 256
Surplus, agricultural, 169; food in wartime, 69; food, sale of, 110
Survey, techniques used, 24
Sweeny, Mary, cited, 86
Sweets, attitude toward, 156
Syrup, and molasses, 160

T

Taboos, on food, 30
Taste and flavor, of food, 46
Tastes, individual, 41
Techniques, to change food choices, 85; used in nutrition studies, 24
Telephone, spread of food news, 79
Temperature, of food, 46
Tenants, canning, 241; dairy products, 236; defined, 27; deviations from basic diet, 247; food drying, 243; food storing, 243; foods not produced at home, 241; foods produced at home, 240; foods sold, 239; gardens, 233; meat, 234; poultry and eggs, 235; saving leftovers, 245; typical Westmore menus, 256; wild foods, 238
Texture, of food, 46
Thoms County, Georgia, 8, 22, 24, 27, 57, 71, 78, 82, 84, 88, 93, 96, 110, 113, 118, 141, 144, 146, 157; food production, 230; population, 229; social and economic data, 229; typical menus, 256
Tradition, and food habits, 95; *vs.* science, 105

U

U. S. Dept. of Agriculture, cited, 7, 26
Urban innovation, in foodways, 106
Urban society, conflicts of value, 50
Urban superiority, rural expression of, 109

V

Vance, Rupert P., cited, 101, 104
Vegetables, remarks about, 59
Verbatim case material, and foodways, 53
Visiting, and hospitality, 118
Vitamins, deficiency, 165; in diet, 57; use of, 138

W

Wage-laborers, and communication, 81; and diet, 64; attitudes toward meat, 155; attitude toward rural foodways, 112; canning, 143, 241; dairy products, 236; defined, 27; deviations from basic diet, 247; food drying, 243; food habits, 102; food storing, 243; foods not produced at home, 241; foods produced at home, 240; foods sold, 239; gardens, 142, 233; meat, 234; nutritional knowledge, 141; poultry and eggs, 235; relations between, 71; saving left-overs, 245; typical Westmore menus, 256; wild foods, 238; work attitudes, 119
War, effect on food, 197; food surplus during, 69
Weaning, methods of, 44, 122
Westmore, *see* Thoms County, Ga.
Wheat, production, 143
White landowner, classification, 25
White owners, and diet, 64
Whites, attitude toward Negroes, 71; canning, 241; dairy products, 236; deviations from basic diet, 247; food drying, 243; food storing, 243; foods not produced at home, 241; foods produced at home, 240; foods sold, 239; gardens, 233; meat, 234; poultry and eggs, 235; saving left-overs, 245; typical Westmore menus, 256; wild foods, 238
Wild foods, supply and use, 238
Wilkins, cited, 86
Witches' brew, Shakespeare, 32
Women's food, and men's, 37
Work, and diet, 253; attitudes, 119

Y

You Can't Eat Tobacco, movie, 25, 28
Young, Paul Thomas, cited, 42, 55

Z

Zimmerman, Carle C., cited, 26, 55